The Development of Social Knowledge: Towards a Cultural-Individual Dialectic

A Volume in:
*History and Society: Integrating Social,
Political and Economic Sciences*

Series Editors:
Jaan Valsiner
Søren Dosenrode
Mario Carretero

History and Society: Integrating Social, Political and Economic Sciences

Series Editors:

Jaan Valsiner
Aalborg University

Søren Dosenrode
Aalborg University

Mario Carretero
FLACSO-Argentina and Autonoma University of Madrid

Books in This Series:

Sensuous Unity of Art and Science: The Times of Rudolf II (2023)
Jaan Valsiner

Sticking Together: How Local Politicians Make Sense of and Respond to International Crises (2022)
Martin Mølholm

Educational Justice: Challenges For Ideas, Institutions, and Practices in Chilean Education (2022)
Camila Moyano Dávila

Reproducing, Rethinking, Resisting National Narratives: A Sociocultural Approach to Schematic Narrative Templates (2022)
Ignacio Brescó de Luna, & Floor van Alphen

Beyond the Dichotomy Between Altruism and Egoism: Society, Relationship, and Responsibility (2020)
Emiliana Mangone

The Development of Social Knowledge: Towards a Cultural-Individual Dialectic

José Antonio Castorina
Alicia Barreiro

INFORMATION AGE PUBLISHING, INC.
Charlotte, NC • www.infoagepub.com

Library of Congress Cataloging-In-Publication Data

The CIP data for this book can be found on the Library of Congress website (loc.gov).

Paperback: 979-8-88730-254-6
Hardcover: 979-8-88730-255-3
E-Book: 979-8-88730-256-0

Copyright © 2023 Information Age Publishing Inc.

All rights reserved. No part of this publication may be reproduced, stored in a retrieval system, or transmitted, in any form or by any means, electronic, mechanical, photocopying, microfilming, recording or otherwise, without written permission from the publisher.

Printed in the United States of America

CONTENTS

Foreword vii
Mario Carretero

Introduction: The Development of
Social Knowledge: Towards a Cultural-Individual Dialectic xi
José Antonio Castorina and Alicia Barreiro

1. The Concept of Epistemic Frame: Variety of
   Applications and Challenges 1
   Gastón Becerra and José Antonio Castorina

2. Historical Conditions of Knowledge Construction: A
   Foucauldian Perspective 25
   Tomas Baquero Cano

3. Uses and Meanings of "Context" in Studies on Children's
   Knowledge: A Viewpoint From Anthropology and
   Constructivist Psychology 49
   *Mariana García Palacios, Paula Shabel,
   Axel Horn, and José Antonio Castorina*

4. The Contribution of Social Representations Theory to the Study
   of Moral Development 71
   José Antonio Castorina and Alicia Barreiro

5. **Dialectical Inferences in the Ontogenesis of Social Representations** 91
   Alicia Barreiro and José Antonio Castorina

6. **Representation and Silencing of Social Meanings in Cartography: The Case of the Conquest of the Desert** 109
   Cristian Parellada, José Antonio Castorina, and Alicia Barreiro

7. **Cognitive Polyphasia, Social Representations and Political Participation in Adolescents** 131
   Daniela Bruno and Alicia Barreiro

8. **The Government, the President, and the Police: Politics According to Children Living in a Squatted House** 145
   Paula Nurit Shabel

9. **The Right to Privacy in Secondary School: Ideas of Adolescents** 163
   Mariela Helman, Axel Horn, and José Antonio Castorina

   Biographies 183

FOREWORD

Mario Carretero
Autonomous University of Madrid and Researcher at FLACSO (Argentina)

I am writing this Forward in the context of a war, Russia against Ukraine, which was unexpected and unthinkable just some months ago. Some of my reflections have a particular relation to this book, which does not address specifically the topic the wars, but is deeply related to the explanations that we social scientists can offer to account for how the human species links and conceptualizes social phenomena, cultural and educational like the casus belli we are living nowadays. Unfortunately, what only months ago might have turned out to be science fiction and Hollywood dystopia seems to be very close, unless planetary responses are generated. My brief comments on these pages will not deal with the possible consequences of the war, which I find quite difficult to predict, but rather with the present or, in any case, with the immediate past. In other words, I propose to take the development of the war itself as a possible example of the issues addressed in this book edited by Castorina and Barreiro.

As the Castilian saying goes, first things go first. So let's go to the first days of the war. That is, when that was an unobservable reality but at the same time unobjectionable. The confrontation approached us silently but relentlessly. How is it possible that the West as a whole, societies, authorities and political scientists, had not warned before, with very few exceptions? How is it possible that

---

The Development of Social Knowledge: Towards a Cultural-Individual Dialectic, pages vii–x.
Copyright © 2023 by Information Age Publishing
www.infoagepub.com
All rights of reproduction in any form reserved..

the obvious alarm signals from the data itself and from statements did not receive the necessary credit? As of today it seems clear that there were at least two cognitive barriers in which this book abounds and develops with a happy and original theoretical result. On the one hand, the enormous difficulty that our societies have, with all their baggage of supposed scientific and culturak progress, to admit that it is not omnipotent.

Or in other words, the verification bias, acted once again by assuming that we are living in omnipotent societies, although the opposite hypothesis advanced leaving a more than threatening number of mortal victims. On the other hand, the human species, as it is organized, at least in the West has demonstrated in this case an enormous capacity to negate the vulnerability of our societies, and that negation is united, and probably sustained, by the expansion of conspiracy theories, precision and a pre-modern, insolidary, banal and self-destructive authoritarianism. It is possible that these statements seem exaggerated and perhaps produced by the impact of the moment we are living, but I will try to show the reader that I am only describing a state of things as real as the effects of the war itself. For example, Andersen's excellent book (2017) shows and documents that a huge amount of American society, composed of nearly three hundred million from one of the richest countries on the planet, holds creationist theories about the origin of the world, and profoundly deniers of many scientific conclusions, as well as many others that are absurd, pilgrim, or simply overwhelming, but that are firmly rooted in the minds of millions of people. This state of affairs, obviously of a social nature -and which has a very close relationship with the theories and developments of this book- is really alarming. In other words, neither numerous natural phenomena, as the COVID pandemic one, has an exclusively natural origin, since it has occurred as one of the negative consequences of the inadequate management of resources on the environment, nor is it a pandemic comparable to others that have happened in history. It could well be that this pandemic represented a point of no return, or at least of no return easily accessible, as we have so far conceptualized the interaction between the phenomena of nature and social phenomena (Chakrabarty, 2009), which have traditionally been seen as separate areas, no longer in their consequences but in their causes.

Thus, this book makes a complex, original and reflective contribution on the possibility that we human persons and societies have to understand the social world, including and even emphasizing its ontogenetic process, which is conceived only in continuous interaction with the sociogenetic. I think that this work is extremely timely at the moment because it abounds in an issue that seems simple but in fact it is not. In other words, the social issues and problems-poverty, inequality or the social impact of the pandemic itself, for example-are difficult to solve because of political obstacles, but they are actually easy to understand. Unlike natural phenomena-gravity which are supposed to be very difficult to understand. The different chapters of this book refute this position and show how many of the social issues that surround us have causes and effects of great complexity, as well as major obstacles to their understanding, both in school and in the general public. One of them is undoubtedly the social representations (RRSS), rooted in the consequent practices that sustain them and give them a daily sense, apparently truthful. In this sense, this work contributes to a very detailed analysis of what these obstacles are and how the functioning of the ideas of the student and the citizen in general about the social world operates. In this same sense, the analysis of the influence of the idea of epistemic framework, within the Piagetian genetic epistemology, is also very useful for these purposes. I believe that this compilation has outstanding merits. On the one hand, the breadth and relevance of the social phenomena addressed ranging from moral ideas, representations about political activity, legal issues such as the right to privacy, political ideas on the role of the presidency of the nation or the role of the police and even the use of cartographic representations and their use in the symbolic and political construction of nations. In all of them, the authors of this research team demonstrate a profound and useful reflection on how social notions, and their associated theories are often inadequately understood by individuals and societies, paving the way both to understand the causes of this difficulty, especially from the theoretical point of view, and to eventually be able to contribute to applied developments that can establish better forms of teaching. The work does not address applied issues since its nature belongs to basic research, but I think it is important to point out its more than possible usefulness for the didactic field. Firstly, one of its most relevant conclusions is precisely the central idea that representations of social phenomena, including the way in which they subsequently become actions, come from our social practices. And that implies, in my opinion, that education in general, and particularly the teaching of the social and political world as a whole, should abandon its traditional verbalism and conceptual elitism, in order to bring students closer to a complex reflective activity, but practical and daily at the same time, on specific social problems.

As we have pointed out elsewhere, just as it is impossible to conceive of science teaching without doing actual scientific activities, in or outside the laboratory, in the same way I do not think it makes sense to try to teach social sciences without approaching the real areas where society looms its conflicts. That is, the thoughts of people through surveys or interviews, the comparative analysis of the media, the democratic management of schools, the unmasking of political falsehoods of different signs, the promotion of dialogue through respect for the opinion of others, criticism of the processes of historical silence, pointing out the hidden conflicts in our societies and many other possible activities that could make social science teaching an attractive and truly enriching activity for students and the general public.

Finally, I would like to thank the editors for the invitation to write this prologue as it is a work that represents the continuity of the research tradition of a team led by J.A. Castorina for decades, with the most recent support of A. Barreiro, which has undoubtedly been key in Latin America, and in Spanish in general, which links with the work of thinkers such as E. Ferreiro and R. García that has been decisive in the contribution of constructivist theory. As is known, the work of these last two authors has had and has full recognition in the world for its great originality and relevance of its approaches, in pursuit not only of the search for theoretical solutions in the study of the construction of knowledge but also of new questions and specific research contexts.

For all these reasons, I believe that a work like this reflects the vigour of constructivist approaches, which is far from the conformity that provides a supposed definitive solutions to the questions about the study of the genesis of knowledge, but it investigates, criticizes and renews the theoretical reflection on the same one, trying to open new theoretical, methodological and empirical ways, through the interdiscipline and the meaningful relation with nearby positions.

REFERENCES

Andersen, K. *The fantasy land. How America went haywire. A 500-year history.* Random House.

Chakrabarty, D. (2009). The climate of history: Four theses. *Critical inquiry, 35*(2), 197–222.

INTRODUCTION

THE DEVELOPMENT OF SOCIAL KNOWLEDGE

Towards a Cultural-Individual Dialectic

José Antonio Castorina and Alicia Barreiro

INTRODUCTION

This book contains works by authors of the same research team, that for more than two decades has been steadily researching the construction of social knowledge from a constructivist perspective inherited from Piagetian thought, complementing empirical investigations, theoretical elaborations, and meta-theoretical analysis (Castorina, 2005a, 2007a, 2010a; Castorina & Barreiro, 2014; Castorina & Lenzi, 2001)[1]. Throughout these years of work, the dialogue with different col-

---

[1] Most of the works gathered in this book were produced within the context of the projects UBACYT 2018-2021 20020170100222BA: Constraints to conceptual construction processes in the domain of social knowledge: possibilities and challenges for the constructivist research programme, and UBACYT 2014–2017 20020130100256BA: Empirical research on knowledge of the social domain and its theoretical-methodological implications, PI José Antonio Castorina, Co-PI Alicia Barreiro. However, these projects are the most recent part of a series of research projects dating back to 2001.

leagues (either in person or through reading their publications) and the knowledge we produced, have allowed us to revise the Piagetian programme, while maintaining essential elements of its core: an epistemological perspective when approaching the construction of the subject and object of knowledge (referring to both children's construction of knowledge regarding the social world and the construction of knowledge by social and scientific groups); and the implementation of a relational or dialectical epistemic framework when defining the units of analysis, the methodology to approach them, and in the elaboration of an explanatory theory on the formation of novel knowledge.

With regard to the constructivist epistemological perspective (difficult to characterize given the diversity of currents historically claimed as such), the Piagetian current, underlying this team's research, focuses on the constitutive relation between subject and object of knowledge, understood as two inseparable poles of the constructive activities carried out on the world. In the development of knowledge, the organizations produced in the interactions between them are not included in the previous organisations; that is to say, they are novelties. In this sense, constructivist theses were elaborated in an attempt to overcome the classic dichotomies in the study of knowledge: subject-object; individual-society; theory and observable; *a priori* and *a posteriori*, facts and values, etc. In other words, these theses make up the epistemological side (as opposite to the ontological side) of a dialectical or relational worldview, contrary to the one based on the split epistemic framework, which has guided a good part of classic development studies of social knowledge (Castorina, 2007b). The analysis of the interrelations, conflicts, and articulations between the components intervening in knowledge construction processes, in order to overcome such dichotomies, and the search for a meta-theoretical background, have explicitly oriented this team's research. That is, the very posing of research problems (increasingly focused on how individual and culture are related in the development of social knowledge), the choice of the units of analysis (the dynamic interdependencies between social practices and individual knowledge construction) or research methods (e.g., clinical interviews, ethnography. Precisely, the intervention of a dialectical framework allows for the compatibility—in their diversity—between social representation theory and Piagetian psychology, both reconsidered and revised, as well as between Piagetian psychology and social anthropology. For this reason, for example, it is relevant, when exploring the construction of adolescents' ideas regarding their right to privacy, to examine institutional practices; or study the way in which the ontogenesis of social representations of justice is enabled by what social groups constitute as 'reality', or how the practices of children and adolescents intervene in the way in which they think about politics and religion, based on their experiences with them.

It is important to clarify that focusing on the contextual conditions of knowledge construction and the appropriation of social representations does not imply leaving aside constructive processes taking place at an individual level, that is, it does not mean abandoning the subject's active character in this process, which is another of the central theses of Piaget's theory. Likewise, in its works, this team analyzed the way in which the genesis of ideas about justice, the right to privacy, gender or the president, requires that individuals reconstruct structures of collective meanings, expressed in the practices and social contexts in which they participate. In order to clarify this process, we resort to the proposal of Jean Piaget (1982/1996, 1975/1990) regarding dialectical inferences, which do not repeat the assumptions in the conclusion, and give rise to the construction of novel meanings. These inferences correspond to the equilibration mechanism (Piaget, 1975/1990) that explains knowledge transformations through the individuals' cognitive activity with the objects of knowledge. Specifically, we argue that dialectical inferences are cognitive instruments that may explain the transformations of collective knowledge during its appropriation by individuals, and can be a useful theoretical tool for researchers to advance in the clarification of the ontogenetic process of knowledge regarding the social world.

On the other hand, as we have already stated in this team's previous productions, the way in which we delimit and study the cultural conditions of the individual social knowledge construction has led us to opening up the constructivist research programme to philosophy (Castorina, 2020), social psychology (Barreiro, 2013a,b; Castorina, 2010b, 2017), and social anthropology (García Palacios et al., 2015; García Palacios, 2014; García Palacios & Castorina, 2014), thus enabling the development of joint researches. This openness supposes the explicitness of the common epistemic frameworks, as well as the articulation of their conceptual perspectives and methodological procedures, critically assuming mutual contributions in order to, in turn, consolidate the constructivist research programme itself. Thus, collaborative work with other disciplines has led us to transform the research process itself, considering it as a dynamic whole, in which the epistemic framework and the theories being elaborated interact, together with methods and constructed phenomena, articulated through the researchers' creativity; a true methodology cycle, in the words of Valsiner (2012). Contrary to the positivist stance that attributes the achievement of knowledge to methods, our research programme shows the conception of an interaction between theoretical construction, the researchers' creative invention, and empirical verification. Any one of these may change, due to their being connected; not only theories, when falsified by facts or by controversies with other theories, or methods when faced with the requirements of novel problems, but also the epistemic frameworks. In our case the dialectical epistemic framework was 'dialectized', if we may use this expression, since the basic relations have become more diversified and complex, moving progressively, for example, from the study of a dual interaction between subject and object to ternary relations between subject-object-other.

In this sense, the meta-theoretical or epistemological reflection on the characterization of theories, the methodological choices, and the explicitness of a dialectical epistemic framework able to justify the *in vivo* dialogue between different disciplines, were of vital importance to produce the theoretical elaborations and empirical studies presented in this book. What is more, the originality of the works gathered in this work lies, to a great extent, in the search for the articulation of meta-theoretical reflections with other levels of research: carrying out empirical studies and theoretical elaborations on the collective construction process and individual appropriation of social knowledge. Evidence of this effort is that most of this book's chapters argue or suggest a revision of the units of analysis: whether in terms of the context's incorporation to the cross-disciplinary research of developmental psychology and anthropology, or in research on the right to privacy in adolescents; or in an approach to a ternary and dynamic unit made up by social subject, object of knowledge, and *alter* (individuals, groups, or normative practices with adolescents at school), specific to each research. Thus, throughout the development of our research programme, we progressively started to leave behind the epistemic subject, typical of classic Piagetian tradition, in pursuit of a psychosocial subject, constituted through participation in social practices, in which the relations between subject and other, expressed in collective beliefs and practices, play a constructive role. This has been our perhaps most significant revision of the classic constructivist research programme on social knowledge, a revision of one of its nuclear theses. In turn, this revision enabled collaborative research with other disciplines. It is worth mentioning that this openness was made possible by the multidisciplinary quality of this research team's members, coming from different fields within social sciences: psychologists and developmental psychologists, sociologists, philosophers, anthropologists, social psychologists, and graduates in educational sciences.

In addition, as a result of the dialogue between different disciplinary approaches, we were able to advance in the delimitation and understanding of the 'social dimension' of knowledge. To us, this thesis is far from obvious—as it does seem to be for many researchers—but rather is a matter that requires conceptual discussion and the production of empirical knowledge in order to be fully interpreted. In this sense, we think that our work has contributed to the definition and clarification, not only in a conceptual, but also in an epistemological and methodological manner, of the specificity of the construction processes of social knowledge in a broad sense, which in our opinion encompasses different dimensions that have unfolded; that is to say, as we progressed in our research, they have become visible and necessary to us.

One of the dimensions of the construction processes of social knowledge, discerned and addressed by this team since its beginning (Castorina & Faigenbaum, 2003; Castorina & Lenzi, 2001), has covered the study of the way in which children think about the social world's objects, this is, what today's developmental psychology calls the 'social domain' of knowledge (Smetana & Villalobos, 2009; Turiel, 1983, 2008). This perspective assumes that social and cultural context influence the content of knowledge, but do not determine the cognitive process; that is, the trajectory of ever-increasing complexity of the judgments and arguments elaborated by individuals (Castorina, 2005b, 2014). More specifically, we maintain the perspective that understands the domain of social knowledge as the field of phenomena and relations in which individuals formulate ideas, constituted during their social experiences (Castorina, et al., 2010; Castorina & Faigenbaum, 2003). Thus, the social domain does not refer to the specific application of general individual thought systems, as it does in classic Piagetian tradition. Therefore, it is possible to identify constructive pathways belonging to each specific field of experience with society. Along these lines, in previous works (Castorina, 2017).

Castorina (2005b) we have defined a 'critical' version of Piagetian psychology, modifying certain aspects of the original tradition, based on progress in the research of social notions in children, as well as in the search for relations with other disciplines. Basically, we have carried out a research programme displaying a variety of objects of knowledge, all sharing the same epistemological perspective regarding the specificity of social knowledge: a renewed constructivist thesis that allows research on moral, political, or juridical experience. In this respect, a result of the collaboration with other disciplines is the consideration of social practices as inseparable from their meaning for the individuals' group of belonging. Likewise, the constitutive character of such practices in the individuals' elaboration of notions is simultaneous to and enabling of the appropriation of collective beliefs, as well as their construction and maintenance over time. As we have stated in previous works, the revised perspective of the constructivist programme framing these studies, affirms that the objects of the social world are constituted through the practices of individuals, therefore, without these practices, there would be no social thought and, in turn, these practices constrain what is thinkable regarding social phenomena (Castorina, 2005b, 2014; Castorina & Faigenbaum, 2003). Hence, there is a 'tension' between the pole of constructive activity and that of the cultural conditions constraining it, since both cannot be conceived independently. In this sense, for example, the chapters of this book reveal how the participation of children and adolescents in social practices typical of school contexts or political groups constrain the conceptualisation of their own right to privacy and politics in a specific way.

The second constitutive dimension of knowledge's 'social dimension' refers to the way in which 'social factors' (e.g., beliefs, values, power relations) intervene in the construction of scientific knowledge itself. It is important to mention that social conditions intervene in our team's research, as in any other's. These refer to worldviews (our epistemic, ontological, and epistemological framework) conditioning the development of scientific research (García, 2001). Due to its connection to a sociocultural background, research must include non-epistemic values, referring to moral and political normative aspects, since it expresses the relations and social disputes in which research practice is embedded. In this sense, and in order to achieve a relative and historical objectivity of the research results, the modalities of intervention of ontological and epistemological assumptions are a problem that should be examined, together with the values making up the genuine components of an epistemic framework, in the 'methodology cycle' (Valsiner, 2012). It is necessary to establish the research practice's conditions of possibility, and to critically determine values that may pose an obstacle, such as denying the political meaning of research, 'value neutrality', or a controlling attitude regarding the subjects' behaviours. Finally, what remains for a future endeavor is the study of institutional, quasi-administrative, and political acts, or those derived from the researchers' positions in the academic field, which together impose a constitutive social regulation of certain manners to 'practice good science', an institutional norm under specific historical conditions.

The third dimension, which we believe is starting to unfold in some of the works gathered in this book, and which allows us to advance in the clarification of the constitutive relations between individual cognitive processes and culture, is a sociogenetic dimension, addressing the study of knowledge construction processes of social groups in the context of historical and political tensions (Barreiro, 2020; Barreiro & Castorina, 2016; Barreiro & Endsleff, 2021). In other words, while in the first dimension we referred to the constraints that culture and social practices impose on thought, or on the conceptual construction of social knowledge, in this dimension we focus on the social construction of these constraints themselves. For example, the sociogenesis of school practices intervening in the conceptualisation of the right to privacy, or the way in which social representations expressed in cartographic representations are the result of political disputes; or the historical formation of ethical beliefs that have conditioned the ideas on justice in our society. In this regard, different chapters of this book address the way in which tensions between different social groups may shape the constitution of objects of knowledge—even denying the possibility of their existence—as we will illustrate with regards to the construction of cognitive tools such as maps, which in turn determine the representation of indigenous people and national territory. We believe that, although this dimension exceeds the levels of analysis considered by traditional Piagetian theory, it is of vital importance to understand the potentiality of the object's action on the subject in the knowledge construction processes, something that in previous works we have called "the vengeance of the object," inspired by Habermas (2015). We wish to underline that, for some years now, this team has used the category of constraint (Castorina, et al., 2010; Castorina & Faigenbaum, 2003) to account for the way in which collective beliefs and practices enable, while at the same time limit, individual processes of knowledge construction. However, due to the aforementioned openness of constructivist psychology with regard to other disciplines compatible with constructivism, in this book we include the study of the processes through which these constraints are socially constructed, and the way in which the particularities of their construction processes may intervene in cognitive development, either by legitimizing certain social relations (such as the domination of indigenous people), or a certain distribution of wealth (by constituting a retributive and punitive representation of justice as "real," over a distributive representation).

ORGANISATION OF THE BOOK

Most of the reflections and considerations raised in this introduction derive from the chapters in this book. In the first part, we address meta-theoretical aspects, related to the clarification of the research's epistemic framework, as well as to the relations between the disciplines involved, and to the common epistemic framework. In the first chapter, Becerra and Castorina specify the concept of epistemic framework, originated in Piagetian epistemological constructivism, especially from the works of Piaget and García onwards. In the first place, they compare the concept of epistemic framework with that of paradigm proposed by Kuhn in the elaboration of his philosophy of science, since both converge in the approach of the problem of the relation between scientific knowledge and its social context, although with important differences. Secondly, the authors progress in the reformulation of constructivist epistemology using the theory of complex systems, developed by García, in which the concept of epistemic framework acquires its clearest, but also broadest formulation, as different uses beyond science can be distinguished, such as psychogenetic analysis, meta-theoretical reflection, or interdisciplinary research oriented to addressing complex problems. They argue that the term's ambivalence derives from the centrality acquired by the problem of the relation knowledge-society in the constructivist programme. Finally, they point out the challenges that have emerged in the past few years for the constructivist programme, calling for future exploration.

In the second chapter, Baquero Cano places Foucauldian archaeology as a possible meta-theoretical tool for analysis in the research on knowledge construction, focusing on the reflection regarding its historical conditions of possibility. He elaborates the difference, specific to archaeology, between *science* and *knowledge*, in order to situate the way in which historical contingency giving rise to the possibility of certain knowledge does not imply its contingency as scientific knowledge. Secondly, following Piaget and García, he reconstructs some of the key issues regarding the relation between scientific disciplines and the social contexts enabling them. Through the concept of epistemic framework, he situates the way in which both authors conceive the revision of the implicit assumptions given by the researchers' context. Finally, based on these two ways of thinking the relation between science and its social and historical context, he points out some contributions of the Foucauldian *critique of the present*, concerning the following question: how to conceive a critical reflection on one's very historical conditions of possibility of knowledge, when, at the same time, the reflection itself is constrained and is part of the conditions it seeks to revise?

In the third chapter, García Palacios, Shabel, Horn, and Castorina analyse the various uses and meanings of the concept of 'context' in studies on children's knowledge construction. They articulate the contributions of developmental psychology with those of social anthropology in order to progress in the understanding of the relation between the individual processes of knowledge construction and the context in which they take place. They point out that, although the 'context' is mentioned in studies of both disciplines, a unanimous definition has not yet been achieved. They also highlight the meta-theoretical, theoretical, and methodological problems resulting from the analysis of this concept in both disciplines. Finally, through the analysis of empirical studies carried out by this research team, the authors reflect on the extent to which research methods of Piagetian psychology and social anthropology can incorporate the context into empirical studies on knowledge construction.

In the fourth chapter, Castorina and Barreiro analyse the contributions of social representations theory to studies on moral development. First, they propose four possible levels of analysis when addressing the mutual relations between philosophy and psychological research: academic philosophies that have influenced developmental psychologists in the formulation of psychological theories, moral philosophies based on ideas deriving from the results of psychological research, the epistemic frameworks underlying moral psychologies, and finally, the worldviews of society's hegemonic sectors becoming the philosophies of ordinary men and women. Next, they examine the specific contributions of interdisciplinary dialogue with social representations theory in the study of moral development, addressing its relations with the four levels of analysis previously considered. They then examine the way in which empirical research that draws on social representations theory and developmental psychology in a complementary manner, and that, furthermore, makes specific reference to its philosophical assumptions, leads to a reconsideration of the concept of 'moral development', traditional of constructivist psychology.

Continuing with the articulation between social representation theory and developmental psychology, in the fifth chapter, Barreiro and Castorina address a possible collaboration between them in the study on the ontogenetic process of social knowledge construction. The theory of social representations focuses on the study of their ontogenesis, even though the explanation of this process is still inadequate. The authors' objective is to analyse the potential found in the category of dialectical inferences, as formulated by Piagetian psychology (Piaget, 1982), to act as a tool in the explanation of the psychological dynamics implied in the ontogenesis of social representations. They first present dialectics in the sense of an inferential process in the individual's construction of new meanings or concepts. Secondly, they analyse research that has studied the ontogenetic processes of SRs of gender and justice, interpreting its results by appealing to dialectical inferences. Finally, they examine the theoretical meaning of including dialectical inferences in research on the ontogenesis of SRs.

In the sixth chapter, Parellada, Castorina, and Barreiro address the way in which a society's power tensions enable certain cartographic representations in which specific matters regarding national territory are visualized or denied, thus impacting on the way in which individuals consider this territory. They propose a dialogue between the cartographic silences present in the map production process and the different modalities that the presence of 'nothingness' can acquire in the construction of social representations. In order to do this, they first develop Brian Harley's ideas regarding political and social discourses as constructors of silences in cartographic representations. Secondly, using a relational conception of the social construction of 'nothingness', they argue that cartographic silences not only are a part of the construction process of cartographic images, but also belong to the process of shaping and expressing the social representations of the territory depicted on these images. Thirdly, based on this team's previous studies, they reveal the way in which the elites ruling at the moment of the Argentine national territory's construction, contributed to the legitimacy of the development of the 'Conquest of the Desert', by producing several empty spaces on the official map, meanwhile inducing the population's idea that the Patagonia was 'empty' territory. They also address the way in which these cartographic representations and silences are still in force today.

In the second part of this book, a set of empirical works is introduced that illustrate the approach to social knowledge construction from the different disciplinary perspectives making up the productions of this research team. In the seventh chapter, Bruno and Barreiro study adolescents' social representations regarding politics. The authors take up national and international research of the last decades, which indicates that adolescents value politics negatively, relating it to conventional forms of participation. In this context, the authors carried out a study in order to describe the social representations of politics through narratives constructed by adolescents from the City of Buenos Aires, regarding their experiences with it. Their results indicate the coexistence of two representations of politics: conventional and unconventional. The representation in which politics is understood mainly as conventional forms of participation (e.g., voting or membership of a political party), was found to be hegemonic, although a controversial representation was identified, referring to unconventional types of participation (e.g., involvement in neighborhood associations). Furthermore, in many of the subjects, both representations coexist in a state of cognitive polyphasia, revealing a relation of selective prevalence between them, which depends on the discursive context in which they are invoked during the interview.

In the eighth chapter, Shabel, from an anthropological perspective, studies knowledge constructions regarding politics, in a group of children between 8 and 15 years old living in a house that was squatted by a social organisation in the City of Buenos Aires. The author points out that with the arrival of neoliberalism to Argentina, thousands of families have had to resort to the occupation of buildings as a strategy of struggle and survival, especially in the larger cities. From then on, these squatted houses have transformed into daily life spaces where children are born, grow up, and construct meanings regarding the world, having their own experience of squatting interact with what adults say and do (and what not), with schooling, media discourses, etc. Specifically, she conducted an ethnographic study that, through participatory observation, allowed the recording of social practices in which the subjects give meaning to the reality that surrounds them, and the categories of government, president, and police acquire relevance and meaning. In her research, this approach is combined with the clinical method of Piagetian psychology, enabling, through individual interviews, a deeper understanding of the reasoning children use in the process of knowledge construction.

Finally, in the ninth chapter, Helman, Horn, and Castorina present the results of a study on the ideas of adolescents regarding their right to privacy at school, from a revised constructivist perspective. They argue that all social knowledge construction occurs while subjects participate in specific social practices, conditioning their cognitive elaboration. For this reason, they perform a thorough analysis of the characteristics of middle school, as well as the most frequent ways adolescents tend to participate in it, using a selection of available bibliography. They then describe the ideas regarding the right to privacy elaborated by the adolescents participating in their study, and obtained through the Piagetian clinical method, and compare them to those found in previous studies on the same object, but in younger children. They highlight that in adolescents they found characteristics suggesting a continuity with regard to those studies directed to subjects of primary schools; particularly, concerning the conditioned nature of rights. At the same time, some features of the adolescents' ideas may suggest significant differences in the way they conceive the issue. Specifically, the arguments they propose when it comes to the right to privacy at school, recognizing and demanding it is respected, and considering more institutional elements and actors when reflecting on situations involving privacy.

It is our hope that this book may contribute to the understanding of the processes of social knowledge construction; through the introduction of research topics and problems, the proposal of a collaborative research modality between different disciplines for their study, and for its potential interest to the different social actors studying and intervening in them.

REFERENCES

Barreiro, A. (2013a). The appropriation process of the belief in a just world. *Integrative Psychological and Behavioral Sciences, 47,* 431–449.

Barreiro, A. (2013b). The ontogenesis of social representation of justice: Personal conceptualization and social constraints. *Papers on Social Representations 22,* 13.1–13.26.

Barreiro, A. (2020). A developmental approach to remembering: The dialectical relation between collective memory and identity construction. In B. Wagoner, I. Brescó, & S. Zadeh (Eds.), *Memory in the wild* (pp. 127–142). Information Age Publishers.

Barreiro, A., & Castorina, J. A. (2016). Nothingness as the dark side of social representations. In J. Bang & D. Winther-Lindqvist (Eds.), *Nothingness: Philosophical insights into psychology* (pp. 69–88). Transaction Publishers.

Barreiro, A., & Endsleff, I. (2021). Remembering and forgetting: A crossroad between personal and collective experience. In M. Lyra, B. Wagoner, & A. Barreiro, (Eds.), *Imagining the past, constructing the future* (pp. 71–88). Springer.

Castorina, J. A. (2005a). *Construcción conceptual y representaciones sociales. El conocimiento de la sociedad.* [Conceptual construction and social representations. The understanding of society]. Miño y Dávila.

Castorina, J. A. (2005b). La investigación psicológica de los conocimientos sociales. Los desafíos a la tradición constructivista [Psychological research on social knowledge. Challenging the constructivist tradition]. In J. A. Castorina (Ed.), *Construcción conceptual y representaciones sociales* [Conceptual construction and social representations. The understanding of society] (pp. 19–44). Miño y Dávila.

Castorina, J. A. (2007a). *Cultura y conocimientos sociales. Desafíos a la psicología del desarrollo.* [Cultural and social knowledge. Challenges to Developmental Psychology]. Aique.

Castorina, J. A. (2007b). El impacto de la filosofía de la escisión en la psicología del desarrollo. In J. A. Castorina (Ed.) *Cultura y conocimientos sociales. Desafíos a la psicología del desarrollo.* [Cultural and social knowledge. Challenges to Developmental Psychology] (pp. 21–44). Aique.

Castorina J. A. (2010a). *Desarrollo del conocimiento social. Prácticas, discursos y teoría.* [The development of social knowledge. Practices, discourses, and theory]. Miño y Dávila.

Castorina, J. A. (2010b). The ontogenesis of social representations: A dialectic perspective. *Papers on Social Representations, 19,* 18.1–18.19.

Castorina, J. A. (2014). Introducción. [Introduction] In J. A. Castorina & A. Barreiro (Eds.), *Representaciones sociales y prácticas en la psicogénesis del conocimiento social* [Social representations and practices in the psychogenesis of social knowledge] (pp. 19–35). Miño y Dávila.

Castorina, J. A. (2017). Relationships between revisited genetic psychology and the theory of social representations. A critical analysis. *Papers on Social Representations, 2*(1), 5.1–5.22.

Castorina, J. A. (2020). The importance of worldviews for developmental psychology. *Human Arenas.* doi.:10.1007/s42087-020-00115-9

Castorina, J. A., & Barreiro, A. (2014). *Representaciones sociales y prácticas en la psicogénesis del conocimiento social.* [Social representations and practices in the psychogenesis of social knowledge]. Miño y Dávila.

Castorina, J. A., Barreiro, A., Horn, A., Carreño, L. Lombardo, E., & Karabelnicoff, D. (2010). La categoría de restricción en la psicología del desarrollo: revisión de un concepto [The category of constraint in developmental psychology: revisiting a concept]. In J. A. Castorina (Ed.), *Desarrollo del conocimiento social. Prácticas, discursos y teoría* [Development of social knowledge, practices, discourses, and theory] (pp. 237–255). Miño y Dávila.

Castorina, J. A., & Faigenbaum, G. (2003). The epistemological meaning of constraints in the development of domain knowledge. *Theory & Psychology, 12*(3), 315–334.

Castorina, J. A., & Lenzi, A. (2001). *La formación de los conocimientos sociales en los niños.* [Development of children social knowledge]. Gedisa.

García, R. (2001). *El conocimiento en construcción.* [Knowledge in construction] Gedisa

García Palacios, M. (2014). Going to the churches of the *Evangelio*: Children's perspectives on religion in an indigenous urban setting in Buenos Aires. *Childhood's Todays, 8*(1), 1–25.

García Palacios, M., & Castorina, J. A. (2014). Studying children's religious knowledge: Contributions from ethnography and the clinical–critical method. *Integrative Psychological and Behavioral Science. 48*(4), 462–478.

García Palacios, M., Horn, A., & Castorina, J. A. (2015). Social practices, culture and children's ideas. Convergence between anthropology and critical genetic psychology. *Estudios de Psicología, 36*(2), 211–239.

Habermas, J. (2015). *La Lógica de las Ciencias Sociales* [English edition: (1990) On the logics of Social Sciencias: Welley]. Tecnos.

Piaget, J. (1975/1990). *La Equilibración de las Estructuras Cognitivas. Un problema central del desarrollo.* Madrid: Siglo XXI. [English edition: (1985). *The equilibration of cognitive structures. The central problem of intellectual development.* University of Chicago Press.]

Piaget, J. (1982/1996). *Las formas elementales de la dialéctica.* [The elemental forms of dialectics]. Gedisa.

Smetana, J., & Villalobos, M. (2009). Social cognitive development in adolescence. In R. Lerner & L. Steinberg (Eds.), *Handbook of adolescent psychology: Vol. 1. Individual bases of adolescent development* (pp. 187–228). Wiley.

Turiel, E. (1983). *The development of social knowledge. Morality and convention.* Cambridge University Press.

Turiel, E. (2008). The development of children's orientations toward moral, social and personal orders: More than a sequence in development, *Human Development, 51*, 21–39.

Valsiner, J. (2012). La dialéctica en el estudio del desarrollo [Dialectics in the study of development]. In J. A. Castorina & M. Carretero (Eds.), *Desarrollo Cognitivo y Educación. Los orígenes del conocimiento* [Cognitive development and education. The origins of knowledge] (pp. 137–164). Paidós.

CHAPTER 1

THE CONCEPT OF EPISTEMIC FRAME

Variety of Applications and Challenges

Gastón Becerra and José Antonio Castorina

INTRODUCTION

In this work we want to propose some clarifications, reinterpretations, and reprocessing regarding the concept of "epistemic frame" (EF), originated in Jean Piaget's epistemological constructivism, particularly from Piaget and Rolando García's works of the '70s and '80s onwards, and continued by the latter during the following decades.

This concept acquires its meaning in the context of genetic-constructivist epistemology, defined by Piaget (1970) as the study of the passage from stages of less knowledge towards a more rigorous knowledge. This approach includes matters such as the constructed knowledge's validity as well as matters of genesis and constitution (Kitchener, 1985). The former typically belong to normative epistemology, which was treated extensively by logical positivism and detractors such as Karl Popper. The latter correspond to research—as yet at an early stage—in a variety of domains related to cognitive activity, such as developmental psychology, biological processes, and the history of science. This programme confronted genetic-constructivist epistemology with speculative and aprioristic, as well as positivist and empiricist philosophies.

The theoretical core of genetic-constructivist epistemology is the equilibration theory, which postulates that all knowledge uses schemes to construct meanings, and that the constant exchange with reality (observable) and with other schemes (coordinations), generates disturbances, which, under certain conditions, may lead to a restructuring of these schemes (Piaget, 1985). The stability of the cognitive system's new organisation is defined as an equilibrium of mutual preservation of the whole and parts, which is momentary, since equilibration is a constant and incomplete reorganization process within the knowledge systems. It is important to notice that, according to these authors, the equilibration of knowledge involves the integration of preceding structures into new ones (Piaget & García, 1982). Therefore, in retrospective, it can be reconstructed as being progressive (Boom, 2009), or rational with a directional tendency in the case of the progress of scientific knowledge (Kitchener, 1987).

By the end of the '70s, it became clear that it is impossible for a constructivist epistemology to reach, in its attempt to show a dialectic and constituent relation between objects and cognitive instruments, a comprehensive synthesis focusing only on the subject, and without problematizing the object of knowledge (Piaget & García, 1982, p. 227). This reasoning lead them to observing how social surroundings offer an object loaded with meanings to the individual, thus conditioning its cognitive assimilation.

> A subject faces the world of experience with an arsenal of cognitive instruments that allow him to assimilate, and therefore interpret, the data he receives from surrounding objects, but also to assimilate the information transmitted by the society in which he is immersed. This information refers to objects and situations previously interpreted by this society. Form adolescence onwards, when fundamental logical structures forming the basic instruments of later cognitive development have been developed, the subject already has… a "worldview" conditioning the later assimilation of every experience. (Piaget & García, 1982, p. 232)[1]

Thus, the general and invariant cognitive instruments and mechanisms proposed by the equilibration theory are linked to the social and historically changing meanings of the objects of knowledge.

> Society modifies the latter, but not the former. … The way in which a subject assimilates an object depends on the subject himself; what he assimilates depends, at the same time, on his own capacity and on the society providing him with the contextual component of the object's meaning. (Piaget & García, 1982, p. 245)

---

[1] Translated by the authors from the Spanish edition

The concept of "epistemic frame" is introduced to address this relation between assimilation and social meaning.

The objective of this work is to clarify and propose specifications regarding this concept. In order to do this, in the first part we will propose a comparison with the concept of paradigm proposed by Thomas S. Kuhn in his philosophy of science. Both concepts converge, in very general terms, addressing the relation between scientific knowledge and its social context. However, when Piaget and García mention Kuhn's paradigms, they bring forward two points of criticism: that the concept of paradigm is narrower that of EF; and that it does not correspond with an epistemology as such, but rather with a sociology of knowledge. Although we concluded that this criticism is debatable, we believe that the counterpoint may be useful to clarify the reach and specificity of the concept of EF in the broadest context of Piaget and García's epistemological programme (Becerra & Castorina, 2016a).

The second part of this work addresses the reformulation of Piaget's constructivist epistemology by Rolando García, considering the relations between domains as diverse as the psychogenetic, biological, socio-historical, and logical domains. Such integration requires a meta-conceptual framework, elaborated by García from a systemic perspective and resulting in an approach of knowledge as a "complex system." Through this reprocessing, the concept of EF acquires its clearest, and at the same time most extensive formulation. From here it is possible to trace its different uses in other contexts, in addition to an analysis of the history of science. In this article we will review another three of these levels: psychogenetic analysis, where EF is related to worldviews or conceptions conditioning the meaning that individuals give to social phenomena in psychogenesis; in meta-theoretical reflection, where it is defined as the social values and ontological and epistemological assumptions conditioning a theoretical or disciplinary programme; and in contemporary scientific reflection, as the basis of interdisciplinary research focused on complex issues. We believe that this diversity of uses, far from being the product of the concept's ambiguity, is the result of the centrality the problem of the relation between knowledge and society has acquired in the constructivist programme.

Finally, we introduce a brief discussion upon the relevance of the thesis of EF in the constructivist programme reviewed here, pointing out some of the challenges that have emerged over the past few years, and that are worthy of exploration.

EPISTEMIC FRAME IN A COMPARATIVE CHARACTERIZATION

The concept of EF appears in the work *Psicogénesis e historia de la ciencia* [Psychogenesis and the History of Science] (Piaget & García, 1982)[2], whose objective was to examine whether the mechanisms of passing from a certain level of sci-

---

[2] English edition: Piaget, J., & García, R. (1989). *Psychogenesis and the history of science*. Columbia University Press.

entific development to a more advanced one—focusing on the history of physics and mathematics—were comparable to those found in psychogenetic research. In this problem domain, the "predominance of the influence of the social environment on the cognitive process" becomes an inevitable issue. It is addressed in the chapter "Ciencia, Psicogénesis e Ideología" [Science, Psychogenesis and Ideology], which introduces the concept of our interest, along with the hypothesis that "scientific revolutions," such as that of mechanics in the 18th century, arise from the reformulation of those problems that were the study object, and of the questions guiding research, rather than from technical or methodological refinement. The clearest example proposed by Piaget and García is a comparison between Chinese and Western science:

> Aristotle, as well as all mechanics from him to Galileo, not only did not achieve the formulation of the principle of inertia, he also rejected the idea of continuous motion not caused by the constant action of a force, considering it absurd. On the other hand, we found the following statement by a Chinese thinker from five centuries BC: "The cessation of movement is due to an opposite force. If there is no opposite force, motion will never cease." More than two thousand years had to go by before Western science reached this concept. More surprising still is the fact that the above-mentioned statement was not considered to be a discovery, but a natural and evident fact. (…) The Aristotelian worldview was completely static. (…) To the Chinese, the world was constantly evolving. (…) Two different worldviews (Weltanschauungen) lead to different physical explanations. The difference between one explanatory system and the other was neither methodological nor did it regard the understanding of science. It was an ideological difference translated into a different epistemic frame (Piaget & García, 1982, pp. 232–233).[3]

From this we can deduce that in science practice the EF functions in relation to the outlines of reality, in such a way that some phenomena are problematized and become "subject of questioning," whereas others are subject to some kind of "epistemological obstacle—as described by Gastón Bachelard—as a result of which they are considered as obvious or absurd, impeding their problematization. This distinction, of social and ideological origin, later appears as a judgment upon a problem or approach's "scientism."

> It took more than thirty years for Newton's mechanics to be accepted in France. The French did not find any calculation errors, nor did they argue that experimental results contradicted Newton's statements. It was simply not accepted as "physics," as it did not offer physical explanations of the phenomena. It was the very concept of physical explanation that was challenged. (...) A few decades later, Newtonian "explanations" were not only universally accepted, but they became the very model of scientific explanation. (Piaget & García, 1982, p. 231)[3]

---

[3] Translated by the authors from the Spanish edition

Years later, García offers a clearer formulation in his work *El conocimiento en construcción* [constructing knowledge], defining it as "a system of thought, rarely made explicit, that permeates the notions of a given time and culture, and conditions the type of theorizations arising in different fields of knowledge" (García, 2000, p. 157). This system of thought refers to a very general worldview—a notion or vision of nature and society—that is part of the ideological pillars of a particular era.[4]

From the first times it is mentioned, the EF, as related to scientific revolutions, is introduced in tension with the concept of "paradigm" proposed by Thomas S. Kuhn[5,6]. This reference is significant since it situates the debate between constructivism and a tradition in philosophy of science that, far from considering theories understood as linguistic and formal organisations as its unit of analysis, focuses on the epistemic and social dynamics in the scientific communities generating them.

---

[4] We should clarify that we refer to ideology in a very broad sense, not limited to Marx's version of a legitimisation of the social order, but rather referring to the symbols and meanings we comprehend natural and social life with (for a broader discussion of the different meanings of ideology, see (Eagleton, 1997). It should be noted that until this work, Piaget always advocated a conception of science as opposed to ideology. In this sense, we can assume that this significant shift in Piaget's approach is a result of his collaboration with García.

[5] There are several meeting points between Piaget's constructivism and Kuhn's philosophy of science. For example, in the preface to *The structure of scientific revolutions*, Kuhn describes how his approach to the history of science occurred simultaneously with his exploration of other fields, in which he encountered similar problems, highlighting Piaget's psychogenetic studies (Kuhn, 1970, p. viii). Especially, certain "parallels" between the concepts of causality, space and movement in children's thought and the concepts sustained by scientists of earlier times, as described in *The Copernican revolution* (Kuhn, 1985, p. 285). Finally, in *The essential tension* Kuhn states "I have learned part of what I know about asking questions to dead scientists from examining how Piaget interviews children" (Kuhn, 1977, p. 22). These references are not free of criticism. In an interview included in *The road since the structure*, Kuhn says that "these children develop ideas in the same way scientists do, except—and I believe Piaget himself did not get to fully comprehend this, I am not even sure I myself had realized it before—that children have been educated, they have been socialized, thus knowledge is not spontaneous, but involves learning what is already known" (Kuhn, 2000, p. 279). References along the same lines can be found in his paper on thought experiments (Kuhn, 1977, pp. 243–247, 251, 264). Meanwhile, according to Piaget, the problem of novelty emerging in the history of scientific thought, is at the core of the question of scientific revolutions as described by Kuhn (Piaget, 1970, p. 14), although he seems to doubt that this project advances beyond mere description and historical analysis (Piaget, 1971, p. 113).

[6] Here we will consider only those aspects of Kuhn's work that focus on theses introduced in *The structure of the scientific revolutions* with its *PostScript* of 1969 (Kuhn, 1970), and some other texts compiled in *The essential tension* (Kuhn, 1977). We did not take into account any subsequent shifts, such as the "linguistic" and even the "structuralist" shifts observed in *The road since the structure* (Kuhn, 2000) which—as Alexander Bird well pointed out (2002)—distances itself from a "naturalistic problematization of philosophy of science, informed by science. We believe that with this shift towards a prioristic approach of epistemology, Kuhn's programme loses—in several aspects—its point of comparison with genetic epistemology.

Before we proceed, it is necessary to clarify the meaning of the concept of paradigm. Kuhn himself acknowledges, in his *PostScript* of 1969, in the first edition of *The Structure of the Scientific Revolutions*, that there are two main uses. In a broad sense, paradigms refer to the constellation of beliefs, values, techniques, and agreements shared by the members of a scientific community; in a narrower sense, it denotes a particular element of such constellation, specifically, concrete solutions to problems—puzzle-solutions—which, when used as models or examples, can replace explicit rules for the application of theory (Kuhn, 1970, p. 175). Kuhn himself calls the broader sense "sociological," and points out that it harbors a certain circularity, insofar as "A paradigm is what the members of a scientific community share, and, conversely, a scientific community consists of men who share a paradigm" (Kuhn, 1970, p. 176). Leaving aside the meaning of paradigm as the group of scientists using and defining it, Kuhn prefers to call it a "disciplinary matrix," containing different types of agreements shared by the team (Kuhn, 1970, pp. 182–187). These agreements include symbolic generalizations (abstract, formal or formalizable expressions introducing general laws and enabling definitions), metaphysical components (ontological and heuristic models, metaphors and allowable analogies to contemplate the problems of the team's interest), and paradigmatic examples (concrete—historical—puzzle solutions, accepted through community consensus). The assumption that certain specific problems may be solved adequately according to previous (exemplary) achievements, is a constituent part of paradigms, and since they indicate "how the work should be done," they are the main source of identification in this puzzle-solving approach. Thus, the exemplars are the essence of the (narrow) meaning of paradigm.

As mentioned above, when Piaget and García introduce the concept of EF, they are discussing scientific revolutions and explicitly referring to Kuhn's concept of "paradigm." This connection introduces two points of criticism: on the one hand, Piaget and García claim that the concept of EF is broader than that of paradigm; on the other, they suggest that the concept of paradigm does not correspond to the objectives of an epistemology as such, but, at most, pursues the objectives of sociology of knowledge. In the authors' words:

> Kuhn developed a theory of scientific revolutions according to which each time period was characterized by what he calls a "paradigm," that is, a particular notion establishing the ideal kind of scientist, a model to follow in scientific research. The criteria for a scientifically acceptable research, determining the lines of investigation, are, according to Kuhn, determined by this specific place and time. In essence, we agree with Kuhn, and from certain point of view, our concept of "epistemic frame" includes the Kuhnian paradigm. However, *the concept introduced by Kuhn is more related to sociology of knowledge than to actual epistemology, to which our concept of epistemic frame belongs* (Piaget & García, 1982, p. 229).[7]

---

[7] Translated by the authors from the Spanish edition

The preceding quotation, referring to the "ideal kind of scientist, the model to follow," and other subsequent passages, suggests that Piaget and García are discussing with the narrower meaning of the concept of paradigm, therefore, the criticism does not apply to the first meaning, which would not be of much value after Kuhn's reformulation. It could even be argued that the agreements and exemplars on which the reformulation of the paradigm is based, fulfil the same functions of outlining and solution criteria indicated in the EF. Given the proximity of these concepts, we should look for the difference on a deeper level. In our view, the difference lies in how these concepts represent the objectives and limits of each epistemological programme.

We should recall that Piaget's constructivism recovered the use of "epistemology" as a theory on the constitution of general knowledge, including the science domain. The central element of this theory is the problematization of generative mechanisms of knowledge. The concept of EF is related to this objective, insofar as it implies the assimilation of social conditions into the process of knowledge construction. A supposed lack of this treatment by Kuhn is the reason of the criticism:

> The problem of the action mechanisms of these conceptions or beliefs of a certain social group (in this case the scientific community) regarding the individual's cognitive development, is not clarified by Kuhn nor by any of the authors addressing ideology in science. On the contrary, this is the central issue of our concerns (...) because it is the exact point where sociology of knowledge transforms into sociogenesis of knowledge (Piaget & García, 1982, p. 231).[7]

However, it is true that Kuhn also wonders how paradigmatic agreements are acquired and how they operate. Just like Piaget and constructivist epistemology, he resorts to the developments of psychology of his time. Nevertheless, it is also true that Kuhn's researches in the field of psychology rather aimed at drawing analogies between the functioning of perception and the way paradigms operate, than at problematizing the transformation mechanisms of individual knowledge. In addition, his referents in psychology lead the opposite way than that of Piaget's constructivism (Brunetti & Omart, 2010): at first he is guided by Gestalt (Kuhn, 1970, pp. 85, 150), and later, by behaviorism and its neural reprogramming of stimulus processing (Kuhn, 1977, pp. 307–310). In the second case, Kuhn remains in psychological empiricism[8], with little or no space for the individual's elaboration. In this case, learning is understood as being characterized by the passive reception of stimuli and corrections in the manner of Skinner's behaviorism.

---

[8] Kuhn explicitly states that his proposition does not manage to detach itself from this tradition: "But, is the sensory experience fixed and neutral? Could theories perhaps simply be interpretations manufactured from given data? The epistemological perspective, which has guided Western philosophy for three centuries, responds with an immediate and unequivocal "yes." As long as an alternative is not developed, I find it impossible to completely abandon such a point of view" (Kuhn, 2000, p. 233)

The instructor takes the active and constructive role. In the first case (Gestalt), the basis is a structuring mechanism not implying genesis nor transformation by the subject (Piaget, 1971, p. 55).

More importantly, the difference between the central theses of the epistemology research programmes of Piaget and García on the one hand, and Kuhn on the other, lies in the outlining of the social space considered by each programme. In *The Structure of the Scientific Revolutions*, Kuhn divides the states of (some) sciences in two moments: the paradigmatic state, in which the previously mentioned agreements remain stable, and the moments of crisis, when these agreements are modified and new theoretical options proliferate. Later, in *Objectivity, value judgement and theory choice*, Kuhn (1977) points out that the confrontation of rival theories at a time of crisis revolves around historically established epistemic values, such as simplicity and parsimony, fertility of their hypotheses, explanatory scope and adequacy, coherence and consistency of their theoretical system, as well as the predictability of the facts. This confrontation of values is eventually solved by means of intersubjective agreements on the level of the scientific community, and on the basis of "good reasons," the ultimate guarantee of their rationality (Newton-Smith, 1981).

In comparison with these values of evident epistemic nature, the EF includes non-epistemic values, of moral and political nature. However, it would be unfair to say that Kuhn did not mention them, since the author, when evaluating and organizing the abovementioned epistemic values, points out the influence of subjective factors such as personality and formation. He even suggests that "the external environment" may influence the different communities, clarifying that he is referring to intellectual, ideological, and economic conditions. He even claims that a change in this environment may have productive effects on research (Kuhn, 1977, pp. 335–338). It is sure that Kuhn, apart from this brief reference to the conditions of the "external environment," does not seem to consider social factors beyond the scientific community itself[9]. If this interpretation is correct, the social space of the EF is, in comparison, much broader. Constructivism aims to cross these lines, maintaining that great scientific changes are possible when exploring into those new questions enabled by an ideological change in society (Piaget & García, 1982, p. 236). As a result, the epistemic agreements that constructivism takes into account, stem from a much broader social context than those of the scientific

---

[9] Critics such as Steve Fuller (2005) or George Reisch (2005) suggest this is due to the fact that Kuhn's vision on science was formed during the success of the Manhattan project: science financed by industrialist-military corporations but self-regulating because of its high specialisation. A concept of science operating within the walls of the academy, and with an autonomous community as acting subject. In the words of Fuller: "To Kuhn, there can be no proper science if the community of researchers cannot set its own standards (…). One could say that such elitist vision has no place in today's world, where science's costs and benefits are as high as those of any other public policy. Nevertheless, Kuhn managed to prevail by simply ignoring this fact, and leaving his readers with the impression—or perhaps, the confusion—that, say, a particle accelerator of several trillions of dollars is nothing but a scientific toy" (Fuller, 2005, p. 27).

community itself. In fact, a possible point of criticism concerning the EF is that it shows a certain indeterminacy in its limits, as is the case of concepts like "culture" and "civilisation," as acknowledged by García himself (García, 2000, p. 157).

In short, while there are several similarities between Kuhn's developments and those of Piagetian constructivism, such as the argument that the way in which scientists observe the world depends to a large extent on the theories they have accepted, or that the philosophical analysis of science should include epistemic and social dynamics of scientific communities, the considerations of both programmes do not correspond in a narrow sense, since the EF takes a broader social framework into account, into which scientific developments are integrated. This social framework includes worldviews, religious views, normative and moral aspects, ethical and political values, expressions of conflicts and social relations, all conditioning scientific development. In this sense, the concept itself may be considered as an attempt to break with the internalism/externalism dichotomy present in the reflection of philosophy of science since before and after Kuhn[10].

However, we believe that what has been said so far cannot justify Piaget and García's criticism identifying Kuhn's epistemology with a "sociology of knowledge." At the very least, it underestimates Kuhn's enormous contribution to the discussion of central problems in this field, such as the role of the community and (mostly epistemic) values in theoretical shifts, the relevance of history of science for its philosophy, and the relation between observation and theory, among others. In fact, given the proximity of these issues, and the paths explored in both programmes, it can hardly be argued that Kuhn does not address the epistemological problem.

THE EPISTEMIC FRAME IN THE REVISED CONSTRUCTIVIST PERSPECTIVE

The concept of EF is reformulated in the setting of Rolando García's revision, which proposes the understanding of knowledge transformation as a "complex system" (García, 2000). This reformulation revises the wide range of cognitive activities explored and conceptualized by genetic epistemology, now approached from the perspective of the relation between three subsystems: biological, cognitive, and social. Each subsystem corresponds to a semi-autonomous level of organisation, governed by its intrinsic activity and relative to its own material domain. It shows transformations of its elements and internal states that are inseparable from the "boundary conditions" presented by the other subsystems. The complex systems' evolution model is characterized by the reorganization in

---

[10] It could be argued that the concept of EF, by managing to focus on the epistemic connection between science and society, escapes the externalist view, characteristic of the strong programme of sociology of science. This programme claims that social production conditions determine scientific developments. At the same time it evades the internalist view, characteristic of the concepts inherited from logical positivism, which reduce theories to statements, and remove epistemological meaning from the study of those relations.

successive states, in line with the developments of dissipative structures by Ilya Prigogine. This connection was already explored by Piaget himself while producing his equilibration theory (Inhelder et al., 1981).

As mentioned above, the main purpose of the equilibration theory is to explain the emergence of cognitive novelties. For this explanation, Piaget proposes a causal mechanism: "Equilibration only makes sense as a model with causal significance. In a system of self-regulation, disturbance is already a causal phenomenon, while compensation is another causal phenomenon tending to neutralize the disturbance, etc." (Inhelder et al., 1981, p. 132). The characteristic aspect of Piaget's programme is that he places these mechanisms in a genetic and evolutionary perspective, where self-regulation does not derive from a predetermined mechanism of linear causality, but rather stabilizes and destabilizes throughout the history of interaction between a system and its environment (Boom, 2009, p. 137; Inhelder et al., 1981, p. 34). García's systemic revision assumes the same causal intention[11] observed in the self-regulation between system and environment, as formulated by Piaget. However, he adds self-regulation of mutually dependent subsystems, on each other and on the total system. Far from being a minor contribution, the result is a greater indeterminacy regarding the development of the system, which eventually seems to avoid the immanentism of the equilibrium as originally formulated by Piaget (Castorina & Baquero, 2005).

This perspective, while only explored at a programmatic level, permits the questioning of some common criticisms of Piaget's theory, such as the leading role of structures in cognitive processes, or the secondary role of "social" factors, when compared to others, such as biological factors. Although Piaget himself already responded to the criticism regarding the structures' leading role, this reformulation deepens the dynamism of these structures, now understood as the organization's stationary states, whose equilibrium is dynamic since it is influenced by the relations of other systems. The role of social and cultural aspects is strongly revalued, as it is precisely the social environment's conditions that modulate psycho-cognitive activities. This results in an indeterminacy of the direction in which the progress of knowledge is headed, as already claimed by several followers of Piaget, such as Chapman (1992). In fact, the complex system perspective forces us to explore, with the same level of importance, all the possible relations between subsystems. Not only the relation between the biological and psychological subsystem—the reason for the "biologist" criticism of the Piagetian programme— nor the relation between the psychological-cognitive and the social-cultural subsystem enforced by García, but also the relation between biological and social

---

[11] It is a non-traditional causality, where linearity is exchanged for a circular linkage mechanism between levels (balancing the relation between parts and emerging commands) and within them. In later years, the "dynamic system" models were standardly incorporated into explanations of human psychological development, including those adopting a post-Piagetian perspective (Castorina, 2014a; Overton, 2014; Witherington, 2007).

processes, in line with the new developments in cultural neuroscience (Chiao et al., 2010; Kolstad, 2015).

Together with this reformulation of the constructivist theory in terms of a complex system, the conceptualisation of the EF acquires a higher abstraction and precision level than the one introduced in *Psychogenesis and the History of Science*. This allows for a generalization and diversification regarding its scope and implementations, in addition to the analysis of the sociogenesis of scientific knowledge. In the remainder of this section we would like to highlight three specific contexts:

1. that of psychogenetic analysis, as a worldview framing the construction of meaning and re-elaboration of knowledge throughout an individual's life;
2. in meta-theoretical reflection, as ideological assumptions to be analyzed in the methodology cycle of theoretical or disciplinary programmes; and
3. in the context of interdisciplinary research, as social values and basic epistemological and ontological assumptions guiding the construction of the research problems (Becerra & Castorina, 2016a).

(1) Regarding the level of psychogenetic analysis, focused on the development and transformation of children's elementary schemes and ideas into adult thought, the EF refers to the social and ideological context of meanings framing the objects of knowledge, enabling the orientation and limits of the individual's cognitive actions. This level of analysis is not treated in García's work.

In recent years, some of the psychogenetic research has pointed out the need to diversify and specify the cognitive relation, moving from a dyadic subject-object relation to a triadic one. The latter includes the possible relations and practices in which the subject is involved with others while relating to the object of knowledge, as well as the context of social and cultural meanings framing these practices (Castorina, 2008, 2014b; Martí & Rodríguez, 2012). This way, there have been research programmes seeking to complement developmental psychology's research, beyond what was proposed by Piaget, with social or psychosocial theories regarding shared imaginaries, such as the social representations theory developed by Moscovici, Jodelet, or Duveen, among others (Psaltis et al., 2009; Zittoun et al., 2007). These collaborative efforts involve abandoning the Piagetian epistemic subject, and replacing it by a psychosocial subject involved in asymmetric social relations with other subjects. Through the exchange of the social representations guiding the individual, his constructive activity may be constrained or conditioned. Leman and Duveen's research illustrates this (Leman, 1998; Psaltis & Duveen, 2006): different pairs of boys and girls were faced with the conservation of liquid experiment, and asked to reach a joint conclusion after discussing their evaluations. One of this research's results is that representations and expectations regarding gender condition the conclusions reached by these boys and girls when arguing upon their disagreements. That said, even these researches, focused on social representations, have not considered the broader social space referred to by the concept of the EF, as related to worldviews or ideology.

A very clear example of the relation between the ontogenesis of social concepts, social representations, and ideological beliefs, is found in the empirical research of Barreiro and one of us (Barreiro & Castorina, 2015). The objective was to specify and provide evidence regarding the relation between the belief in a just world—specifically, the characterization of the world being a place where one gets what one deserves, concealing social mechanisms generating injustice—and social representations of justice (see the chapter by Castorina and Barreiro in this book). Results indicate that, in our society, social representation of justice would be preponderantly retributive, in line with the belief in a just world. This involves the rejection of a more distributive conception of justice, associated with the search for equity and equality through rights and laws. Now, beyond this shared representation, we observed some differences when dividing the answers into two groups, according to the level of attachment to the belief in a just world. Individuals less attached to this belief consider justice to be a social institution, with errors and problems in its daily functioning, generating order and regulating the individuals' freedom. This idea is absent in those more attached to the belief in a just world, who, in turn, associate justice with a more individual experience. This is clearly an ideological idea, since it supposes an inverted or fetishized image of justice, concealing its historical and social character, in which justice presents itself to individuals as a naturalized idea, enabled by an ideological perspective that justifies our society's *status quo* and inequality (Barreiro & Castorina, 2015; Castorina & Barreiro, 2006).

Without referencing EF, other studies, like those by authors such as Wainryb or Turiel, point out that the development of moral concepts and judgments is conditioned by beliefs that vary across cultures (Wainryb, 1991; Wainryb & Turiel, 1993). In this way, the differences between moral evaluations of individuals from different cultures are influenced by the different information taken into account by the individual when evaluating these judgments. It has been argued, for example, that a culture that evaluates certain practices as morally relevant, such as adhering to a dress code, is influenced, unlike another culture that would not consider it as a moral practice, by different informational assumptions, such as the belief, in the first culture, that ancestors suffer as a result of the actions of their living relatives. In this sense, the moral judgment of a dress code violation does not mean a different concept of harm, but does imply a different consideration of the social actors most probable of being harmed (Elliot Turiel et al., 1987).

(2) Another level of analysis is the one related to the meta-theory of disciplinary research. This involves the critical examination of ontological and epistemological assumptions, as well as non-epistemic values that, indirectly and without determining them, condition the interactions between the components of the methodology cycle of research in a particular field. We believe that the purpose of this particular approach is to explore the ways in which the EF is assimilated into

the methodology cycle: the formulation of research questions and problems; the construction of the units of analysis; the evaluation of the explanatory models to be used; the selection and design of empirical methods and techniques; and even the scope of the theories' use or application in the social world. This type of analysis continues and advances upon García's approach[12] regarding today's physics' discussions (García, 1997), now considering new problems.

This line of analysis has been thoroughly explored by one of us in order to clarify the participation of EFs in the research process of developmental and social psychology, as well as the way in which they interfere in the study of social knowledge (Castorina, 2003, 2007, 2008, 2010, 2019). In these fields we observe the hegemony of an EF heir to modern and Cartesian thought, dissociating mind from body, representation from reality, and—more relevant to our discussion—individual from society. Facing this EF stands an opposite one, whose strategy is to establish dialectical relations between the components of these—and other—dualities. The first EF, for example, had an influence on large part of the history of developmental psychology, particularly on computational psychology, as well as cognitive social psychology. In both cases, the unit of analysis is the individual, isolated and split from his social conditions and cultural context, thus focusing on his internal information processing. Where methods are concerned, the research looks for dependent and independent variables, without mayor interest in subjective or cultural qualities, and undervaluing qualitative methods. The second EF underlies—among others—social representations theory and knowledge development theories such as the post-Piagetian perspective, the socio-historical school continuing Vygotsky's work, and some cultural psychologies. In these cases, and in others, knowledge is constructed in relation to other social agents; therefore it is important to explore the subjectivities within the networks of relations and shared social meanings. Finally, these EFs can also be differentiated by the political and ethical values guiding them. The former establishes the promotion of individualism or control of behaviours as a value, or desirable course of action, while the latter seeks to give voice to subordinate groups. In the case of Barreiro's research mentioned above, these values are linked to the hegemony of subordination mechanisms, such as the affirmation of retributive justice (Castorina, 2019).

---

[12] García offers a good definition, related to sociology, regarding the direction of these analyses: "The first problem of the epistemologist analysing the work of sociologists, consists—for specific cases and authors— in the establishing of: (1) the empirical domain referred to by the sociologist; (2) the empirical material accepted by the sociologist as an "objective" referent to describe the specific situations characterising the topics to be explained; (3) the types of conceptualisations and theoretical constructions used by the sociologist, and his explanatory theory (in particular, the explicit or underlying basic assumptions). From there, the epistemologist needs to consider the theory's explanatory scope, which means confronting the offered explanations, as well as their implications, with the facts the theory is trying to explain. (…) Which means finally getting to the heart of the problem. Because this is where the researcher's epistemic frame becomes clear" (García, 2001, p. 618). In this regard, you may consult the very fine works of Fernando Cortés (Cortés, 1991, 2001).

At this level of analysis, the exploration of the EF requires a certain degree of reflection from the researchers, since they are the epistemologists of their discipline, critically analyzing the social conditions in which their research takes place, and connecting them to the difficulties of knowledge production in the field itself. In this sense, the orientation of the EF's analysis is related to concepts such as "theoretical framework" and "meta-theory," developed by Willis Overton (2012), or even Valsiner's "axioms" and their influence on the methodology cycle's interactions (Valsiner, 2014). Although, unlike Overton, and coinciding with Valsiner's conceptualisation, the characterization of the EF particularly emphasises the link of these meta-theoretical aspects with the social and political conditions of science production that, as we said, refer to a broader social space than that of scientific communities.

(3) A third point we would like to mention is the study of the intervention of the EF in interdisciplinary research, such as those formulated by García in *Sistemas complejos* [Complex Systems] (2006). This kind of research is a challenge for scientific knowledge, since it involves problems implying situations where it is essential that their different processes or components be considered in an "interdefined" way (García, 2006, p. 21). In order to do this, they require the integration of conceptual frameworks from physical-natural disciplines, as well as from social sciences. Here, "interdiscipline" acquires a particular meaning: it involves a methodology—a way to proceed in research, consistent with a theoretical and epistemological approach—that aims to achieve an integrated analysis of the processes taking place in a complex system, explaining its behaviour and evolution as an organized totality (García, 2006, p. 88).

According to this author, the construction of the research problem involves drawing outlines (of the empirical material to be considered, of the possible states of the system to be modelled, etc.). Interdisciplinary research is defined by questions implying the team members' political-evaluative stance and social experience of the problem, rather than by theoretical, methodological or empirical outlines associated with a disciplinary perspective. The questions behind this approach are clearly of an evaluative, ethical, and political nature. What aspect of reality appears to us as problematic? What do we want reality to be like? Why do we want to intervene? We believe this implies the most obvious form of the relation between science and society: what kind of science do we want, and at the service of what kind of problems? García calls this approach the research's EF, which he defines as .".. the set of questions or enquiries that a researcher asks himself regarding the domain of the reality he intends to study. This EF represents a certain worldview, and on many occasions expresses the researcher's value hierarchy" (García, 2006, p. 36). Thus, the ideal state of the problems to be explored in interdisciplinary research, that is, the social values and political objectives guiding research, plays a central role in the regulation of the dynamics of interaction between disciplinary contributions. We should recall that, at least in García's Complex Systems Theory proposal, the explicit objective of interdisciplinary research is "… to reach an integrated diagnostic, providing the basis for the proposal of concrete actions and alternative general policies that enable the influence on the system's evolution" (García, 2006, p. 94).

In this sense, the EF of the interdisciplinary research is expressed both in the way of posing the problem—including the consideration of possible courses of action—and in the construction of a representation of the system, including the evaluation of and the relation between different disciplinary contributions. It is also reflected in the decisions guiding the project's development, both of an epistemic nature and regarding organisational issues, even extending to political action.

REMAINING CHALLENGES FOR THE CONCEPT OF EPISTEMIC FRAME

To conclude this work, we would like to briefly point out some challenges for the abovementioned four levels of analysis using the concept of EF: (1) the study of sociogenesis of scientific knowledge; (2) the study of psychogenetic analysis; (3) meta-theoretical reflection in research processes; and (4) the context of interdisciplinary research. Particularly, we want to specify some challenges whose possible answers would contribute to progressing in the conceptualisation and the use of this category.

(1) In the first place, we refer to the initial intellectual space in which the concept of EF was developed: that of genetic epistemology, a theory of knowledge that draws on the history of scientific knowledge. This approach, original of Piaget's work, later developed in collaboration with García and in the work of the latter after Piaget's death, has—as far as we know—not been continued nor updated.

In the 1960s and '70s, García engaged in a debate with the brightest supporters and detractors of empiricism, such as Carnap, Quine, or Russell, or, as referred to above, Kuhn, in the field of philosophy of science and epistemology. Today the context of epistemological debate is different. Two fields with an overwhelming presence over others are a strong scientific experimentalism, and new forms of naturalism in neurosciences, as well as predominant empiricism in studies using *big data*. Also, since then, new actors have come up in epistemology and philosophy, such as social studies of science and feminist epistemologies, focusing on the relation between science and society, and problematizing the role of (non-epistemic) values (Gómez, 2014; Longino, 2015). Even postmodern relativistic versions questioning the legitimacy of epistemology itself, and of any objectivity other than that established by each culture, among others, the version of the pragmatist philosopher Rorty. It should even be mentioned that the constructivist epistemology itself has been transformed into a heterogeneous field with programmes that, although sharing a "family resemblance," deal with very different problems referring to the processes of knowledge in different branches of science—from biology to psychology and cognitive sciences, through social sciences—involving, in many cases, clearly opposite philosophical theses and assumptions (Becerra &

Castorina, 2018). These transformations in philosophy and epistemology enable the emergence of new problems, dialogues, and controversies, which could renew the genetic-constructivist epistemology, originated and remaining in a world of rather classic debates.

Considering one of the topics mentioned above, we will briefly refer to feminist epistemologies' contributions to the problem of the role of non-epistemic values in science, and the resulting consideration of scientific knowledge's objectivity (Anderson, 2012; Douglas, 2007; Harding, 1995; Longino, 2015). In these developments, knowledge is usually understood as "more objective" if it is the product of intersubjective agreements and arrangements regarding the critical debate of different perspectives and evaluative positions of the scientific community. In these cases, appealing to political and moral values does not imply predetermining the results or conditioning the acceptance or rejection of evidence. It does, however, imply the rejection of value-neutrality as an ideal, which is actually desirable when scientific activity involves high risks and enormous social costs. In this regard, the concept of EF may contribute to the debate, since it strongly criticizes the positivist dissociation of facts and values. Researchers' non-epistemic values, political objectives and moral standards are considered to be components of research in any discipline, and these values are linked to the different components of the methodology cycle, hence the need for epistemological supervision.

(2) Secondly, analyses of the EF of psychogenetic study, developmental psychology, and particularly of social knowledge, should be broadened and specified, based on empirical investigation.

In this analysis, the EF refers to worldviews and ideologies covering the objects of knowledge, while conditioning its transformation by the subject. The challenge is greater on this level, since this is the less extended use of the concept of EF in research. It seems, in fact, that, apart from Castorina and Barreiro's research, and Turiel and Wainryb's perspective we mentioned earlier, this concept is not taken into account by developmental psychology. The lack of empirical studies does not contribute to the solution of a true challenge on this level of analysis: determining the mechanism through which ideological aspects operate on cognitive processes.

A few authors have brought forward possible hypotheses regarding this matter, referring to the relation between ideological beliefs and social representations. Jodelet (1985) proposes two considerations: first, she points out that, when faced with the necessity to make sense of novel phenomena, social representations may "mobilize" ideological contents or cultural models, in order to provide structure. Secondly, since they are part of an elaboration in communication and interaction, between groups and regarding an object in question, social representations depend on the subjects' position in society, expressing an ideological function, legitimizing or criticizing social positions. These remarks arise from the idea that social representations are constructed upon a background of broader ideas, an ideological horizon on which to draw the outlines. Aiming to continue this intervention's mechanism, and following research on the belief in a just world, Doise referred to a "filter," operating on the representational object and protecting more basic illusions, such as that the world is orderly and predictable. In their work, Barreiro and Castorina go one step further by suggesting that collective ideological beliefs linked to social order not only serve as a background for the social representations' outlines, but also actively condition their production.

Even so, research into the mechanism through which ideological conditioning operates on cognitive aspects is still in a very programmatic state. It might be appropriate then to broaden the question and begin by specifically exploring this conditioning of cultural beliefs and collective practices. In this field we find other concepts, somewhat more elaborate and widespread in psychology, such as the concepts of "obstacle" or "constraint" (Castorina et al., 2010), understood in a double sense: positive, when allowing for the development of knowledge by pushing it in a certain direction; and negative, when limiting the development of ideas. These categories may contribute to the specification of the EF's intervention modalities. However, this call for dialogue with social sciences seems difficult when considering the hegemonic direction of psychology's conceptual and methodological interests, today under strong institutional impositions of an EF closer to natural sciences—through neurosciences—than to social sciences. Thus, an analysis of the discipline's EF is important, as addressed in the next level.

(3) A third level of study of the EF consists in critically examining the scientific work. It is clear that this programme does not come with a set of defined concepts, or with a clear procedure for analysis. In some works dedicated to analyses from this perspective, such as the ones gathered by Fernando Cortés and Manuel Gil Antón in *La epistemología genética y la ciencia contemporánea* [Genetic Epistemology and Contemporary Science] (Cortés & Antón, 1997), it is pointed out that the purpose is to reflect upon "the fundamental dilemmas (…) at the heart of the development of diverse disciplines" (1997, p. 73), later covering issues such as, for example, what has been understood by "social aspects" in different historical contexts of Latin American social sciences (Yocelevszky, 1997), or whether it is possible to consider society on a different level than that of interaction and intersubjectivity, as proposed by the post-humanist view of Luhmann's sociology (Torres Nafarrate, 1997).

Here we propose a concept that is broader than the analysis of the disciplines' central categories, given that we understand that the EF is present in the assumptions, assimilated in the components and relations within the methodology cycle of a particular discipline or theoretical programme, conditioning their practice. As mentioned before, this includes everything from the formulation of questions and research problems, the analysis and clarification of their central concepts, methodological choices, relations with other disciplines, and even the intentions of applying the theories. At this level of analysis, the EF becomes an essential category when it comes to explaining how these different aspects are linked to social worldviews, ideological and philosophical assumptions, and to the ethical and political values mobilizing the communities' research. In this regard, we would like to point out two challenges.

The first one is to specify the concept of the EF, in order to define some meta-theoretical guidelines allowing the characterization of the analysis, starting by the formulation of some questions[13]: what are the central concepts of a research programme? Within which framework of philosophical assumptions and ontological agreements are they embedded? What emerging concepts account for their main challenges? How is the unit of analysis constructed? What analysis techniques and methods are used in empirical research? What new data sources might be considered? What other developments or disciplines could it interact with, and to what purpose? What are the theory's intended use and fields of application? What political projects and social actors does it question or give voice to? To our knowledge, there has barely been any research into several of these questions. We dare say that addressing these challenges will be an impossible task, especially when it comes to psychological disciplines, if interaction with social and human sciences, as well as with philosophies, is not established.

The second challenge arises from the idea that these questions should not merely explore epistemological and ontological assumptions, while neglecting criticism of social, institutional, and regulatory conditions imposed on research practices. Earlier, we mentioned the way in which epistemic frames are inserted into methodology cycles, encouraging a certain outlining of the research objects, and leading to the use of certain techniques over others. For example, we have referred to the predominance of quantitative and experimental techniques, associated with objectivism and scientism, in certain currents of psychological research focused on the individual. It is now a matter of emphasizing that such conditioning gains normative strength through political and administrative regulations in the various institutional spaces where science is practiced, and that they appear in the form of imperatives to practice "true science" or "rigorous science."

An example of this can be observed in the relations between disciplines and some emergent fields. We have already mentioned the emergence of neurosciences and experimental studies whose influence on psychological research and theories cannot be minimized, and whose progress must be critically examined in order to avoid any reductionism of socio-cultural phenomena to biological ones; or in the field of social sciences, to the advance of *big data* and the application of exploratory/predictive techniques based on machine learning, that tend to underestimate the role of theory and explanatory-critical interest. In both cases, these are developments that, by dint of a rhetoric combining promises of objectivity and control, are promoted with a much broader propaganda and dissemination scope than science, and by new actors of knowledge, situated in the private sector, who, exerting pressure from outside the academy, aim to legitimize certain epistemic criteria. We feel the need to mention, as one of us has done in another work (Cas-

---

[13] Some of these have been explored by one of us in the field of psychology, particularly, in developmental psychology (e.g., Castorina, 2016).

torina, 2020), that these demands become institutionalized, as is the case, increasingly common in some North American universities, of including a chapter on neuroscience in any project of psychological research, in order to be considered valid. All this allows for us to demonstrate, as was suggested by Pierre Bourdieu (2000; Bourdieu & Wacquant, 1993), that science is a field of forces, where scientists carrying out the different programmes are in unequal positions regarding the distribution of power—or in this case the distribution of research funding—and the ability to defend a methodological design consistent with a proper EF.

Surely, a critical analysis of these impositions is difficult for researchers, given the institutional conditions of science production, where scientific vices tend to obscure such agreements, and where the dynamics of the "paper factories" leave little room for the creation of ideas, encouraging ritualistic reproduction (Castorina, 2015; González, 2018). To all this, corporatist vices in many universities' research management must be added, preventing the democratization of research institutes and secretariats, and undermining the formation of spaces in which to engage in a mature debate with all the actors involved in research.

Before moving on to the last level of discussion regarding the EF, we would like to briefly return to the issue of the relations between disciplines and emerging fields, in order to pose a question that, as far as we know, has not yet been considered. It addresses the EF's very conceptualisation: is it possible for transformations and innovations in particular aspects of the methodology cycle—for example, new techniques and methods, or new sources of information and data—to lead to changes in the EFs? And regarding the relations between disciplines, can such innovations lead to changes in ideological, evaluative or philosophical matters? Can new methods and techniques, together with new concepts, modify the EF's social space? What is the meaning of the controversies between concepts and arguments defined by the EF, regarding the transformations in research?

(4) Finally, we will refer to the EF in interdisciplinary research. This level is the most widespread and perhaps the most discussed of the four mentioned, due to the broad reception of complex systems theory in the Latin American community (González, 2018). It also faces us with the challenge of addressing some aspects that deserve in-depth elaboration.

Here we could insist on the need for greater conceptual elaboration that we mentioned as a challenge for the other levels of analysis, establishing a dialogue with other concepts proposed in studies regarding interdiscipline, such as "epistemic values" (Boix-mansilla, 2006), or "agreements upon the nature of the world" (Eigenbrode et al., 2007), or especially insist on the need to think about the organisational and institutional conditions of interdisciplinary collaboration. This includes issues such as the publication of results in an academic world in which specialization limits the publication spaces for cross-cutting issues, elaboration periods too short for the correct integration and discussion of different perspectives, and even the problem of the quantity and order of authorship, and its subsequent evaluation for each researcher's career. Moreover, in order to highlight the social and evaluative nature of the EF, we will briefly address the need to "open up" the "expert interdiscipline," proposed by García, to a dialogue with the communities involved in the problem towards which the project is directed. Here the challenge lies in including the perspective of the social actors involved, with the political meanings and objectives they attribute to social situations. This participation is proposed both for the problem's construction and for the debate on and evaluation of alternative scenarios, particularly in view of the eventual transformations of public policies, which are the essential culmination for a good part of interdisciplinary research. In order to facilitate these attempts, other authors have proposed—with different levels of preparation and testing—the incorporation of participatory modelling techniques (Amozurrutia, 2012; Rodríguez Zoya, 2017) or the use of qualitative techniques (Espejel et al., 2011) at the epistemic moment; and the organisation of seminars and working groups with local communities at the prospective moment, in order to ensure that the suggested actions and policies have sufficient legitimacy to be implemented[14]. A subsequent challenge is to start linking the reflection of these experiences and their impact on the concept of EF, to other developments that are being made regarding the study of public participation in the purpose, costs, and risks of scientific research (Collins & Evans, 2002; Gómez, 2014; Kitcher, 2001).

REFERENCES

Amozurrutia, J. A. (2012). *Complejidad y sistemas sociales: un modelo adaptativo para la investigación interdisciplinaria.* [Complexity and social systems: an adaptive model for interdisciplinary research]. UNAM, Centro de Investigaciones Interdisciplinarias en Ciencias y Humanidades.

Anderson, E. (2012). Feminist epistemology and philosophy of science, In E. N. Zalta (Ed.), *The Stanford Encyclopedia of philosophy* (Spring 2020 Edition), https://plato.stanford.edu/archives/spr2020/entries/feminism-epistemology/

Barreiro, A., & Castorina, J. A. (2015). La Creencia en un Mundo Justo como Trasfondo Ideológico de la Representación Social de la Justicia [Belief in a just world as ideological background for the social representation of justice]. *Revista Colombiana de Psicología, 24*(2), 331–345.

Becerra, G., & Castorina, J. A. (2016a). Acerca de la noción de "marco epistémico" del constructivismo. Una comparación con la noción de "paradigma" de Kuhn [About the constructivist notion of "epistemic frame." A comparison with Kuhn's "Paradigm"]. *Revista Iberoamericana de Ciencia, Tecnología y Sociedad, 11*(31), 9–28.

Becerra, G., & Castorina, J. A. (2016b). Una mirada social y política de la ciencia en la epistemología constructivista de Rolando García [A socio political view of the science in Rolando García's constructivist epistemology]. *Ciencia, Docencia y Tecnología, 27*(52), 329–350.

Becerra, G., & Castorina, J. A. (2018). Towards a dialogue among constructivist research programs. *Constructivist Foundations, 13*(2), 191–218.

---

[14] This point is further developed in another work (Becerra & Castorina, 2016b)

Bird, A. (2002). Kuhn's wrong turning. *Studies in History and Philosophy of Science*, *33*(3), 443–463.
Boix-mansilla, V. (2006). Interdisciplinary work at the frontier: An empirical examination of expert interdisciplinary epistemologies. *Issues in Integrative Studies*, *31*(24), 1–31.
Boom, J. (2009). Piaget on equilibration. In U. Müller, J. I. M. Carpendale, & L. Smith (Eds.), *The Cambridge companion to Piaget* (pp. 132–149). Cambridge University Press.
Bourdieu, P. (2000). *Pascalian meditations*. Stanford University Press.
Bourdieu, P., & Wacquant, L. (1993). *An Invitation of reflexive sociology*. Polity Press.
Brunetti, J., & Omart, E. B. (2010). El Lugar de la Psicología en la Epistemología de Kuhn: La posibilidad de una psicología de la investigación científica [The place of psychology in Kuhn's epistemology: The possibility of a scientific research psychology]. *Cinta de Moebio. Revista de Epistemología de Ciencias Sociales*, *38*, 110–121.
Castorina, J. A. (2003). Las epistemologías constructivistas ante el desafío de los saberes disciplinares [Some epistemological problems of psychological theory and psychopedagogical practice]. *Psykhe*, *12*(2), 15–28.
Castorina, J. A. (2008). El impacto de las representaciones sociales en la psicología de los conocimientos sociales: problemas y perspectivas [The impact of social representations on the psychology of social knowledge: issues and perspectives]. *Cadernos Da Pesquisa*, *38*(135), 757–776.
Castorina, J. A. (2007). El significado del análisis conceptual en psicología del desarrollo [Meaning of conceptual analysis in developmental psychology]. *Epistemología e Historia de La Ciencia*, *13*(13), 132–138.
Castorina, J. A. (2010). La Dialéctica en la Psicologia del Desarrollo: Relevancia y Significacion en la Investigación [Dialectic in developmental psychology: Its importance and significance in research]. *Psicologia: Reflexao e Critica*, *23*(3), 516–524.
Castorina, J. A. (2014a). La explicación para las novedades del desarrollo psicológico y su relación con las metateorías [Explanation of novelty in developmental psychology and its relation to meta-theory]. In A. Talak (Ed.), *La explicación en psicología* [Explanation in psychology] (pp. 57–76). Prometeo.
Castorina, J. A. (2014b). La psicología del desarrollo y la teoría de las representaciones sociales. La defensa de una relación de compatibilidad [Developmental psychology and social representations theory. An argument for their compatibility]. In J. A. Castorina & A. V. Barreiro (Eds.), *Representaciones sociales y prácticas en la psicogénesis del conocimiento social* [Social representations and practices in social knowledge psychogenesis]. Miño y Dávila Editores
Castorina, J. A. (2015). Condiciones institucionales y gestión académica de la investigación en la universidad pública [Institutional conditions and academic management of research in the public university]. *Sinéctica*, *44*, 2–14.
Castorina, J. A. (2019). ¿La teoría de las representaciones sociales se puede interpretar como un paradigma? Una discusión crítica [Is the social representation theory a paradigm? A critical discussion]. In S. Seidmann & N. Pievi (Eds.), *Identidades y conflictos sociales* [Identities and social conflicts] (pp. 347–358). Editorial de Belgrano.
Castorina, J. A. (2020). The importance of worldviews for developmental psychology. *Human Arenas*, *4*, 153–171. https://doi.org/10.1007/s42087-020-00115-9

Castorina, J. A., & Baquero, R. J. (2005). *Dialéctica y psicología del desarrollo. El pensamiento de Piaget y Vigotsky.* [Dialectics and developmental psychology. Piaget and Vigotsky's works]. Amorrortu Editores.
Castorina, J. A., & Barreiro, A. V. (2006). Las representaciones sociales y su horizonte ideológico. Una relación problemática [Social representations and ideology. A problematic relation]. *Boletín de Psicología, 86,* 7–25.
Castorina, J. A., Barreiro, A. V., Horn, A., Carreño, L., Lombardo, E., & Karabelnicof, D. (2010). La categoría de restricción en la psicología del desarrollo: revisión de un concepto [Restriction in developmental psychology: A conceptual revision]. In Castorina, J. (Ed.), *Desarrollo del conocimiento social. Prácticas, discursos y teoría* (pp. 237–255). Miño y Dávila.
Chapman, M. (1992). Equilibration and the dialectics of organization. In H. Beilin & P. Pufall (Eds.), *Piaget's theory: Prospects and possibilities* (pp. 39–59). Psychology Press.
Chiao, J. Y., Hariri, A. R., Harada, T., Mano, Y., Sadato, N., Parrish, T. B., & Iidaka, T. (2010). Theory and methods in cultural neuroscience. *Social Cognitive and Affective Neuroscience, 5*(2–3), 356–361.
Collins, H. M., & Evans, R. (2002). The third wave of science studies: Studies of expertise and experience. *Social Studies of Science, 32*(2), 235–296.
Cortés, F. (1991). La perversión empirista [Empiricist perversion]. *Estudios Sociológicos, 9*(26), 365–373.
Cortés, F. (2001). Nociones de la epistemología genética aplicadas a temas de discusión en las ciencias sociales. Un par de ejemplos [Genetic epistemology's notions applied to social sciences' topics. A few samples.]. *Estudios Sociológicos, XIX,* 641–651.
Cortés, F., & Antón, M. G. (1997). El constructivismo genético y las ciencias sociales: Líneas básicas para una reorganización epistemológica [Genetic constructivism and social sciences. Some lines for an epistemological reorganization]. In R. García (Ed.), *La epistemología genética y la ciencia contemporánea. Homenaje a Jean Piaget en su centenario* [Genetic epistemology and contemporary science: Tribute to Piaget on his 100th birthday] (pp. 69–90). Gedisa.
Douglas, H. (2007). Rejecting the ideal of value-free science. In J. Dupre, H. Kincaid, & A. Wylie (Eds.), *Value-free science: Ideal or illusion* (pp. 120–139). Oxford University Press.
Eagleton, T. (1997). *Ideology. An introduction.* Verso.
Eigenbrode, S. D., O'Rourke, M., Wulfhorst, J. D., Althoff, D. M., Goldberg, C. S., Merrill, K., Morse, W., Nielsen-Pincus, M., Stephens, J., Winowiecki, L., & Bosque-Pérez, N. A. (2007). Employing philosophical dialogue in collaborative science. *BioScience, 57*(1), 55.
Elliot, T., Killen, M., & Helwig, C. C. (1987). Morality: Its structure, functions, and vagaries. In J. Kagan & S. Lamb (Eds.), *The emergence of morality in young children* (pp. 155–243). University of Chicago Press.
Espejel, B. O., Berhmann, G. D., Frich, B. A., Antonio, M., Guzmán, E., & González, M. (2011). Sistemas complejos e investigación participativa. Consideraciones teóricas, metodológicas y epistémicas para el estudio de las Organizaciones Sociales hacia la Sustentabilidad [Complex systems and participatory research. Theoretical, methodological and epistemological considerations for studying sustainability-oriented

social organizations]. *Sociedades Rurales, Producción y Medio Ambiente*, *11*(22). 133–150.
Fuller, S. (2005). *Kuhn vs. Popper. The Struggle for the Soul of Science.* Columbia University Press.
García, R. (1997). *La epistemología genética y la ciencia contemporánea: homenaje a Jean Piaget en su centenario.* [Genetic epistemology and contemporary science: Tribute to Piaget in his 100th birthday]. Gedisa.
García, R. (2000). *El conocimiento en construcción: De las formulaciones de Jean Piaget a la teoría de sistemas complejos.* [Knowledge in construction. From Jean Piaget's formulations to the complex systems theory]. Gedisa.
García, R. (2001). Fundamentación de una epistemología en las ciencias sociales [Foundations of epistemology in social sciences]. *Estudios Sociológicos, XIX*(57), 615–620.
García, R. (2006). *Sistemas complejos. Conceptos, método y fundamentación epistemológica de la investigación interdisciplinaria.* [Complex systems. Concepts, methods, and epistemological foundation for interdisciplinary research]. Gedisa.
Gómez, R. (2014). *La dimensión valorativa de las ciencias. Hacia una filosofía política.* [The valorative dimension of science. Towards a political philosophy]. Universidad Nacional de Quilmes.
González, J. A. (2018). *¡No está muerto quien pelea! Homenaje a la obra de Rolando V. García Boutigue.* [He who fights is not dead! Tribute to Rolando Garcías's work] Centro de investigaciones interdisciplinarias en ciencias y Humanidades.
Harding, S. (1995). "Strong objectivity": A response to the new objectivity question. *Synthese*, *104*(3), 331–349.
Inhelder, B., García, R., & Voneche, J. (1981). *Jean Piaget. Epistemología genética y equilibración.* [Jean Piaget. Genetic epistemology and equilibration]. Fundamentos.
Jodelet, D. (1985). La representación social: fenómenos, conceptos y teoría [Social representations: Phenomena, concepts and theory]. In S. Moscovici (Ed.), *Psicología Social II* [Social psychology II] (pp. 17–40). Paidós.
Kitchener, R. F. (1985). Genetic epistemology, history of science and genetic psychology. *Synthese*, *65*(1), 3–31.
Kitchener, R. F. (1987). Genetic epistemology, equilibration and the rationality of scientific change. *Studies in History and Philosophy of Science Part A*, *18*(3), 339–366.
Kitcher, P. (2001). *Science, truth, and democracy.* Oxford University Press.
Kolstad, A. (2015). How culture shapes mind, neurobiology and behaviour. *British Journal of Education, Society & Behavioural Science*, *6*(4), 255–274.
Kuhn, T. S. (1970). *The structure of scientific revolutions.* Cambridge University Press.
Kuhn, T. S. (1977). *The essential tension. Selected studies in scientific tradition and change.* Chicago: The University of Chicago.
Kuhn, T. S. (2000). *The road since the structure.* The University of Chicago.
Leman, P. (1998). Social relations, social influence, and the development of knowledge. *Society*, *7*(1998), 41–56.
Longino, H. (2015). The social dimensions of scientific knowledge. In E. N. Zalta (Ed.), *The Stanford encyclopedia of philosophy* (Spring 2020 Edition). http://plato.stanford.edu/archives/spr2015/entries/scientific-knowledge-social
Martí, E., & Rodríguez, C. (2012). *After Piaget.* Transaction Publishers.
Newton-Smith, W. H. (1981). *The rationality of science.* Routledge.

Overton, W. F. (2012). Evolving scientific paradigms: Retrospective and prospective. In L. L'Abate (Ed.), *Paradigms in theory construction* (pp. 31–66). Springer.
Overton, W. F. (2014). The process-relational paradigm and relational-developmental-systems metamodel as context. *Research in Human Development, 11*(4), 323–331.
Piaget, J. (1970). *Genetic epistemology*. The Norton Library.
Piaget, J. (1971). *Structuralism*. Routledge.
Piaget, J. (1985). *The equilibration of cognitive structures: The central problem of intellectual development*. University of Chicago Press.
Piaget, J., & García, R. (1982). *Psicogenesis e historia de la ciencia*. Siglo XXI. [Piaget, J., & Garcia, R. (1989). *Psychogenesis and the history of science*. (H. Feider, Trans.). Columbia University Press
Psaltis, C., & Duveen, G. (2006). Social relations and cognitive development: The influence of conversation type and representations of gender. *European Journal of Social Psychology, 36*(3), 407–430.
Psaltis, C., Duveen, G., & Perret-Clermont, A. N. (2009). The social and the psychological: Structure and context in intellectual development. *Human Development, 52*(5), 291–312.
Reisch, G. (2005). *How the cold war transformed philosophy of science. To the icy slopes of logic*. Cambridge University Press.
Rodríguez Zoya, L. G. (2017). Contribución a la crítica de la teoría de los sistemas complejos : bases para un programa de investigación [Contributions to the critique of complex systems theory: Foundations for a research program]. *Estudios Sociológicos, XXXVI*(106), 73–98.
Torres Nafarrate, J. (1997). Lineamientos para la comprensión de un nuevo concepto de sistema (la perspectiva de Niklas Luhmann) [How to understand the new concept of system (according to Niklas Luhmann)]. In R. García (Ed.), *La epistemología genética y la ciencia contemporánea: homenaje a Jean Piaget en su centenario* [Genetic epistemology and contemporary science: Tribute to Piaget on his 100th birthday] (pp. 185–202). Gedisa.
Valsiner, J. (2014). Needed for cultural psychology: Methodology in a new key. *Culture and Psychology, 20*(1), 3–30.
Wainryb, C. (1991). Understanding differences in moral judgments: The role of informational assumptions. *Child Development, 62*(4), 840–851.
Wainryb, C., & Turiel, E. (1993). Conceptual and informational features in moral decision making. *Educational Psychologist, 28*(3), 205–218.
Witherington, D. C. (2007). The dynamic systems approach as metatheory for developmental psychology. *Human Development, 50*(2–3), 127–153.
Yocelevszky, R. (1997). Sociogénesis y sociología: el cambio de paradigma en las ciencias sociales latinoamericanas. [Sociogenesis and sociology: Paradigm change in latin american social sciences] In R. García (Ed.), *La epistemología genética y la ciencia contemporánea: homenaje a Jean Piaget en su centenario* [Genetic epistemology and contemporary science: Tribute to Piaget on his 100th birthday] (pp. 153–170). Gedisa.
Zittoun, T., Gillespie, A., Cornish, F., & Psaltis, C. (2007). The metaphor of the triangle in theories of human development. *Human Development, 50*(4), 208–229.

CHAPTER 2

HISTORICAL CONDITIONS OF KNOWLEDGE CONSTRUCTION

A Foucauldian Perspective

Tomas Baquero Cano

(...) To all those agoraphobics of history and time,
to all those confusing rupture and irrationality (...)
—Michel Foucalt, The Archaeology of Knowledge[1]

To us, history is the epistemological laboratory of science.
—Rolando García, The Problems of Knowledge Are One and the Same[2]

INTRODUCTION[3]

Some kind of allegation runs through *The Archaeology of Knowledge* from beginning to end: when it comes to thinking, the habit of assuming so many previous forms of continuity should concern us. A habit that makes us quickly take an ob-

---

[1] Translated by the author from the Spanish edition
[2] Translated by the author from the Spanish edition
[3] Part of the work presented here was included in two articles: "Fetishism of the Disciplines: a Dialogue between Michel Foucault and Rolando García," *Revista Kula. Antropólogxs del Atlántico*

ject as a starting point, a place from which to think its transformations, processes, and limits, as secondary aspects with respect to this object. It is the allegation that what we think, whatever it is, is already a given, as if problematization were a point of arrival and not all the work's starting point. For this reason, Foucauldian archaeology begins by disposing of all immediate evidence of unity, whether in the form of a book, work, an author, a science, or a discipline: it receives them restlessly, suspecting they are merely neutral outlines to be filled with thought. Far from being an invitation to relativism, in which all distinctions would have the same value, there is a concrete question about the historicity of the categories used in thought, taken to the utmost consequences: not categories that also have a history, but always already history, in which modes of thought emerge and are conformed. The depth of this Foucauldian text from the late 1960s may lie here: starting from the question of the historicity of thought modes, we can only verify that the continuous, the identical, what is repeated, as well as the ruptures, "far from manifesting that fundamental and reassuring inertia which we like to use as a criterion for change, they are themselves actively, regularly formed" (Foucault, 1969/2013, p. 227).[4] Thus, the problem with the continuities assumed in thought is not so much whether or not these objects of knowledge "exist" (as some may twist Foucault's words), but the difficulty they pose when it comes to thinking about and knowing novelty. It is a very special way of attending to criticism—both Kantian and anti-Kantian—that does not aim to make us pointlessly suspect of any starting point for knowledge, but rather tries to introduce the consideration of this kind of inertia of forms that many times seem immutable, almost timeless: that "silent and naively motionless basis" upon which we think (1966, p. 18).[5] The book as a form no longer harbors doubts like at the beginning of our era, when the authorship of a writing circulating between schools could only be confirmed by an amicable circle linked to an entire way of life (Hadot, 1995). However, this historical dimension does not lead us to disaggregate it, or stop relying on it: as Judith Revel points out, reading Foucault as an advocacy for the discontinuity of thought would make us lose sight of the presence of a *true thought of the discontinuous* (2010/2014).

The question is the contemporary, the possibility of knowing today. Agamben said in his article "What is Contemporary?" that "the access to the present necessarily takes the form of archaeology" (2009, p. 17).[6] The task begins with archaeology because, in principle, any critical consideration of the present should always begin by verifying the historicity of everything presented as universal or as a naturalized foundation. In other words, the archaeological perspective reveals this absence of foundation, absence of *arché*, to redirect these continuities to their

---

Sur, 2019, and "Crítica práctica y sujetos de conocimiento: de *The Archaelogy of Knowledge* al perspectivismo en la genealogía," *PSocial. Revista de Investigación en Psicología Social*, 2018.
[4] Translated by the author from the Spanish edition
[5] Translated by the author from the Spanish edition
[6] Translated by the author from the Spanish edition

historical character. For this reason, perhaps, our purpose is not so much celebrating coincidences with Foucault's works, or considering him as an authority, but recovering this problem of thought that, as we believe, is not at all speculative work, but rather aims to operate within research and concrete practice. Given certain conditions for knowledge, both individual and at the level of scientific disciplines, Foucauldian archaeology allows for a possible interruption of this historical inertia of ideas, at the level of *knowledge*, seeking something as valuable as is, at a given moment, the establishment of a *possibility* (Foucault, 1969/2013). In short, the question is how it is possible to conceive something novel at a certain moment. Does thought or does it not have a function in the midst of concrete research and practices? We follow—or at least try to—the maxim written by Foucault in his prologue to the English edition of *The Anti-Oedipus*, on the matter of political action, but with the exact same relevance for research:

> Do not use thought to anchor political practice in Truth; do not use political action to discredit, as mere speculation, a line of thought. Use political practices as intensifiers of thought, and theories as multipliers of forms and domains for the intervention of political action. (1983, p. 14)

SCIENCE AND KNOWLEDGE, OR ABOUT THE TWO HISTORIES OF TRUTH

At the time, the canonically called Foucauldian archaeological period was the subject of various criticisms, especially due to *The Order of Things* (1994), influencing the distinction between science and knowledge, to which Foucault dedicates the penultimate section of *The Archaeology of Knowledge* (1982) (Castro, 1995, 2015). Piaget himself would not have been the exception and is perhaps a clear spokesperson for those criticisms: "The last word of the archaeology of reason is that reason is transformed without reason" (1974, p. 154).[7] We soon observe the problem pointed out by Revel, not without good reasons: there is confusion between the discontinuity of thought and the thought of the discontinuous. In order to get out of this quagmire we think it is necessary to reconstruct this difference—existing in Foucault—between science and knowledge, that, four years later, would give rise to what he calls two *histories of truth* (1973/2013).

Knowledge is a strategic concept in Foucault's thought, both in his own work and for those of us who wish to think in his line of thought, with him as a starting point. Overall, it is the specific territory addressed by and at the same time founding archaeology. Defined as "the group of elements regularly formed by a discursive practice" (1969/2013, p. 237),[8] Foucault points out that archaeology does not aim directly at scientific disciplines, but at discourses.[9] He wonders about the

---

[7] Translated by the author from the Spanish edition
[8] Translated by the author from the Spanish edition
[9] To Foucault, discourses are not defined by what "was meant to be said" nor by what "has not been said" (1968, p. 685), but by the formation rules of its objects, the definition of thresholds from

rules giving rise to what can be spoken of at a given time in concrete discursive practices, to the production of its objects and theoretical selections. He addresses the processes and effects that allow for something to be acceptable at a given moment in knowledge, the historical conditions enabling its emergence (1978/2015), "that *from which* knowledge and theories have been made possible" (1966, p. 15, the italics are ours).[10] The task of defining the rules that at a given time defined what was spoken of, how this was preserved, its appropriation by individuals and institutions, and the forms in which discourses of other eras were reactivated, is called the description of the *archive* (1968/1994) by Foucault. Thus, we claim that *knowledge* is a strategic concept since it opens up a territory parallel to the one of scientific disciplines, while conversing with it: within the general and extensive magma of knowledge of a given era, of that what can be spoken of, there are daily practices and, in addition, certain discourses that may become scientific. Science is "located" in the knowledge domain, it is rooted in it as it takes into account certain historical coordinates that make it possible for something to be thought of, but installs its own *thresholds* of epistemologization and scientificity (Foucault, 1969/2013).

An interesting example to illustrate this distinction and to make it tangible—extensively commented in medical science due to its importance—is the case of Ignaz Semmelweis. In the midst of the 19th century, when the existence of microorganisms was unthinkable, medical procedures would be performed without any kind of asepsis method, in hygienic conditions that—inconceivable today—did not trouble anyone at all. Hempel tells us: "Semmelweis was distressed when he saw that a large proportion of the women who had given birth in that division contracted a serious and often fatal disease known as puerperal fever or postpartum fever" (1966/2003, p. 16).[11] In 1844, figures reached 8.2% of deliveries (260 deaths per year), while in another maternity of the same hospital the percentage barely exceeded 2%. After rejecting several hypotheses of the time, including the influence of the atmosphere, psychology, and whether the patients laid on their backs or on their sides, he reached the conclusion that it was the "cadaverous matter" carried by the doctors themselves that caused the disease (they would attend to women in labour after performing autopsies, having barely sanitized themselves). The conditions of possibility of knowledge were different to such

---

which new rules (of scientific validation, for example) may be installed, and the possibility of defining them according to their relation with other discourses and the extra-discursive context in which they operate: "institutions, social relations, economic, and political conjuncture" (1968, p. 676). The latter "are not "reflected," "translated," or "expressed" in concepts, statements or methods (...): they modify the formation rules" (1968, p. 690). During an international event organised by the *Centre Michel Foucault* four years after his death, there was a small debate on the concept of "discourse": the arguments varied between understanding it as a clear structuralist inspiration (stemming from Lévi-Strauss and Saussure), with more or less specificity in his own work, or, as suggested by Paul Veyne, it could simply be a linguistic fashion (Frank, 1988).

[10] Translated by the author from the Spanish edition
[11] Translated by the author from the Spanish edition

an extent that these theories were rejected—understood as an unjustified blame on the medical staff—ruining Semmelweis's life. He drifted away from his profession and lost his mental health. Approximately thirty years later, microorganisms entered scientific conceptualizations and Semmelweiss was vindicated. It is interesting to wonder, then, what it means to ask oneself what was "possible" to think at a given moment? Knowledge in Foucault seeks to deal with a difficult concept, that of *historical a priori*: blowing up Kantian thought, he aims to put a name on how the very conditions of possibility of something being thought are in turn historical (Castro, 2013). As we said before, this limit does not only involve scientific knowledge, but it contains, in a wider sense, the conditions of what can be thought at a given moment in time.

Foucault frequently mentions two historical moments in order to produce some kind of perspective when wondering about the transformation that has taken place: in some way this is what we need to do when approaching Semmelweis's work, to take a distance from the rejection provoked by the absence of hygiene in medical procedures. In a schematic way—and just as an approximation that perhaps we should not take too far—Semmelweis's case illustrates the difference between the historical possibilities of something being thought, the archaeological territory addressing the ways in which discursive practices produce their objects, and the non-discursive ways in which they circulate (for example, the hospital). On the other hand, it reveals how under certain conditions, from a certain territory of knowledge, some knowledge may cross a threshold and thus become scientific knowledge. In this way, explains Foucault, these thresholds of epistemologization imply specific "norms of verification and coherence" that, when reached—no longer depending solely on the territory of knowledge—acquire their own statute, thus also implying certain thresholds of "scientificity" (1969/2013).[12] To Foucault, philosophy "has lost its privileged status in relation to knowledge in general and science in particular" with the appearance of human sciences. "It no longer legislates, nor judges" (1967/1994, p. 580).[13] Archaeology does not address this issue, but rather deals with the ways in which these thresholds have been crossed, under what conditions of possibility. How is it possible that at a given moment microorganisms, unthinkable before, became thinkable, and the possible objects of scientific study? What is with this transformation of what is thought of at a certain moment, that even without precise scientific knowledge, we are now disgusted with this absence of asepsis? A question that is different from both epistemology and the history of ideas, as conceived by Foucault and certainly nourished by them. It is neither a work on the validation rules of scientific knowledge, nor a history of the influences and continuities in knowledge: archaeology is situated in this strange substrate uniting what is transcendental and what is historical.

---

[12] Translated by the author from the Spanish edition
[13] Translated by the author from the French edition

This distinction between science and knowledge is of particular interest to us, since it may allow for the delimitation of scientific knowledge's autonomy and, at the same time, for the analysis of its roots in knowledge, within the broad framework of what is historically possible. This distinction then leads Foucault to speak, as we anticipated, of two histories of truth:

> The first is *an internal history of truth*, corrected through following its own principles of regulation: the history of truth as made in or from the history of *science*. On the other hand, I believe that in society, or at least in our societies, there are other places where truth is formed, where a certain number of game rules are defined, from which we see certain forms of subjectivity arise, object domains, and types of *knowledge*. Therefore, parting from this, we can make *an external, exterior history of truth*. (1973/2013, p. 15, the italics are ours)[14]

Notwithstanding, it is necessary to clarify where we are in Foucauldian thought. Although Foucault's perspective is nourished from the history of science in general, for his work he has chosen "discourses that do not have the strongest epistemological structure (mathematics or physics), but the densest and most complex field of positivity (medicine, economics, human sciences)" (1968/1994, p. 688).[15] This *internal* history, understood as the "epistemological history of sciences," is what Canguilhem and Bachelard carried out, according to Foucault (1969/2013). To him, the purpose was to create a *history of discourse*, therefore his archaeological project was directed either to the analysis of theoretical models common to different discourses from the same era (the *episteme*[16] from *The order of things*), or to the search for the relations between a discourse and its non-discursive domain (medical discourse and its material conditions in *The Birth of the Clinic*) (Foucault, 1967b/1994, p. 590).[17] At this archaeological stage we can already find elements of this "external" aspect, for example, when observing that "clinical discourse is not formulated in the same places, it does not have the same registration procedures, it does not spread, nor accumulate, nor is it preserved or refuted in the same manner as was medical discourse in the 18th century" (1968/1994, p. 678).[18] Hospital care is now a possible place of observation, there are new ways of teaching medicine, and a new role for medical discourse in population policies (1968/1994, p. 690). However, one of the main methodological limitations of archaeology is its difficulty to understand the ways in which these transformations

---

[14] Translated by the author from the Spanish edition
[15] Translated by the author from the French edition
[16] The *episteme* corresponds to what Foucault has called an interdiscursive space of analysis, "it is the set of relations that can be discovered, for a given time, between sciences, when analysing them at the level of discursive regularities" (1969, p. 249). It is therefore "an open and without doubt indefinitely describable field of relations" (1968, p. 676). This is accurate to the point where, two years after *The order of things*, Foucault mentions that he is working on *another* archaeology of human sciences, since he has written only *one* (1968, p. 676).
[17] Translated by the author from the French edition
[18] Translated by the author from the French edition

occur (Dreyfus & Rabinow, 2001). It is the subsequent genealogical period—introducing concepts such as the *dispositive*—that makes it possible to conceive them, with the growing consideration of what is extra-discursive.

Our purpose is to address the transition towards that period, in order to pose questions regarding this transformation. Even so we wish to preserve this specific register of archaeology since it allows us to address the domain of scientific knowledge. We believe that here, we may find the elements allowing us to address the idea of an "external history of truth," but we would like to use these tools for a re-reading of his archaeological writings, trying, at the same time, to take into account the transformation and specificity of scientific knowledge.[19] In this way, we can think about how contingency at the level of the "external" history of truth, that is, at the level of knowledge, may coexist without coming into tension with the validation modes of a given scientific knowledge. Certainly there was no need for the possibility to think about microorganisms at a given moment. No historical law led to this point, which does not imply that scientific knowledge built on this modification of knowledge is in any sense a mere relativity. The contingency of its historical existence does not imply the contingency of its knowledge status.[20]

We believe these brief considerations enable us to introduce some of the reasons why these archaeological questions might contribute to the constructivist perspective, particularly concerning two points. On the one hand, the importance of disciplines when thinking about knowledge production, and their connection to the constraints of the social context. On the other hand, the ways of considering subjects of knowledge. We will now address both points, proposing certain coordinates that may enable the *use* of Foucauldian thought.

CHALLENGING THE DISCIPLINES

How is it that, at certain times, under certain circumstances, along with certain practices, one thinks what has not been thought before? How do researchers of different disciplines interfere? With this question, and following Foucault in his concern about the way in which forms of continuity numb thought, we suspect the disciplines may be a departure point. A suspicion that, as we would like to propose, might be a point of approach to some of the problems raised by Rolando García: without comparing theoretical models, we believe it poses some challenges and questions that could be taken as a reference in one sense or the other.

---

[19] Ilya Prigogine and Isabelle Stengers refer to "an "external" history of science in a similar way, that is, the description of the relation between form and content of the scientific corpus and social context" (1979/2004, p. 74).

[20] To illustrate using the words of Foucault himself: "What was a dead end for a long time, one day becomes a way out; a lateral test becomes a central problem around which others begin to gravitate; a slightly divergent approach becomes a fundamental rupture: the discovery of non-cellular fermentation—a marginal phenomenon in the domain of Pasteurian microbiology—did not imply an essential rupture until the day physiology of enzymes was developed" (1985, p. 770).

In a way, wondering about the disciplines involves wondering on how we converse with what has already been thought, how a certain knowledge is inscribed in relation to what has already been said. As a background, it may be useful to recall Heidegger's observation (1988) regarding the history of thought. He said that penetrating these forces, that what has already been thought, is not merely about gaining momentum from the place seemingly reached in the projects and the intentions of past times, as if they were finished things, closed upon themselves: what is already thought is merely a preparation of what is not yet thought of. Far from being somewhat abstract, it means that knowledge is produced on something that did not previously exist in the disciplines addressing it.

In his work *Sistemas complejos* [Complex Systems], Rolando García explains that the difficulty of starting from the disciplines as a given, arises from concrete problems in the research on complex systems, far from originating in speculative reflections. In the face of a complex study object—in his case climate systems and drought—a great impotence in knowledge production arises from the "impossibility of considering particular aspects of a phenomenon, process or situation from a specific discipline" (2007, p. 21).[21] The impossibility of this labelling leads to the consideration of a certain problem as a *complex reality*, requiring for its scientific treatment a reconsideration of the way in which the link between disciplines and their objects is conceived. Interdiscipline is a possibility to research complex systems, given that due to their heterogeneity they belong to various disciplinary fields. It does not imply the mere sum of perspectives when addressing an object, but involves a reformulation of the object itself through the reconsideration of the questions leading to research (2007). The gathering of disciplines is not only about the approach, but also about the planning of what is researched: "the integration of these different approaches in order to—that is, prior to—the delimitation of a problem" (2007, p. 33).[22] The first challenge of this specific strategy is to define the problem it is addressing, to focus on *what* will be studied, which is not data available in advance in the disciplines as they are given. The delimitation and differentiation of the totalities to study, in order to reach a possible disciplinary approach and subsequent constructive integration of the object. Also, these problems do not arise in a static manner, but must be constantly reformulated.

In this sense, García points out that one of the fundamental problems of interdisciplinary work does not concern so much the disciplines themselves, but those working with them. It is, in a way, a reflection on one's own belonging to a discipline, in light of interdisciplinary dialogue and the formulation of problems. An interesting consideration is that, given this delimitation problem, "each researcher must take a step back from his discipline's specific study objectives" (2007, p. 68).[23] Both conceptually and through the connection between their research and social relations in general, disciplines have certain scopes and limitations that,

---

[21] Translated by the author from the Spanish edition
[22] Translated by the author from the Spanish edition
[23] Translated by the author from the Spanish edition

ultimately, reflect on their researchers. What appears as an automatism of thought makes us consider them as a naturalized starting point for knowledge, or, in Alicia Stolkiner's words (1987), the fetishism surrounding them. It is not a question, then, of denying or rejecting them, but rather of "not assuming as natural and immutable the categorization of sciences that arose from a certain social demand, and perhaps, is useless for another" (Stolkiner, 1987, p. 315).[24]

Following García, this issue requires at the same time "a common conceptual base, and a shared conception of scientific research and its relations with society" (2007, p. 33).[25] Of course, the need for a study project emerges from its social context, but, at the same time, the latter strongly influences the questions formulated in it. This particularly occurs when it comes to objects in which social factors play important roles, or when the social dimension will directly be influenced by this knowledge. Researchers start from a certain social context, take interests and questions from it, possibilities and limitations to formulate their theoretical problems and, in the case of social sciences, they are also directed at them. Hence, the importance of considering the relation between science and society.

Together with Piaget, García establishes the concept of *epistemic framework*, born from the need to consider this connection, at the same time limiting and enabling. In *Psicogénesis e historia de la ciencia* [Psychogenesis and the History of Science], the authors award a broad meaning to this concept, as a world conception or worldview (*Weltanschauung*), referring in a more or less general way to those concepts emerging from social life, modulating the formulation of research questions (Piaget & García, 1982/1984). To us, the most relevant of this concept is the possibility to think about the connection with social factors, and the role they effectively play in research. This becomes clear in its own definition, quickly situating it as a concept dedicated to thinking about concrete research: it is a "system of thought, rarely made explicit, permeating the conceptions of a certain moment in time in a given culture, influencing what kind of theorizations emerge in various fields of knowledge" (García, 2000, p. 157), such as the "system of implicit or naturalized ideas, expressed as a judgment on what is considered "scientifically acceptable" at a given historical moment" (Piaget & García, 1982/1984, p. 229).[26] To the authors, the epistemic quality and precision of the formulation of problems and questions fundamentally depend on whether teams can—through an effort of clarification—work with a "common" epistemic framework: revising, questioning, and demanding reflection upon oneself and the historical context.[27]

---

[24] Translated by the author from the Spanish edition
[25] Translated by the author from the Spanish edition
[26] Translated by the author from the Spanish edition
[27] Although it is not the central point of our work, we cannot fail to mention the proximity between the concepts of *epistemic framework* in García and Piaget, and Foucault's *episteme*, both from their revisited Kantian perspective, as well as in a general manner, in relation to the question about the social-historical emergence of certain conditions enabling knowledge. When desiring to make the two perspectives work together, we believe it fruitless to seek their equivalence, insofar as it results in the aforementioned misunderstanding between science and knowledge, which confuses

As we have said earlier, certain challenges and questions—if not common, then at least proximate—may allow for an exchange between this perspective and Foucauldian works. In general, it seems to be that there lies the question about the historical and social conditions of knowledge construction, that, in different ways, play an important role and present a task necessary when it comes to understanding scientific knowledge. At the same time, although in a different manner, they are complex formulations of this relation, seeming to head towards a common problem: the need to understand these historical conditions as that what enables research, and at the same time, as what may hinder its progress. This supposes a very particular way of reflecting upon or criticizing current knowledge, or in the words of Bachelard: "One knows *against* previous knowledge" (1975/1938, p. 15).[28] Even if to Foucault new knowledge is not strictly *opposed* to previous knowledge (Yuing Alfaro, 2017), that what we know today must still be the subject of possible reflection in order to enable the transformation of knowledge. This is not a task outside of research practice, but precisely internal to it, as we will elaborate in the next section. It seems possible to approximate Foucault's perspective to that of constructivism in this challenge (rather than in ways of evading it): the conditions for knowledge construction do not arise from some kind of pure epistemic subject that has been degraded, but from "limitations" that are, at the same time, the even historical possibility of these formulations. They are *constraints*, limiting and enabling at the same time (Castorina, 2010): both a tool and a task.

CRITICISM AND META-THEORETICAL REFLECTION

> It is not a question of "learning more things," but rather of "thinking differently" about the problems arising in research, that is, of reformulating the conception of science practice.
> —*Rolando García,* Sistemas complejos [Complex Systems]

We will start—in a really broad sense—with the question regarding the historical conditions of knowledge production, both enabling and limiting these exercises. When thinking about meta-theoretical reflection or criticism, perhaps one of the first challenges is to conceptualize the relation with the worldview emerging

---

that what motivates the two perspectives: as in Piaget's above-mentioned criticism of Las *palabras y las cosas*, focusing on the "arbitrariness" of this concept (cf. 1974, "Un estructuralismo sin estructuras" [A Structuralism without Structures]). Following the revisited specific levels of analysis of the *epistemic framework* by Becerra and Castorina (2015), we believe that for each case a dialogue may be established, in accordance to its role in the specific research process, either with the general concept of knowledge or discursive formation, or expressing criticism of the present. That is, that what we understand as the link between internal conditions of the scientific discourses" formation, their social conditions and their connection as a practice with other non-discursive practices.

[28] Translated by the author from the Spanish edition

from social aspects in a way that is not reduced to an ideological domination that we need to "overcome." The question regarding "ideology" is present in both Foucault and García and Piaget, influenced by their era, since it was common currency to wonder about the link between science and social aspects, between intellectuality and power, as seen in Althusser, for example, or even Canguilhem. In a way, both in the case of the *epistemic framework* and in Foucauldian archaeology, this link is not considered as an "imposition" on knowledge, as extrinsic determinations, but rather as conditions of possibility, limiting and enabling at the same time, a starting point (possibly materialistic), and not merely an impurity to dissolve (cf. Piaget & García, 1982/1984; Foucault, 1975/2009).

Both perspectives have their ways of accounting for this issue. Through the concept of *Weltanschauung*, understood as a worldview, Piaget and García argue that while there is no "imposition," the problem posed by the *epistemic framework* is still an ideological problem (1982/1984). On the other hand, Foucault dismisses this concept, considering it part of a history of ideas foreign to his work (1963; 1969/2013). In regard to the concept of "ideology," there is a broad discussion, and it often abounds in interpretations aiming to find a logic of state apparatus, unconfessed in their interpretations on power (e. g. Žižek, 2008), which, in our view, is unfair. Without wanting to enter into this discussion, we wonder whether, perhaps paradoxically, it is not of greater potency to direct this ideological question more to the archaeological phase than to the genealogical one. Particularly to Foucault's comments in *The Archaeology of Knowledge*, for that is precisely where he situates, once again, the relation between discourses and what is extra-discursive. We believe that in these different standpoints regarding this concept (whether characterized as a worldview, or as in Foucault's case that we will develop later), in a sense, the ways of addressing the question of ideology suppose, at the same time, specific ways of thinking strategies to overcome obstacles for the emergence of novelty, that is, ways to deal with it. This is where we would like to broaden the meta-theoretical reflection.

Following Castorina (2007), we believe meta-theoretical reflection is not an extra-disciplinary tool, rather it is internal to the discipline itself; at least this is doubtlessly the case for psychology. There, for example, the concept of *epistemic framework* functions as a concrete tool supporting the revision of implicit assumptions of researchers, of those producing theory (Becerra & Castorina, 2015). Therefore, we are interested in a small comment made by García, saying it is a thought system *rarely made explicit*. It is not necessary to consider he is saying this is actually achievable in order to reveal the problem: what kind of critical connection can we sustain with those obstacles preventing novelty in knowledge, when, at the same time, they are the very conditions enabling our own knowledge? Does the revision of our own conditions of knowledge arise from practices and reflections emerging from those same conditions? How can we take a "distance" to what is limiting and at the same time enabling? In our view, it would be interesting to converse with Foucault upon these questions, based on the way in which he has managed to formulate them and put them to work, in his own project and for his own purposes.

Although Foucault does not comment explicitly upon this, we believe it is possible to think about the question of ideology from his point of view, from his archaeological phase, precisely at the centre of the problem we have mentioned: in *The Archaeology of Knowledge* Foucault states that "if the question of ideology may be asked of science, it is in so far as science, without being identified with knowledge, but without either effacing or excluding it, is localized in it" (1969/2013, p. 241)[29][30]. While distinguishing these two levels, these two histories of truth, how do we consider the effects on science of this second history of truth of the struggles within the field of knowledge, the point of intersection? What does the inscription of a science in the general sphere of knowledge mean to Foucault? First of all, he says, "it is the question of its existence as a discursive practice and of its functioning among other practices" (1969/2013, p. 241).[31] According to the author, discursive practices are inserted within the general domain of all practices, whether discursive or not: appropriations, uses, and incidental interactions are not only not external to them, but are true "formative elements" (1969/2013, p. 92) of knowledge. As we have mentioned, this implies a particular way of thinking the discourses" uses and appropriations, but also modifications as concrete as the questioning of the hospital structure at the beginning of the 19th century for the discourse of medicine (is the hospital or social life the best place to heal?), or the way in which university education is managed or limits the practice of medicine by layman (Foucault, 1963). Hybrid discussions addressing both disciplinary and social aspects, and the questions that medical discourse may pose: it is not about reflections or translations, but rather about modifying the *rules* of formation (1968/1994).

Regarding criticism of this distinction between discursive and non-discursive practices, Laclau and Mouffe (1985) make a very thorough observation concerning a passage by Foucault: if all these so-called non-discursive instances "are not simply juxtaposed by a series of historical contingencies, it is because it [the discourse of medicine] makes use of this group of relations constantly" (Foucault, 1969/2013, p. 74).[32] Even if they play a formative role, all these levels, such as technical and institutional levels, could only be articulated in relation to the discourse of the discipline in question. Partly, the question is the place given to the idea of *discourse*—very costly according to the authors of this observation—but we believe that even preserving this distinction from the non-discursive, there is

---

[29] Translated by the author from the French edition
[30] In the preface of his book *Ideología y racionalidad en la historia de las ciencias de la vida* [Ideology and Rationality in the History of the Life Sciences], Canguilhem himself points out—with regard to *The archaeology of knowledge*—that his "relative analyses have been very useful to him when it comes to scientific ideology" (1977, p. 10).
[31] Translated by the author from the Spanish edition
[32] Translated by the author from the Spanish edition

another nuance: although it participates in transformation, its inscription in the ways in which knowledge is structured, depends on the way in which it manages to articulate them (Laclau & Mouffe, 1985, p. 123). However, the question is considering discursive practice *as a practice* (Foucault, 1969/2013): taking into account the thorough and precise observation, it still comes to the possibility to think about the connection between the discourse of a particular science with the general field of knowledge.

In some way, the reflection on research practice may be considered as that what, at the level of knowledge and not in its internal character, allows bringing scientific problems closer to political ones. In the case of the reflection of interdisciplinary researchers, the permanent task of making the epistemic framework explicit, for example, "produces interactions within the research team" (García, 2007, p. 67).[33] This results in "an openness to unfamiliar methods, concepts, and languages" that, while allowing the elaboration of a common conceptual framework, contributes to "the development of a convergent *practice*" (2007, p. 67, italics in the original).[34] Our point of interest is that the character of the reflection on the role as a discipline member in a specific social and political context, and its implications for the formulation of hypotheses and theories, belongs to both the discipline and to the historical context in general. The concept of epistemic framework tries to name this task of clarification of "an extradisciplinary normativity of social content that involves what 'should be done', based on its "practical implications" (2007, p. 106).[35] Far from being merely a methodological discussion, this addresses García's concern regarding the formation of those working in social sciences, and the way in which they conceive their work, particularly in Latin America (2007).

In a way, as an approximation attempt, we could bring together both concerns. On the one hand, what is the place of the research practice in which I participate within the general set of practices? On the other hand, when trying to conceive it, how can I sustain a critical connection to that what enables me what to think and what not, when these are the same conditions from which I formulate my criticism? We believe that this *rare explicitness* may be considered as a critical demand. As in the constant problematic reformulation pointed out by García, it is a question never to be considered as answered, and it implies a permanent task of reflection and rehearsal. At this point, perhaps, some of Foucault's reflections

---

[33] Translated by the author from the Spanish edition
[34] Translated by the author from the Spanish edition
[35] García distinguishes between this type of "implicit" normativity and the one that, for example, is established by a Minister of Economy, imposing a certain rationality to research: "normativity works in two ways: on the one hand, it is implicit in the epistemic framework from which a theory is generated; on the other hand, theory is then used to justify the "legitimacy" or "rationality" of the applied rules" (2007, p. 107). Although they are parallel problems, what interests us is addressing the implicit aspect, to which García dedicates the problem of researchers "taking a distance."

regarding the possibility of working on our own conditions of thought and knowledge could be useful to expand certain questions and research possibilities.

We would now like to address a way of thinking the "critique of the present," introduced by Foucault in his work *What is Enlightenment?*, around 1984. Although it might seem like a leap that is not consistent with the predominance of the archaeological period we are utilizing, Foucault (1985/1994) said that, in his opinion, the history of science as practiced by Canguilhem and Bachelard is inspired on this question, as an exercise to delimit the current possibilities of science after the role played by reason in the despotisms at the beginning of the last century. Here Foucault offers elements to analyse and reflect on the limits of what is possible to think today, for "a critique of what we say, think, and do, through a historical ontology of ourselves" (1984b/1996, p. 104).[36] This work on the present starts by renouncing the "complete" explanation of our historical limits. Together with research producing new knowledge it may help advance this critical attitude, since "this historical-critical attitude must also be an experimental attitude" (1984b/1996, p. 105).[37] This turns more profound when, taking up the archaeological aspects we mentioned (pointed out by Foucault in 1984) this "limit" is formed by the conditions of what is possible to think of at a given time. Once again, Kant appears: whereas Kant explored the limits of the conditions under which we obtain knowledge as to avoid exceeding them, to avoid mistakes[38], Foucault, in opposition to this criticism, proposes the possibility of considering these limits not in order to respect them, but to test their possible crossing. To do so, he seeks to situate the contingency that made us who we are, through historical work (both archaeological and genealogical), to, from there, obtain the possibility of conceiving its transformation (1984b/1996). To Foucault, this criticism cannot be merely speculative, but must be connected to practice. It does not have a universal role, since "it is not possible to judge the scientificity of a science in the name of a political practice" (1968/1994, p. 691).[39] Rather, the question is to consider the articulation of a scientific discourse with its context, the way in which both—being discursive practices—"are in a system of correlations with other practices" (1968/1994, p. 693).[40]

---

[36] Translated by the author from the Spanish edition
[37] Translated by the author from the Spanish edition
[38] With regard to this criticism: "Its usefulness, as far as speculation is concerned, shall really truly only be negative; it will serve not for widening, but only for the purification of our reason, and will keep it free of errors; with this, we already gain a lot" (Kant, 1787/2014, p. 79).
[39] Translated by the author from the French edition
[40] While the Kantian problem is present in Foucauldian problems from the outset, Poster points out that when Foucault ends up defining *practice* as a determining place of criticism, "he is closer to Marx than to Kant" (1988, p. 303). Cf. "The results and all the products of consciousness do not emerge through the work of spiritual criticism (...), but can only be dissolved by the practical overthrow of real social relations" (Marx & Engels, 1932/1970, p. 40). As mentioned above, Foucault disagrees with what he calls "University Marxism of France," but even so, the introduction of the dimension of practice would seem to confirm Poster's comment.

As we mentioned, this type of work on one's own historical conditions does not aim at their being made explicit, but at the possibility of their transformation. A critical practice, of the present, that through relating to other practices may contribute to the multiplication of lines of work. Having reached this point, we believe there is one last consideration to try to work with this mode of criticism. Just as it allows for the possibility to think about one's own conditions of knowledge, its radicalness also implies that in them not only what we know is constructed, but also we ourselves as subjects. To Foucault, this "taking a distance" from naturalized modes of knowledge is also taking a distance from ourselves. What happens with the subject while maintaining a critical connection to those historical conditions from which his knowledge is constructed?

THE PROBLEM OF THE SUBJECT OF CRITICISM

As we move towards the so-called genealogical stage, towards the possibility of thinking transformations, the place of this "practice among practices" acquires a more specific character. In 1973, in *La verdad y las formas jurídicas* [Truth and Juridical Forms], Foucault points out that the work on discourses has two sides: one that refers to linguistic facts and their construction rules (closer, perhaps, to the preceding years) and, on the other hand, one that seeks to reveal the struggle that operates there, a "strategic game of action and reaction" (1973/2013, p. 13).[41] A dynamism is introduced that seeks to think not so much about the synchronic terms of archaeology, but rather about transformations, giving rise to the so-called genealogy in which knowledge always appears linked to power, as in knowledge-power (1975/2009, p. 37). As he will later say, this is the study on "the games of truth in relation to each other (...), followed by the games of truth in relation to power relations" (1984/2016, p. 12).[42]

In this sense, the concept of *power* is introduced gathering the complete series of discourses" dynamisms: their relation as a practice among other practices, their link with institutional and political elements, among others. It is also here that Foucault wants to think of a relation between social practices and knowledge production that does not reduce the latter to being a mere reflection of the former. He aims to reject what he calls the *University Marxism* of France, that violence-ideology opposition. To Foucault, "any place of power exercise is at the same time a place of formation, not of ideology, but of knowledge" (1973b/2016, p. 269).[43] In a way, even if "genealogy" is introduced as a method, these problems are no different than those we mentioned earlier. Without a doubt, the question of this game of forces is introduced as a result of Foucault reading Nietzsche, and, as he points out, it makes him wonder about this dynamic characteristic of social

---

[41] Translated by the author from the Spanish edition
[42] Translated by the author from the Spanish edition
[43] Translated by the author from the Spanish edition

practices (1973/2013). But the relation with power is by no means that of the exteriority implied in an imposition on knowledge.

Here, as he initiates the specific task of thinking these transformations, Foucault introduces a new observation on subjects. Up until this point, around *The Archaeology of Knowledge*, Foucault had used the concept, perhaps still too structuralist, of *subject positions* (1969/2013), as part of the possible statements at a given historical moment: "The subjects move within the discursive field—they have a place there (and possibilities of movement), and a function (and possibilities of functional mutation)" (1968/1994, p. 680).[44] Now, in his text of 1973, he adds, with the same relevance, a reflection on the appearance of new historical subjects of knowledge, based on social practices, to the reflection on the emergence of new objects of knowledge. Thus, we arrive at the consideration that the subjects of knowledge are not a given before their historical constitution, that they are also linked to conditions of possibility. However, it is very important—despite having introduced the concept of *power*—to sustain the perspective addressed at the beginning: just as power does not "impose" itself on knowledge, neither does it on subjects. It is not a question of trying to "break free" from this framework of knowledge-power, since it is not an imposition, but rather the same historical conditions of possibility we mentioned earlier, which now also have dynamism. Regarding the subjects, it will also be a question of wondering what it means to maintain a critical connection to that what is at the same time limiting and enabling, although no longer with respect to the knowledge of an object, but concerning the subject's own place.

Again, the main point is that practices and social relations should not be considered as an obscuration for the subjects, but as their condition of possibility. But, in addition, it is the subjects of knowledge that are the point in which, in a very concrete way, context and knowledge construction are connected: they are the ones producing knowledge. Thus, the subjects are situated in a place triangulating with power and knowledge in a very precise manner: "there is no truth if you cannot find a perspective from which it is possible" (Deleuze, 1986/2006, p. 143). It is the contingent emergence of certain conditions in which something can be said, in which the truth can be said. It is extremely important though to emphasise that this is not relativism, but rather, as Foucault pointed out (1972/1992), a "perspectivism" referring to Nietzsche, and ultimately, to Leibniz. This does not mean that all knowledge is contingent and that it can simply be forced through certain power relations: the encounter with power is not at the level of science and epistemology, but at the level of knowledge. Of course, there is sometimes a "very direct" relation, since a policy is capable of dismantling an entire research (through persecution or underfunding), but what this concept of power-knowledge tries to introduce implies certain "indirect relations," since "the statements of a scientific discourse can no longer be considered as the immediate expression of a social

---

[44] Translated by the author from the French edition

relation or an economic situation" (1968/1994, p. 691).[45] Power does not aim at the internal history of truth, proper to science, but at the external history, of knowledge as a condition of possibility of scientific knowledge: "neither to Nietzsche nor to Leibniz perspectivism meant "each one with his truth," they place the perspective as a condition for the expression of truth" (Deleuze, 1986/2006, p. 143).[46] Of course, our purpose is not to add a last word to these discussions based on the "external history," but rather to advance in a perspective that can sustain and open up these questions while still maintaining the limit of the autonomy of scientific knowledge.

The question is not whether or not a subject is arbitrary in his exercise of power: it is about the concrete conditions enabling a subjectivation process. First there is the perspective, that is, the framework of knowledge and power that, secondly, allows for the constitution of the subject within it. As Deleuze points out: "the perspective is more profound than who is in it" (1986/2006, p. 34).[47] Strictly, this only emphasises that thought is always constituted within the limits of its historical possibilities of existence, but to this we add that subjects themselves are included in these historical transformations. It is no longer them who, with their lucidity and fresh minds, articulate new knowledge: every emerging novelty arises from a transformation in which they themselves are transformed, since "no one is responsible for emergence, no one can take credit for it, it always occurs in the interstitium" (Foucault 1971/1992, p. 17).[48] In a certain way, the last element of criticism is that for something new to be said, a new subject is necessary, a new subjectivation process.

BY WAY OF CLOSING

We have tried to reconstruct some problems regarding the historical conditions for knowledge construction that may be useful to bring certain Foucauldian reflections closer to constructivist tradition. Without wanting to validate them or generate controversies between them, we intended to bring them closer in the way in which they formulate and work on aspects of the relation, in a broad sense, between knowledge and its connection with political and social factors.

In order to situate this connection, this relation between disciplines and their social contexts in Foucault, we have first tried to reconstruct the place of science in Foucauldian archaeology, differentiating it from the concept of knowledge. In regard to the latter, we tried to restore its connection with Kantian heritage in order to specify the idea of a "historical condition of possibility," of what can be thought at a certain time, to locate the inscription of science at this point, with its own thresholds of epistemologization. There, we tried to locate the historical

---

[45] Translated by the author from the French edition
[46] Translated by the author from the Spanish edition
[47] Translated by the author from the Spanish edition
[48] Translated by the author from the Spanish edition

question regarding science's "internal" conditions (belonging to epistemology or the history of science), differentiating it from an "external" history, in order to situate the possibility to think about contingency and transformations in such a way that they do not contradict the autonomy of scientific knowledge. Then, we mentioned some fundamental characteristics of the way in which Rolando García conceives the relation between disciplines and their social context. Starting from his observations on interdisciplinary research, we tried to reinstate the reasons leading to the importance of the researchers" reflection and working on this connection (especially in the case of social sciences). Then, we mentioned some of the fundamental characteristics of the concept of epistemic framework, as formulated by Piaget and García, and its place when thinking this relation. Thirdly, we tried to reconstruct—based on the authors" observations regarding "ideology"— some characteristics and difficulties regarding the question of one's own historical conditions of the possibility of knowledge. In García's case, we approached this problem through the task of "making the epistemic framework explicit," and in Foucault, through a possible link between archaeology and his concept of critique of the present. At the same time we have tried to highlight the importance—even political and social—of sustaining this task as a permanent requirement, and the paradoxical nature of the fact that this reflection or criticism of the historical conditions we use when thinking, arises, in turn, from those same conditions. To do this, we tried to bring Foucault's question marks closer to the problems posed by the concept of *constraints* in knowledge construction (referring to the part of the context that is both limiting and enabling). Finally, parting from Foucault's perspective, we have tried to briefly reconstruct the subject's place in this type of critical reflection. That, we believe, is a central point of the problem: if every possibility of novel knowledge implies a transformation of the conditions making it possible, Foucault adds—from his perspective—the need for transformation of the knowing subject himself, as part of these conditions. If we follow Foucault, we come to the conclusion that all knowledge production comes with the possibility of a subjectivation process.

Although it is not novel to bring Foucault closer to these problems, we would like to explain, by way of conclusion, where our interest comes from. In her recent work *Los usos de Foucault en la Argentina* [The Uses of Foucault in Argentina], Mariana Canavese points out that Foucault's acceptance is intermittent in the early stages of his work, reaching a certain massiveness only in the early eighties, with *Discipline and Punish* (1975). "The appearance of an analysis focused on power, like the one offered in this book, provoked a local appropriation of Foucault's ideas determined by state terrorism, bound to devices of repression and social control" (Canavese, 2015, p. 97).[49] Perhaps this is why it is common to find in Foucault an arrival point of thought: the use of his concepts to point out disciplinary measures, devices, and the omnipresence of power. Of course, most

---

[49] Translated by the author from the Spanish edition

of the time these allegations are essential and activate practices, but other times they might close the possibility to keep thinking, as if, when speaking of "power," we draw conclusions too quickly, and the issues close around it, as a last word. Perhaps, if we were to read Foucault without knowing what we would find, today we might not conclude—or at least not this quickly—that he is the philosopher of power. That is why we have tried to head in this direction, focusing our reconstruction on *knowledge*: starting from its questions and moving forward according to its needs.

In this work we have tried to bring the discussion regarding the concept of *epistemic framework* closer to research practice, but of course the Foucauldian perspective may be used as a tool to raise general questions about knowledge construction, even in everyday life. When considering *knowledge*, the question regarding historical conditions of possibility, a statement such as the following is perhaps more stabbing and less obvious: from a Foucauldian perspective, "the ability to constitute oneself as a subject of knowledge depends on the intervention in the present" (Poster, 1988, p. 301). It is the possibility—not at all romantic and with great historical density—of saying that things, sometimes, under certain conditions, can be otherwise. Not that they "could be" or that "we would like" them to be otherwise: it is about conceptualizing a historical possibility, of a transformation that is possible today, and a way of working with it, of pointing it out and cherishing it. As Blanchot (1986) said, the possibility of "timing" current threats, not to wonder if anything else could be possible, but rather to think how to intervene in the present just as it is. Hence, this is not about a subject fighting within a web of power, and managing, by himself, to acquire another position or knowledge. The present opportunity of *constituting* oneself as a subject of knowledge supposes a perspective including both the regularities of what is known, the framework of the practices in which it is carried out, the ideas we have regarding what could or should be carried out, and institutional, political, and economic dimensions. It is only as a whole that they enable certain (and not other) ways of knowing and subjecting oneself. It is clear, then, why exploring these conditions is not about an accomplished "explanation," but rather a permanent task of trying to locate a possible point of transformation.

In order not to leave "subjectivation" as an abstraction, perhaps we can illustrate it with Foucault's participation in the *Prisons Information Group*, bearing in mind that although this was above all a political intervention, it occurred precisely in the period of his work on which we are focusing. In 1971, he had been asked to coordinate an "inquest commission" to investigate a situation of detention for political reasons. He accepted, on the condition that it be an information group, "a way of insisting both on the collective thought experience and giving voice to the detainees" (1971b/2012, p. 169).[50] As Judith Revel (2010) observes, the purpose of the experience was not so much the achievements forced from power, but the

---

[50] Translated by the author from the Spanish edition

possibility of returning the word, of generating conditions so that other ways of constituting oneself as a subject be enabled. This is why Deleuze has said in an interview that if we have learned anything from Foucault, it is "the indignity of speaking on behalf of others" (Foucault, 1972/1992, p. 86).[51]

How far do we extend the reading of the conditions enabling a certain way of knowing and not another? How do these elements, at the same time individual, disciplinary, social, and historical, come together in a unit of analysis? How broad is the spectrum used to evaluate possible interventions to transform these ways of knowing and thinking? How much do we trust in the subjective transformations we can produce—in ourselves and in others—and in catalyzing ways of knowing, even if not foreseen in advance? What possibilities do we have to "take a distance" when necessary, to give rise to new ways of thinking our practice and our discipline, based on the challenges we encounter? How willing are we to abandon the ways we think when the situation demands it? How much energy do we spend on the inertia of the ideas we already know, instead of on the thoroughness of a transforming discipline, or to what is possible to be thought in a given era?

ACKNOWLEDGEMENTS

I would like to thank Tono Castorina and Matías Abeijón for their attentive, friendly and extremely valuable reading.

REFERENCES

Agamben, G. (2009). ¿Qué es lo contemporáneo? In *Desnudez*. Adriana Hidalgo. [English edition: (2010) What is contemporary? In *Nudities*. Stanford University Press].

Bachelard, G. (1975/1938). *La formación del espíritu científico. Contribución a un psicoanálisis del conocimiento objetivo*. Siglo XXI. [English edition: (1986). *The new scientific spirit*. Beacon Press]

Becerra, G., & Castorina, J. A. (2015). El condicionamiento del "marco epistémico" en distintos tipos de análisis constructivista [The conditioning of the "epistemic framework" in different types of constructivist analysis]. In *Filosofía e historia de la ciencia en el Cono Sur: Selección de trabajos del IX Encuentro y las XXV Jornadas de Epistemología e Historia de la Ciencia* [Philosophy and history of science in the Southern Cone: a selection of papers from the IX Meeting and XXV Conference on Epistemology and History of Science] (pp. 101–107). Universidad Nacional de Córdoba.

Blanchot, M. (1986). *Michel Foucault tel que je l'imagine*. éditions fata morgana. [English edition: (1989). *Michel Foucault as I imagine him*. Zone Books].

Canavese, M. (2015). *Los usos de Foucault en la Argentina: recepción y circulación desde los años cincuenta hasta nuestros días* [The uses of Foucault in Argentina: Reception and circulation from the 1950s to the present day]. Siglo XXI.

---

[51] Translated by the author from the Spanish edition

Canguilhem, G. (1977). *Idéologie et rationalité dans l'histoire des sciences de la vie.* VRIN. [English edition (1988). *Ideology and rationality in the history of life sciences.* Mit Pr].

Castorina, J. A. (2007). Introducción [Introduction]. In Castorina, J. A. (Ed.), *Cultura y conocimientos sociales. Desafíos a la psicología del desarrollo.* [Culture and social knowledges. Challenges to developmental psychology]. Aique.

Castorina, J. A. (2010). La investigación de los conocimientos sociales: la crítica de sus condiciones sociales y sus supuestos filosóficos [Social knowledge research: Critique of its social conditions and philosophical assumptions]. In J. A. Castorina (Ed.), *Desarrollo del conocimiento social. Prácticas, discursos y teorías* [Development of social knowledge: practices, discourses, and theories]. Miño y Dávila.

Castro, E. (2015). *Introducción a Foucault* [Introduction to Foucault]. Siglo XXI.

Castro, E. (2013). Foucault, lector de Kant [Foucault, Kant's reader]. In Foucault, M. *Una lectura de Kant. Introducción a la antropología en sentido pragmático* [A lecture of Kant. An introduction to de antropology in a pragmatic way]. Siglo XXI.

Castro, E. (1995). *Pensar a Foucault. Interrogantes filosóficos de La arqueología del saber* [Thinking Foucault. Philosophical questions on the archaeology of knowledge]. Biblos.

Deleuze, G. (1986/2006). *El Leibniz de Deleuze. La exasperación de la filosofía* [Deleuze's Leibniz. The exasperation of philosophy]. Cactus.

Deleuze, G. (1985/2013). *El saber. Curso sobre Foucault I* [Knowledge. Course about Foucault I]. Cactus.

Dreyfus, H., & Rabinow, P. (2001). *Michel Foucault: más allá del estructuralismo y la hermenéutica.* Nueva Visión [English edition: (1983). *Michel Foucault: Beyond structuralism and hermeneutics.* University of Chicago Press].

Foucault, M. (1963). *El nacimiento de la clínica. Una arqueología de la mirada médica.* Buenos Aires, Siglo XXI. [English edition: (1994). *The birth of the clinic: An Archaeology of medical perception.* Vintage].

Foucault, M. (1966). *Las palabras y las cosas. Una arqueología de las ciencias humanas.* Buenos Aires, Siglo XXI. [English edition: (1994). *The order of things: An archaeology of the human sciences.* Vintage].

Foucault, M. (1967/1994). La philosophie structuraliste permet de diagnostiquer ce qu'est "aujourd'hui" [Structuralist philosophy makes it possible to diagnose what is "today"]. In *Dits et écrits I. 1954–1969* [Sayings and writings I 1954–1969]. Gallimard.

Foucault, M. (1967b/1994). Sur le façons d'écrire l'histoire [On ways of writing history]. In *Dits et écrits I. 1954–1969* [Sayings and writings I 1954–1969]. Gallimard.

Foucault, M. (1968/1994). Réponse à une question. In *Dits et écrits I. 1954–1969.* Gallimard [English edition: (1972). History, discourse, discontinuity. In *Salmagundi* (vol. 20), 225–248].

Foucault, M. (1969/2013). *La arqueología del saber.* Siglo XXI. [English edition: (1982). *The archaeology of knowledge.* Vintage].

Foucault, M. (1971/1992). Nietzsche, la genealogía, la historia. In *Microfísica de poder.* La Piqueta. [English edition: (1977). Nietzsche, Genealogy, history. In *Language, counter-memory and practice: Selected essays and interviews.* Cornell University Press].

Foucault, M. (1971b/2012). Manifiesto del GIP [GIP's manifest]. In *El poder, una bestia magnífica. Sobre el poder, la prisión y la vida*. [Power, a magnificent beast. On power, prison and life] .Siglo XXI.
Foucault, M. (1972/1992). Los intelectuales y el poder. In *Microfísica del poder*. Madrid, La Piqueta. [English edition: (1973). The intellectuals and power: A discussion between Michel Foucault and Gilles Deleuze. In *Telos. Critical theory of the contemporary* (vol. 16), 103–109].
Foucault, M. (1973/2013). *La verdad y las formas jurídicas*. Gedisa. [English edition: (2000). In Truth and judicial forms. In J. D. Faubion (Ed.), *Power* (vol. 3 , pp. 1–89).
Foucault, M. (1973b/2016). *La sociedad punitiva*. Fondo de Cultura Económica [English edition: (2018). *The punitive society: Lectures at the collège de France, 1972–1973*. Picador]
Foucault, M. (1975/2009). *Vigilar y castigar. Nacimiento de la prisión*. Siglo XXI [English edition: (1995). *Discipline & Punish: The Birth of the Prison*. Vintage]
Foucault, M. (1976/2012). *Historia de la sexualidad I: La voluntad de saber*. Buenos Aires, Siglo XXI. [English edition: (1990). *The history of sexuality, Vol. 1*. Vintage].
Foucault, M. (1978/2015). *Que 'est-ce que la critique?* [What is critique?]. VRIN.
Foucault, M. (1983). Preface. In G. Deleuze & F. Guattari (Eds.), *Anti-Edipus: Capitalism and schizophrenia*. University of Minnesota.
Foucault, M. (1984/2016). *Historia de la sexualidad II: El uso de los placeres*. Siglo XXI [English edition: (1990). *The history of sexuality, Vol. 2*. Vintage].
Foucault, M. (1984b/1996). *¿Qué es la Ilustración?* La Piqueta [English edition: (1996). *What is enlightenment?: Eighteenth-century answers and twentieth-century questions*. University of California Press].
Foucault, M. (1984c/1994). Le style de l'histoire [The style of history]. In *Dits et écrits IV. 1980–1988* [Sayings and writings IV 1980–1988]. Gallimard.
Foucault, M. (1985/1994). La vie : l'expérience et la science. In *Dits et écrits IV. 1980–1988*. Gallimard. [English edition: Life: Experience and science. In *Aesthetics method, and epistemology. Essential Works of Foucault 1954–1984. Volume Two*. The New Press].
Frank, M. (1988). El concepto de discurso en Foucault. In AA.VV. *Michel Foucault, filósofo*. Gedisa [English edition: (1992). On Foucault's concept of discourse. In *Michel Foucault philosopher*. Harvester Wheatsheaf].
García, R. (2007). *Sistemas complejos* [Complex Systems]. Gedisa.
García, R. (2000). *El conocimiento en construcción. De las formulaciones de Jean Piaget a la teoría de sistemas complejos* [Knowledge under construction. From Jean Piaget's formulations to the theory of complex systems]. Gedisa.
Hadot, P. (1995). *¿Qué es la filosofía antigua?* México, Fondo de Cultura Económica. [English edition: (2004). *What is ancient philosophy?* Belknap Press].
Heidegger, M. (1988). *Identidad y diferencia*. Editorial Anthropos. [English edition: (2002). *Identity and difference*. University of Chicago Press].
Hempel, C. G. (1966/2003). *Filosofía de la ciencia natural*. Alianza. [English edition: (1996). *Philosophy of natural science*. Prentice Hall].
Kant, I. (1787/2014). *Crítica de la razón pura* (Mario Caimi, Trans.). Colihue. [English edition: (2008). *Critique of pure reason*. Penguins Classics].

Laclau, E., & Mouffe, Ch. (1985). *Hegemonía y estrategia socialista. Hacia una radicalización de la democracia.* Siglo XXI [English edition: (2014). *Hegemony and socialist strategy: Towards a radical democratic politics.* Verso.]

Marx, K., & Engels, F. (1932/1970). *La ideología alemana.* Grijalbo. [English edition: (2016). *The German ideology.* Intl. Pub. Co. Inc.].

Piaget, J. (1974). *El estructuralismo.* Oikos-Tau. [English edition: (1976). *Structuralism.* Basic Books].

Piaget, J., & García, R. (1982/1984). *Psicogénesis e historia de la ciencia.* México. [English edition: (1988). *Psychogenesis and the History of Science.* Columbia University Press].

Poster, M. (1988). Foucault, el presente y la historia. In AA.VV. *Michel Foucault, filósofo.* Gedisa. [English edition: (1987–1988). Foucault, the present and history. In *Cultural critique* (vol. 8), 105–121.].

Prigogine, I., & Stengers, I. (1979/2004). *La nueva alianza. Metamorfosis de la ciencia.* Alianza. [English edition: (1984). *Order out of chaos.* Bantam New Age Books.].

Revel, J. (2010/2014). *Foucault, un pensamiento de lo discontinuo* [Foucault, a thought of the discontinuous]. Amorrortu.

Stolkiner, A. (1987). De interdisciplinas e indisciplinas [Of interdisciplines and indisciplines]. In N. Elichiry (Ed.), *El niño y la Escuela-Reflexiones sobre lo obvio.* [The Child and the School—Reflections on the Obvious]. Nueva Visión.

Yuing Alfaro, T. (2017). *Tras lo singular: Foucault y el ejercicio del filosofar histórico.* [Pursuing singularity. Foucault and the exercise of historical philosophizing]. CENTALES Ediciones.

Žižek, S. (2008). El espectro de la ideología. In *Ideología: un mapa de la cuestión.* Buenos Aires, Fondo de Cultura Económica. [English edition: (2012). *Mapping ideology.* Verso].

CHAPTER 3

USES AND MEANINGS OF "CONTEXT" IN STUDIES ON CHILDREN'S KNOWLEDGE

A Viewpoint From Anthropology and Constructivist Psychology

Mariana García Palacios, Paula Shabel,
Axel Horn, and José Antonio Castorina

INTRODUCTION[1]

For more than a decade, our research team of psychologists and anthropologists has studied the construction of diverse types of social knowledge among children, focusing on topics like the building of religious knowledge and children's ideas

---

[1] This work was originally published in García Palacios, Mariana; Shabel, Paula; Horn, Axel y Castorina, José Antonio (2018) Uses and meanings of 'context' in studies on children Knowledge: A viewpoint from Anthropology and constructivist Psychology. *Integrative Psychological and Behavioral Science* (ISSN 1932-4502), 52: 191–208. DOI: https://doi.org/10.1007/s12124-018-9414-1

of intimacy and justice. This work has involved an interdisciplinary dialogue between social anthropology and constructivist psychology that takes a critical approach to the contributions of Piagetian psychology (1997). In fact, we have addressed the relationship between children's knowledge and social practices in both psychology and anthropology in several of our previous works, based on the idea that children construct diverse meanings about the social world and modify them as active participants in social practices (García Palacios & Castorina, 2010, 2014; García Palacios et al., 2015; Horn & Castorina, 2010; García Palacios et al., 2014, 2015). This work departs from the theoretical assumption that knowledge is constructed *in context*. However, although the vast majority of studies on children's knowledge incorporate the idea of context, we found that the scope and limits of this notion are not unequivocally defined (with a few remarkable exceptions we will discuss in the following sections). In this regard, we believe that it is necessary to clarify how the myriad definitions of context influence research on cognitive construction. To paraphrase Althusser (2005), context appears to be a concept *in a practical state*. For this reason, an interdisciplinary dialogue is imperative to examining the meaning of this category and the unresolved issues it poses for psychology and anthropology researchers at the meta-theoretical, theoretical and methodological level.

With this aim, we will attempt to define context, its scope and its connections to "individual constructions." In general terms, although "context" was a concern from the very beginning of anthropology, constructivist psychology initially chose to focus instead on either individual or universal aspects in cognitive construction. We understand, however, that the first groundbreaking studies on cognitive construction within constructivist psychology and existing frameworks in social anthropology must be reexamined in light of this new point in question. In this regard, we set out to create a common conceptual framework and a methodological strategy based on the contributions of both disciplines.

To start, we will describe how the notion of context has been understood in social anthropology before delving into the meanings of context in psychology. Based on previous analyses of this concept in both disciplines, we will then analyze possible ways of associating context with the construction of knowledge before arguing that the notion of context can either limit the construction of knowledge or serve as its catalyst. Finally, following this same line of thought and based on our own empirical studies, we will examine how the consideration of context can influence the methodological procedures of constructivist psychology and anthropology research and its potential for different types of collaboration between the two disciplines.

THE USES OF CONTEXT IN SOCIAL ANTHROPOLOGY AND CONSTRUCTIVIST PSYCHOLOGY[2]

Context in Social Anthropology

At the start of the twentieth century, an idea of context began to develop soon after the founding of social anthropology,[3] an academic field strongly rooted in functionalism. This notion became essential for an anthropological analysis of the rituals, the institutions and indeed, the very lives of *others* on their own terms. A common belief in anthropology was that in order to understand the *natives*, it was necessary to travel and live amongst them, studying the different human groups *in context*. Direct observation thus became the only possible research method (Krotz, 1988). From the time of Malinowski's pioneering work (1922/2001), traveling to villages, speaking local languages and sharing the day-to-day lives of a people became the basis for modern anthropology. The contexts for knowledge production were at the core of this research, though they were never conceptualized in a systematic way. Even so, we can infer that according to this line of thought, context is closely associated with the laws and norms that regulate a society's institutions. "Context" acquires a homogeneous form in every culture/society that anthropologists study. Subjects appear to have no effect on context, which is external and all-encompassing, and serves as a point of reference for each subject's individual actions.

By the second decade of the twentieth century, the new trend of historical particularism incorporated history to the analysis, producing a novel understanding of context within anthropology. Boas (1981) and his disciples challenged the idea that genetics play a decisive role or condition human development, placing the emphasis on the particular historical development of each group instead. Historical particularists posit that although human thought is universal, the historical development of each group depends on its unique cultural context.

In contrast, structuralists invoke universal mental structures when explaining social phenomena, structures that exceed any contextual examination, historical analysis or particular features of a people. Levi-Strauss (1977) argued that univer-

---

[2] Different branches within the social sciences have also approached the question of context, like the works on cognitive sociology by Cicourel (1973). Reflections on context can also be found in certain branches of anthropology and psychology (see notes 2 and 4). While some of these trends are relevant and will be mentioned here, the focus of our discussions is on social anthropology and genetic psychology.

[3] Influenced by the development of pragmatics, the linguistic anthropologist Duranti (Duranti, 2001; Goodwin & Duranti, 1992) proposed rethinking the notion of context created by speech acts that not only involve saying things but also doing them. Along these same lines, the works by Hutchins and Goodwin (2011) introduce the category of embodied interaction to analyze social interaction and shared cognition, based on the assumption that contexts are comprised of these social interactions and the materiality of the bodies and cultural elements which form them.

sal human thought works by categorizing the world in binary terms and that each social group *fills* these cognitive compartments with its own particular meanings. Context here could be considered a cultural framework that produces such meanings, filling categories of thought with specific contents. Structuralists, however, only consider these contents relevant when examining the mental mechanisms involved in thought.

In another branch of anthropology developed in the 1960s based on Geertz's work, symbolic anthropology, the emphasis is on the meaning that *native* social actors themselves attribute to social events. Anthropologists thus began to study symbols as entities of collective meaning without losing sight of the subjects who produce this meaning as the functionalists had. Context here can be understood as the interwoven meanings that a group jointly attributes to *social events*. These shared symbols transform local culture into "a context, something within which they can be intelligibly —that is, thickly— described." (Geertz, 2001, p. 14). Throughout the 1960s, anthropologists set out to interpret meanings in order to understand diverse cultural contexts. This new take on reality made the notion of context more heterogeneous but provided no insight into the unequal social relations at work in these day-to-day contexts and as a result, each cultural configuration continued to be presented as a single harmonious unit.[4]

In the 1970s, however, Marxist approaches in anthropology systematically focused on social inequalities. This gave a macro-level perspective to the notion of concept, acknowledging the existence of a social structure that generates inequalities associated with class, gender, age, etc. (Boivin et al., 2006; Godelier, 1974). In this regard, the Marxist notion of scales made an important contribution to the study of context (Ortner, 1984). By placing capitalism at the center of the global scene, researchers began to consider how a dialogue begins within each social group at the local level and is influenced by processes such as colonial relations, imperialism and international trade that necessarily influence the day-to-day lives of each group. To cite Wolf, "The world of humankind constitutes a manifold, a totality of interconnected processes, and inquiries that disassemble this totality into bits and then fail to reassemble it falsify reality," (Wolf, 1982, p. 3). The idea of context in the discipline was thus modified to include the power relations of each group studied in both past and present, given that any group is part of social contact networks that influence their processes of production and social reproduction.

---

[4] Postmodern anthropology appeared in the 1980s and took this interpretation to an extreme by affirming that every social interaction produces a context of meanings so particular that an external analysis becomes impossible. The context thus becomes a whole once again but for the opposite reason as the functionalism described earlier; here the individual subject becomes the epicenter where meaning is created outside any general social principles. This explains why "instead of context, postmodern scholars speak of intertextuality," (Reynoso, 1991, p.55) suggesting that ethnographic narrative is more of a literary work than a scientific text.

In keeping with this line of thought, which also draws on the Weberian tradition in the social sciences, the Marxists drew up a theoretical framework in relation to *practice/praxis*. The premise of this approach is that unequal structures foster power disputes, though Marxists also return to the notion of agency as a producer, reproducer and potential transformer of this structure. By focusing on human practices without losing sight of the circumstances of their production, the notion of context becomes profound enough to understand both the material and symbolic conditions of a certain group and the ways in which these form the structures of each society by influencing individual human actions.

As briefly seen here, anthropology is teeming with references to context. Although researchers have explored the different sociocultural aspects of context since anthropology emerged as a discipline, the meanings and scope of this concept—which has been employed in reference to "culture," "social relations," "interactions," "the socioeconomic system," etc.—have not always been clear. In order to further develop and clarify context, we will review how constructivist psychology has dealt with this concept and identify points in common between the two fields.

Context in Constructivist Psychology

In most classical research in constructivist psychology,[5] little if any attention is paid to context. According to Lave (1996), although the different branches of psychology may incorporate context in their analysis of individual cognitive processes, this is nothing more than an unsuccessful "enhancement," since all of the assumptions surrounding the concept are based on the study of internal, individual processes. In particular, these considerations are a red flag for Piaget's constructivist psychology, where the question of how context influenced the development of knowledge systems was overlooked entirely. In keeping with this dialectical approach to subject-reality, the post-Piagetian psychologists successfully introduced context in their theories without it representing a strange or artificial addition (Psaltis et al., 2009).

In his first works, Piaget (1997) skirted around context without ever proposing a specific focus on the topic. The Swiss psychologist argued that individual thought and social relations were "two sides of the same coin," (Psaltis et al., 2009) that is, two different expressions of coordinated actions. In keeping with Psaltis, Duveen

---

[5] As indicated earlier, there are mentions of context in other branches of psychology (such as discursive psychology) in which language is understood as constitutive rather than referential of knowledge constructions. This marks an important divide with genetic psychology that merits mention. One influential researcher in this area, Potter (2000), addressed the rhetorical nature of a world defined through the discursive practices among participants in a dialogue. Discursive constructions here are examined as situated constructions in the context in which they occur with a focus on the social action that researchers and participants are describing. According to this perspective, the analysis deals with the way an individual constructs a representation and then acts accordingly, obtaining an invitation, for example, or attributing guilt.

and Perret Clermont, one could argue that thoughts are indissociable from social actions, though Piaget avoided examining the specific features of the social relations in question. By overlooking the cultural contexts which limit yet also enable cognitive processes, Piaget was able to emphasize the constructivist activity of an epistemic subject detached from the fluctuating social and cultural conditions in which knowledge is elaborated. Subsequently, post-Piagetian theorists such as Psaltis et al. (2009) strived to situate cognitive construction in what could be considered contextual settings, identifying three generations of studies that altered the original Piagetian tradition (Psaltis et al., 2009; Psaltis & Zapiti, 2014). The first generation of studies emerged in Geneva in the early 1970s, and focused on socio-cognitive conflicts (Doise et al., 1975; Doise, 1985; Carugati & Mugni, 1988), emphasizing that the conflicts arising from social interactions are as important to knowledge construction as socio-cognitive conflicts. Specifically, these authors showed how dialogue among children—a dialogue that reveals the different levels of conceptualization in children's thought process—invariably helped the less advanced subjects make progress. This cognitive dissonance resulted from an exchange with more advanced children. In other words, cognitive development cannot be explained solely by the conflicts that the subject experiences individually at different moments in an observation; the inconsistencies that appear during interactions with others are equally important.

Another generation of post-Piagetian studies in Neuchâtel (Schubauer-Leoni et al., 1992; Schubauer-Leoni & Grossen, 1993) opened up "a black box" of interactions and their contextual expectations to reveal how the context of communicative exchanges between interviewer and interviewee affects how children work through the interaction (Psaltis & Zapiti, 2014). Accordingly, interviews can no longer be seen as a culturally neutral interaction and a child interprets not just the questions interviewers pose during a communicative exchange but also their intentions.

During this same period, Donaldson (1979) was conducting studies in Great Britain that would influence that generation of constructivist psychologists and the next, reaching all the way to today's discussion. Basing on a critical review of 'Piaget's researches, Donaldson argued that his tested situations were too abstract for the children participating in the interviews and bore no relation to their everyday life. After outlining the effects of different presentations of classic Piagetian tasks on the cognitive stages attributed to children, Donaldson argued that a more genuine approach to what children know and understand required familiar circumstances that made "sense" to them. Context, then, became a fundamental element in the study of knowledge constructions.

More recently, another generation approached cognitive construction by examining the social representations that limit the construction of knowledge. For example, Leman and Duveen (1996) analyzed how gender representations condition the cognitive process, showing, for example, that a girl more advanced in her acquisition of a certain notion will have to use several arguments to convince a boy who is not as advanced as she is. In the inverse scenario— that is, when a boy who is more advanced tries to convince a girl who is less advanced—he convinces her more quickly. These studies revealed that social representations are part of cognitive development and that they contextualize (limiting or enabling) it; on the other hand, by considering the broader context of social representations and social practices, these studies modified the very notion of the epistemic subject, who went from an abstract being to a social actor with her own expectations and identifications. Cognitive activity structures and is structured by the triadic relationship between the object of knowledge, the social individual and the others (Psaltis et al., 2009).

In schools of thought inspired by Vygotsky, researchers are also concerned with incorporating context in post-Piagetian studies. However, as Cole (2003) notes, the concept of context is polysemic even within cultural psychology, sparking confusion in sociohistorical trends and cultural psychology and yielding highly different approaches. In Cole's first description, context is presented as separate from the individual although she interacts (and can influence) it in different ways. In this regard, it is possible to refer to both the "family context" as well as the "historical context" that influence psychological development. In the author's second version (Cole, 2003), child and context are constructed together through their relations with one another, making them two parts of a whole. In this characterization of the concept, it becomes analytically challenging—if not impossible—to separate the child from the context. In any case, there is still no precise definition for context.

Inspired by Vygotsky's work, other authors (Lave, 1996; Rogoff, 1995) developed the theory of situated activity. "Contexts are activity systems. An activity system integrates the subject, the objects and the instruments (material tools as well as signs and symbols) into a unified whole (...) that includes production and communication, distribution, exchange and consumption" (Lave, 1996, p. 30). We believe that this perspective, unlike Cole's, places more emphasis on the specific relationships between the components of a dynamic whole, that is, an activity system that is constructed historically. Rogoff (1995) focused on a triangular relationship between student, contents and context to study learning. For this author, context was all of the elements involved in situated learning. Here context is not comprised of external factors separate from cognitive activity; instead, the situation or school event is taken as the learning "text." This focus underlines the interdependence of learning components, which are woven into an inextricable whole. In this regard, individual thought cannot be examined separately from actions, circumstances and goals. If context is not external, then, and instead constitutive of human actions, the unit of analysis is guided participation, that is, culturally organized activities where active individuals encourage less experienced members to participate in a more mature way.[6]

In short, even taking into account these conceptual developments, several questions associated with context and the construction of knowledge—in terms of both operating structures and specific concepts—remain unanswered. What are we referring to precisely when we speak of the context of cognitive construction? How does context affect production? Is this a causal relationship, a simultaneous influence or is it a condition of the *surroundings*? Another question might be the following: if we clarify the notion of context, what consequences will that have for research methodology? To address these questions, we will draw on contributions from anthropology to further analyze the meaning of context and its relationship to cognitive construction.

RELATIONSHIPS BETWEEN CONTEXT AND KNOWLEDGE CONSTRUCTION

Now that we have reviewed different understandings of context in each discipline, we will introduce our position on how context relates to knowledge construction.

In some of our previous works (García Palacios et al., 2014, 2015), we have emphasized the dialectical framework of context and knowledge construction, connecting individual cognitive processes with the social surroundings in which they are produced at both the macro-historical and micro-social level of each situation. From this perspective, knowledge construction cannot be analyzed "independently from the meaning that the context has for the participants," (García Palacios et al., 2014, p. 55).

From this framework of relational epistemology, we join Valsiner (2014) in questioning studies that emphasize the division between context and psychological phenomena. These studies, which can be divided into two groups, introduce other theories. In the first group, the focus is solely on psychological phenomena that occur outside the social context, as can be seen in certain literal interpretations of constructivist psychology (Delval, 1989) and some trends within cognitive anthropology and psychology (Hirschfeld, 1994). Within anthropology, the evolutionist paradigm and the naturalists took a similar approach, considering cognitive developments separately from context based on the idea that human thought is determined by the so-called "race" of the person in question.

The second group of studies separates contextual conditions from the psychological process, which is determined externally. Here cognitive processes are not

---

[6] Though he does not belong to the genetic psychology tradition, Engeström (1999, and Engeström & Middleton, 1996) influenced the field with his situated cognition approach. According to this activity theory derived from Leontiev's ideas, the activity components are the subject, the tool, the object, the community (those who share the activity), the division of labor and the community rules. Activity theory in this regard "is contextual and is oriented at understanding historically specific local practices, their objects, mediating artifacts, and social organization" (Cole & Engeström, 1993, p. 377).

autonomous but fully determined by cultural phenomena; this is the position of certain schools within culturalism and sociologism. Thus, studies on socialization, for example, present society as a set of rules and meanings that supposedly exist independently of individuals, who are then passively "socialized" (Pires, 2010). This perspective would be compatible with Cole's initial version, as described in the first section.

For our perspective on the relationship between context and knowledge construction, we borrow arguments from anthropology (Toren, 2012) and psychology (Valsiner, 2014). Inspired by the Vygotskian holistic perspective when examining the conditions for psychological changes within the field of semiotics, Valsiner' emphasizes an interaction, a mutual articulation between psychological phenomena and the sociocultural context in which context conditions psychological life and vice-versa (Cabell & Valsiner, 2014; Valsiner, 2014; Winegar & Valsiner, 1992). Unlike studies that separate context from psychological phenomena with a dualist epistemic frame, this approach posits that catalysis occurs in a semiotic process typical of cultural psychology. The way in which meanings are transformed varies according to the conditions for such catalysis.

This allows us to posit that context that does not determine development linearly but instead paves a certain path within development; this only occurs when certain material and symbolic conditions are in place, though said conditions do not necessarily guarantee that development will in fact go in a certain direction. One of the most original facets of this concept is that it allows these catalyzing conditions to be defined. By limiting or enabling cognitive activity, then, the context lays the groundwork for the transformation of the meaning garnered by subjects. For Valsiner, "It is important to note that the concept of semiotic catalysis is a process that highlights the systemic relations between parts, and specifies how the relationship of these parts construct, as a gestalt, the conditions necessary, but not themselves sufficient, to bring about a qualitative transformation of a psychological phenomenon," (2014, p. 12). This proposal allows the concept of catalysis to be separated from causality, given that the relations posited here are not linear: instead, catalysis suggests the conditions for possibilities, not for givens (Cabell & Valsiner, 2014).

This proposal has points in common with Toren's research in anthropology (1990, 1993, 2006, 2012). This author argues that we are all active subjects in cognitive constructions "Other people have structured the conditions of your existence (...) but it was you who made meaning out of the meanings they presented you with" (2006, p. 8). This information, however, is always mediated by the social relations in which we are immersed. In our view, these conceptualizations contribute to the historical debate within this field on the relationship between nature and culture; affirming that our ability to produce culture is innate but also that everything we know about our own nature is cultural. It is thus necessary to abandon the binary terms of the debate to produce a more encompassing perspective for studies of knowledge construction. Furth explains that for Toren, knowledge is "endogenously acquired in development" (1994, p. 977), in other words, not innate or imposed externally. In keeping with constructivism, men and women thus have the ability to symbolize, and human minds generate knowledge and base their interpretations of the world on this knowledge. These interpretations, however, are always associated with the way that we "make meaning out of meanings that others have made and are making," (1993, p. 267) and must therefore be analyzed at their convergence point. The focus on socialization is at stake here, since the analysis has shifted from abstract concepts like "culture" and "society" to people, who are both active and historical subjects as well as the object of others' actions; they are the products and producers of signifiers that can be infinitely diverse but never arbitrary (Pires, 2010).

Based on these reflections, we can assume that while children learn "grownup culture," they also have a hand in reshaping it. Children are thus attributed with a whole new role in building the social world, and we believe that this should be a tenet in future research in both disciplines. Context can thus be thought of as *sociality*—a concept that includes the dynamic social processes in which people are immersed (Pires, 2010)—opening up a dialectic between subjects. Rather than forfeit agency as knowledge is constructed, subjects are influenced by social processes that allow them to generate meanings of the world, meanings which they then use to build knowledge in a necessarily creative effort. The meanings culled through *sociality* are not replicated but appropriated with minor, gradual and always historical changes (Wagoner, 2008) that develop and evolve through social relations; social meanings can also be modified in a similar way.[7] The knowledge construction processes pose the question "of what we are capable of discovering" as social beings (Toren, 2012, p. 22). This departs from an analysis centered on possible information-processing mechanisms that the individual human mind utilizes, given that the mind itself is an ongoing social production.

This notion of context leads us to posit that the meanings constructed in any social scenario vary according to the subject but are never arbitrary because they bear the mark of their origin. At the same time, this analysis is not limited to the social relations and objects at present but instead assumes that children are historical subjects with a collective past in their respective communities. This past materializes in circulating meanings—even when adults avoid explicitly stating things—that children then appropriate to form knowledge. In this schema, history is presented as "what is past, but persistent, as inhering in the products of human action," (Toren, 1990, p. 979), which adds a time dimension to context that must be considered when analyzing knowledge construction because it affects the production of meaning in specific ways. What represented a problem, conflict or damage within the group will have some negative charge for the next generations,

---

[7] In the field of anthropology and education, Rockwell (1995, 1996) proposed the concept of appropriation, which draws attention to the network of meanings constructed from the different knowledge circulating in a certain space (school, family, etc.) and to what subjects do with these meanings, consciously or otherwise, based on their own needs and possibilities.

even if no one talks about it in a clear or conscious manner. That negative charge, however, will be resignified to a certain degree by the present-day events.

In this regard, Toren says that "humans are dynamic and transformative products of their past, which comes to bear on every aspect of their being. Moreover, humans are situated in relation to others (young and old, alive or dead), whose ideas and practices help structure the conditions for their existence in the present," (2012, p. 22) Context, we insist, has diverse diachronic and synchronic scales that must be considered in cognitive studies, as suggested by the Marxist anthropologists cited above (Wolf, 1982). In this regard, Achilli underlines that the notion of "context" goes beyond the *external* surroundings of everyday relations and processes, insisting on the need to consider in relational terms ."..the interaction between different mutually configured contextual levels that also establish the conditions and limits of the processes and relations that interest us," (2013, p. 44).

DIALOGUES ON RESEARCH METHODOLOGY BETWEEN SOCIAL ANTHROPOLOGY AND CONSTRUCTIVIST PSYCHOLOGY

The approach to the concept of context in the previous section has consequences for our research methodologies and analysis units. It is important to note that the choice of methodological procedures depends not only on the issue at hand but also on the meta-theoretical framework chosen for the research. In studies centered on individual activities independent of their discursive contexts or, depending on the theme, of the social practice contexts, there is a certain type of unit of analysis. However, if a framework of relational epistemology is used, the units of analysis have components which are defined in a system of interactions. In this regard, in both constructivist psychology and social anthropology, the emphasis is on articulating previously dissociated components such as individual knowledge, social practices and cultural contexts. These articulations reveal the interrelations and/or contradictions resulting from the researcher's approaches and units of analysis should thus also be considered part of the topic of study.

As proposed in this chapter, the reference to context implies a transformation in the methodology with regards to several factors, including the units and scales of analysis. The units of analysis for the relationship between knowledge and context are particularly complicated, as they are not limited to the interactions between subject and object but instead include three components: the subject and object of knowledge, and the social practices that situate its production. In other words, it is necessary to construct units of analysis that consider the particular aspects of children's ideas in terms of the processes of constructing meanings in a dialectic of integration and conceptual differentiation; the object of this knowledge, which may or may not emerge from the subjects' own social experience; and the social practices carried out at a certain institution, based on certain norms, or in a social context, which also includes social representations (García Palacios et al., 2015), though we do not address these to any length here.

In an attempt to manage these challenges and understand these interrelations, in our respective empirical research we have incorporated methodological strategies which are uncommon in the traditions of our respective disciplines, specifically in studies in the field of psychology on how children construct their right to intimacy (Horn) and anthropology research on the construction of religious knowledge (García Palacios).

As noted by Weisner and Gallimore (1977), one of the main challenges associated with articulating the knowledge produced by psychology and anthropology has to do with the range of methodologies employed in the two disciplines. Most literature in psychology is based on indirect measurements (often tests and questionnaires) of very specific phenomena, while anthropology produces general ethnographic data based on direct observation and interviews with informants. Despite the disparities in the research variables, a few important works have contributed to understanding children's constructions by focusing on traditional topics of analysis within both disciplines. Whiting and Whiting (1979) authored a pioneering study of this sort, treating cultural values as crucial variables to be examined both on their own and in conjunction with other variables in cognitive development studies. Other interdisciplinary efforts between constructivist psychology and anthropology have analyzed "deviance" from so-called normal states of cognitive development, as reflected in the socialization processes of children from non-Western societies or different social classes (Feldman et al., 1984). As we have noted in earlier studies (García Palacios, 2012), one of the biggest problems of these works—which harken back to Piaget's research—is that they only offer a linear interpretation of the four states of cognitive development, and they discount the epistemological arguments that form the backbone of Piagetian theory. In addition, by basing their studies on the theoretical universe of psychology, the methodological approach to social reality fails to capture its complexity (Nunes, 1999).

The relationship between ethnographic analysis and developmental psychology continues to be problematic (LeVine, 2007) and there is a clear need for anthropology to do more than warn against universalist pretensions. We believe it is necessary to move from the "anthropological veto" to a more productive, mutual exchange between disciplines. In other words, interdisciplinary exchange cannot be based on the belief that anthropology only serves to place limits on psychological theories (García Palacios, 2012; LeVine, 2007). On the contrary, we argue that anthropology should instead base its contribution on a long tradition of studying sociocultural contexts and in the specific methodology—ethnography—anthropologists developed to approach such contexts. Conversely, perspectives that draw on anthropology but use contextual explanations for subjects' cognitive constructions are equally limited. Such approaches underestimate individual productions of knowledge and lose sight of the multiple dimensions that are equally critical to these processes. The intra-mental and inter-mental should not be merged in studies: instead, the relationship between the two should be one of the research aims (Valsiner, 1998, in Psaltis & Zapiti, 2014).

We believe that the methodological strategies of social anthropology and constructivist psychology can be articulated in a productive way, generating a dialogue between ethnography and the clinical-critical method, as our team has noted in earlier works (García Palacios & Castorina, 2014).

A basic premise of ethnography is that above all else, it is a family of methods involving direct and substantial contact with social agents as well as a process of writing about this encounter. Ethnography textualizes elusive human experience, mostly on its own terms (Willis & Trondman, 2000). The final goal of the process and the product of anthropological research (which are, as a matter of course, *theoretically informed*) on social realities occurring in a specific space and time is the analytical description of their particularity (Rockwell, 2009). In this regard, ethnography has always studied unique sociocultural expressions among humans (Guber, 2008). This goes beyond intercultural analysis and also encompasses the differences that arise within a single group of studies, turning the familiar into something exotic and fostering reflection on the continuities and transformations of one's own cultural practices. This approach gives researchers insight into how subjects conceive of the categories that construct their day-to-day reality within the framework of specific relations that take place in the field, enabling the study of "relations between the construction of children's ideas and social practices" (García Palacios & Castorina, 2010, p. 98). The researcher is positioned in the interstices of this dialectic, forming a particular social relation with the other actors that also contributes to the knowledge constructed in the field (Guber, 2008; Rockwell, 2009).

The clinical-critical method (Piaget, 1997) represented a methodological innovation since it differed from pure observation and psychometric techniques (Castorina et al., 1984). From Piaget to current-day critical perspectives, constructivist epistemology has been the basis for the clinical-critical method. Subjects do not acquire knowledge, according to this perspective, but instead build it and the researcher—originally a psychologist—has the task of interpreting that which the connections a cognizant subject makes within her world of meaning. In other words, "researchers gradually approach the object of study by actively reformulating their hypotheses" (García Palacios & Castorina, 2010, p. 100). Interviews carried out with the clinical-critical method consist of asking the informant questions, "giving her the time necessary to make any associations she sees fit, while the researcher focuses on the connections she is making in order to formulate the next question based on her answer" (García Palacios, 2012, p. 49). The counterarguments researchers propose at each step in the process allow them to delve deeper into the justification for each piece of knowledge brought to bear in the explanation, thus recovering the social nature of thought. Immersed in the sociocultural contexts the ethnography seeks to understand, this method is a particularly useful tool for approaching the questions examined herein.

A STUDY ON CONSTRUCTIVIST PSYCHOLOGY

In keeping with a critical approach to constructivist psychology, Horn's research focuses on children's ideas about the right to privacy, in a public school of Buenos Aires (Horn, 2013; Horn et al., 2012; Horn & Castorina, 2010). This right, recognized in the Convention on the Rights of the Child (UNICEF, 1989), is unconditional and Horn's analysis shows that children between 6 and 12 years old have different ideas about it. For example, younger children (between the ages of 7;3 and 8;6) acknowledge the existence of personal space but not the right to any protection of such space. In other words, in the mind of young students, school authorities have the right to infringe upon an exclusively personal sphere of their lives. Other children (many between the ages of 8;6 and 12;6) have begun to expect adults to respect their privacy, but condition the right to this privacy on good behavior (on the part of the students) or on the teacher's tact. The child understands that their personal information should be safeguarded from grownup meddling; however, they believe this privacy depends on good school performance and can be violated in cases in which a teacher's intervention ostensibly aims to benefit the student. Finally, only a few students, generally a bit older (ages 11;6 to 12;6), seem to understand the right to intimacy independently of a student's adherence to school norms and of the positive or negative consequences the violation of this privacy may have. Even among these subjects, only a few consider this right to be unconditional and only at certain points in the interviews, revealing how students can view this right as both conditional and unconditional.

In addition, Horn (2013) reveals that certain degrees of abstraction can be found in the building process of children's ideas within the parameters of the social practice. The scarce references to notions of an unconditional right to privacy among the students interviewed are compatible with the limited recognition of this same right at the schools they attend. This suggests that ideas are not independent from the social context in which they take shape and that context limits them. In the words of the researchers, "Without the institution's interventions, it would not be possible for any ideas on authority to form. At the same time, this intervention directs the children's construction of knowledge towards notions consistent with the duty to follow school rules," (Horn et al., 2013, p. 201).

Privacy, then, is not an idea that children copy and paste from reality, from the discourses they hear or from a convention they are usually unaware of. Instead, children form their own idea of privacy in relation to a particular object of knowledge (and its history), their own prior knowledge, and the context of production of the new knowledge: "The knowledge children produce and the privacy they build depend on the recognition of their right to these spaces as part of the social practices in which they are immersed," (Horn & Castorina, 2010, p. 197).

In order to analyze the characteristics of the social context in which ideas are produced and the forms these acquire in relation to context, we decided to do a series of clinical interviews, presenting students with summaries or narratives of everyday school events in which a school authority invaded a student's private space.

In any case, the issue of context requires further research. In the first place, the context of the interview continues to be artificial to some degree, as it is never the same context in which the ideas are produced. It would be naïve to base a subject's ideas regarding his or her right to privacy on what he or she says in an interview in response to certain questions about that particular object, without considering that such ideas are necessarily mediated by the interview situation and the presence of the researcher.

This recently led us to accompany the interviews with observations at the schools attended by our subjects in order to start to analyze the relations between children's ideas and institutional practices.

A STUDY ON SOCIAL ANTHROPOLOGY

In a study based on an anthropological approach to the topic, García Palacios (2012, 2014) analyzed the meanings that children from an indigenous (Toba/ Qom) neighborhood associate with going to church. As part of the ethnography, interviews with children were conducted using the clinical-critical method. From the research, it is clear that although going to church is part of everyday life for all the neighborhood residents, children attribute different meanings to the activity than adults. For children ages eight and under, going to church is associated only with singing and dancing. Although these activities are mentioned by the next subgroup of children (ages nine and up), the older children also begin to mention the Bible, Jesus, God and prayer when asked about churchgoing.

One important aspect of the study is that children are exposed to prayer, the Bible and the figure of Jesus from a very early age, long before the age of nine, when they begin mentioning them during the interviews (García Palacios, 2012). In this regard, it is necessary to consider children's developmental experiences, like church worship and other activities, the music that neighborhood residents enjoy, the videos shown at homes, the presence of the Bible, and prayers. By using ethnographic research tools, especially participant observation, to examine these experiences, it becomes clear that children learn to pray from a very young age, for example, when they are frightened. Thus, the fact that the children under age nine did not mention prayer or the Bible when talking about what they did at church does not necessarily mean they aren't aware of them but that they may not associate it with churchgoing. Given that a subject's construction of the proposed social objects is based on their experiences interacting with them (Castorina, 2005), it is not surprising that children do not initially associate prayer as a social object with the church—or at least not exclusively—because prayer could be something that belongs to different spheres in the children's own experience. The process that appears to take place over time here is that of associating the church and its activities (singing and dancing) with religion (the Bible, Jesus, God, prayer). Thus, children effect a reconstruction (Castorina, 2005) in which they associate church activities with new meanings which adult believers would take as a given.

Methodologically speaking, it is critical to note that the anthropological study on religious knowledge was an ethnography and as such, participant observation was planned right from the start. Before conducting the interviews with the children, extensive fieldwork was done, so most of the interview questions stemmed from prior observation of the children and children-adult interactions in the different situations in which knowledge is constructed. Other questions were based on the materials collected during the research such as the children's textbooks, church brochures, etc. What is more, understanding local beliefs surrounding childhood construction proves fundamental, as research is thus sensitive to different social expectations of children and not constructed beforehand based on an age division arbitrarily imposed by the researcher (García Palacios, 2014). Thus, in the study on religious knowledge cited above, the children were organized in two large groups and then subdivided into *nogotshaxac* ("children or youth") based on the Toba/*Qom*'s conceptualization of different phases of development (Hecht, 2010).

In keeping with the tenets of anthropological theory, our first fieldwork phase was an introduction to the universes of meanings of our subjects before delving deeper into some of the themes that stood out and were most compelling for our research in a second phase. After reconstructing the social practices involving children, we opted for the clinical-critical method, since it allowed us to define key aspects in a study focused on the process of constructing certain knowledge. One example of this is the role of justifications and counterarguments in the interviews (García Palacios & Castorina, 2014), a role that helps to establish the degree of certainty children express in their points of view. Ethnography may reveal contradictory perspectives but is unlikely to allow for a deeper examination of these contradictions unless both methodologies are put into practice in a specific case.

Ultimately, the lines of research in constructivist psychology and social anthropology have gradually adopted methodological tools that were traditionally uncommon in either field. In the case of the study on the Toba/*Qom*, instead of the classic approach of considering either children's constructions or social practices, the focus was on understanding the relationship between them. In both disciplines, the same epistemological framework is used to select the units of analysis, making them methodologically compatible: units of analysis are built on the theoretical assumption of a dialectical relationship between subject and context. In this way, the construction of individual knowledge and context can only be understood in their relation to one another and not as mere aggregates. In this regard, the dialectic is not strictly a theory but a methodology for approaching one's research topics (though theory could produce dialectical explanations, according to Castorina, 2005). This way of examining the developmental processes does not stand in for specific empirical research methods in psychology and anthropology; instead, it is an instrument for devising theory, a perspective that guides scientific research and reshapes its results. From this point of view, researchers must be aware of the interrelations and contradictions of the object of their research in order to effectively approach it. For this reason, the study of a knowledge process in context must address its shifting relationship, reconstructing it according to its own history and complex connections. The value of research strategies "in the field" is therefore enhanced since these strategies can reveal people's social relations and the necessary effects of social interactions on individuals as they construct knowledge (Pires, 2010). At the same time, this perspective obliges us to recognize that individuals do not merely reproduce learned cultural patterns but rework them as part of human praxis and their personal reshaping always depends on the material and symbolic context in which these cultural patterns circulate.

CONCLUSIONS

This chapter has reviewed one of the key issues for contemporary social and human sciences, the systematic analysis of context within knowledge construction. Specifically, we have reached a definition of context for constructivist psychology and social anthropology. Based on the arguments and analyses presented here, we argue in favor of a dialectical relationship between context and knowledge, and a methodology that uses dynamic units of analysis to examine its interrelations.

Based on the points in common between the two disciplines, we have compiled certain theoretical assumptions on the processes of children's knowledge construction *in context*. We argue that context functions as a catalyst, enabling and limiting subjects' construction of knowledge; we also show that a good analysis of context goes beyond "visible" social relations to encompass dimensions of space and time which, though not in plain sight, do have concrete effects on reality. In addition, we noted that as construction processes take place in context, subjects transform that context with the knowledge produced therein, yielding a dialectic that obliges us to consider the importance of agency in cognitive developments. Context can be considered a set of social relations in constant movement; it can be argued that "social practices are what situate the future objects of knowledge in existing systems of social meaning" (García Palacios & Castorina, 2010, p. 94). These practices limit or enable the construction of knowledge, sparking interest or dissuading subjects from delving any further. Our thesis is compatible with Toren's notion of context as sociality (2012) and Valsiner's idea of catalysis (2014) and leads us to affirm that context not only influences that meanings we give the world but also the definitions of what is (or is not) worth knowing, what draws (or does not draw) attention, what sparks (or does not spark) curiosity.

As part of the epistemological and methodological discussion, we have established that in both disciplines, a single epistemological framework can be used to define units of analysis, making them methodologically compatible: units of analysis are chosen based on the theoretical assumption that there is a dialectical relationship between subject and context. Even so, many aspects associated with context continue to be problematic and open to conceptual and methodological revisions, especially those related to the construction and analysis of the empirical research data used to contextualize subjects' activities. On the other hand, context is difficult to analyze due to its multiple meanings and its uses in diverse disciplines and branches, and because of the myriad analysis dimensions that it entails. The dialogue between disciplines makes an essential contribution to defining the different characteristics of context and establishing its differences based on the nature of the research questions.

REFERENCES

Achilli, E. (2013). Investigación socioantropológica en educación. Para pensar la noción de contexto [Socio-anthropological research in education. Thinking about the notion of context]. In N. E. Elichiry (Ed.) *Historia y vida cotidiana en educación* [History and everyday life in education] (pp. 89–132). Manantial.

Althusser, L. (2005). *For Marx*. Verso.

Boas, F. (1981). Curso de antropología general [Course On general Anthropology]. *Boletín de Antropología Americana*, *3*(2), 149–170.

Boivin, M., Rosato, A., & Arribas, V. (2006). *Constructores de Otredad* [Otherness builders]. Antropofagia.

Cabell, K. R., & Valsiner, J. (2014). *The catalyzing mind: Beyond models of causality*. Springer Science & Business Media.

Carugati, F., & Mugny, G. (1988). La teoría del conflicto sociocognitivo [The sociocognitive conflict theory]. In G. Mugny. & J. A. Pérez, (Eds.), *Psicología social del desarrollo* [Social psychology of development] (pp. 79–94). Anthropos.

Castorina, J. A. (2005). La investigación psicológica de los conocimientos sociales. Los desafíos a la tradición constructivista [Psychological research on social knowledge. Challenges to the constructivist tradition]. In J. A. Castorina (Ed.), *Construcción conceptual y representaciones sociales. El conocimiento de la sociedad* [Conceptual construction and social representations. Knowledge of society] (pp. 19–44). Miño y Dávila.

Castorina, J. A., & Baquero, R. J. (2005). *Dialéctica y psicología del desarrollo: el pensamiento de Piaget y Vigotsky* [Dialectics and developmental psychology: The thinking of Piaget and Vigotsky]. Amorrortu.

Castorina, J. A., Lenzi, A., & Fernández, S. (1984). Alcances del método de exploración crítica en psicología genética [Scope of the critical scanning method in genetic psychology]. In J. A. Castorina, S. Fernández, A. Lenzi, H. Casavola, M. Kaufman, & G. Palau (Eds.), *Psicología Genética: aspectos metodológicos e implicancias pedagógicas* [Genetic psychology: Methodological aspects and pedagogical implications] (pp. 83–118). Miño y Dávila.

Cicourel, A. V. (1973). *Cognitive sociology*. Penguin.

Cole, M. (2003). V*ygotsky and context. Where did the connection come from and what difference does it make?* Biennial Conferences of the International Society for Theoretical Psychology, Istanbul, Turkey.

Cole, M., & Engeström, Y. (1993). A cultural-historical approach to distributed cognition. In G. Salomon (Ed.), *Distributed cognitions: Psychological and educational considerations*, (pp. 1–46). Cambridge University Press.

Delval, J. (1989). La representación infantil del mundo social [Children's representation of the social world]. In E. Turiel; I. Enesco, & J. Linaza, (Eds.), *El mundo social en la mente infantil* [The social world in the child's mind] (pp. 245–328). Alianza.

Doise, W. (1985). Social regulations in cognitive development. In R. A. Hinde, A. N. Perret-Clermont, & J. Stevenson-Hinde (Eds.), *Social relationships and cognitive development* (pp. 294–308). Oxford University Press.

Doise, W., Mugny, G., & Perret-Clermont, A. N. (1975). Social interaction and the development of cognitive operations. *European Journal of Social Psychology*, *5*(3), 367–383.

Donaldson, M. (1979). *Children's minds*. W. W. Norton & Company.

Duranti, A. (2001). *Linguistic anthropology: A reader*. John Wiley & Sons.

Engeström, Y. (1999). Innovative learning in woks team: Analyzing cycles of knowledge creation in practice. In Y- Engeström, (Ed.), *Perspectives On Activity Theory* (pp. 377–404). Cambridge University Press.

Engeström, Y., & Middleton, D (1996) (Eds.). *Cognition and communication at work*. Cambridge University Press.

Feldman, J., Petersen, M., & Mendoza, M. (1984). La maduración cognoscitiva y perceptual en niños de una comunidad toba del oeste de Formosa [Cognitive and perceptual maturation in children from a Toba community in the west of Formosa]. *Revista fono audiológica*, *30*(3), 166–173.

Furth, H. G. (1994). On childhood cognition and Social Institutions. *Man, 29*(4), 976–978.

García Palacios, M. (2012). Religión y etnicidad en las experiencias formativas de un barrio toba de Buenos Aires [Religion and ethnicity in the formative experiences of a Toba neighborhood in Buenos Aires]. Doctoral Thesis (Anthropology), Faculty of Philosophy and Letters, University of Buenos Aires, Argentina.

García Palacios, M. (2014). Going to the churches of the Evangelio: Children's Perspectives on religion in an indigenous urban setting in Buenos Aires. *Childhood's Todays*, *8*(1), 1–25.

García Palacios, M., & Castorina, J. A. (2010). Contribuciones de la etnografía y el método clínico-crítico para el estudio de los conocimientos sociales de los niños [Contributions of ethnography and the clinical-critical method to the study of children's social knowledge]. In J. A. Castorina (Ed.), *Desarrollo del Conocimiento Social* [Social Knowledge Development] (pp. 83–111). Miño y Dávila.

García Palacios, M., & Castorina, J. A. (2014). Studying children's religious knowledge: Contributions of ethnography and the clinical-critical method. *Integrative Psychological and Behavioral Science*, *48*(4), 462–478.

García Palacios, M., Horn, A., & Castorina, J. A. (2014). Prácticas sociales, cultura e ideas infantiles. Una convergencia entre la antropología y la psicología genética crítica [Social practices, culture and children's ideas. A convergence between anthropology and critical genetic psychology]. *Estudios de Psicología*, *36*(1), 211–239.

García Palacios, M., Horn, A., & Castorina, J. A. (2015). El proceso de investigación de conocimientos infantiles en psicología genética y antropología [The process of researching children's knowledge in genetic psychology and anthropology]. *Revista Latinoamericana en Ciencias Sociales, Niñez y Juventud*, *13*(2), 865–877.

Geertz, C. (2001). *La interpretación de las culturas* [The interpretation of cultures]. Gedisa.

Godelier, M. (1974). *Economía, fetichismo y religión en las sociedades primitivas* [Economics, fetishism and religion in primitive societies]. Siglo XXI editores.

Goodwin, C., & Duranti, A. (1992). Rethinking context: An introduction. In A. Duranti & Goodwin, C. (Eds.), *Rethinking context* (pp. 12–48). Cambridge University Press.

Guber, R. (2008). *El salvaje metropolitano* [The metropolitan savage]. Paidós.

Hecht, A. C. (2010). *Todavía no se hallaron hablar en idioma. Procesos de socialización lingüística de los niños en el barrio toba de Derqui, Argentina* [No language has yet been found to be spoken. Processes of linguistic socialisation of children in the Toba neighborhood of Derqui, Argentina]. Lincom Europa.

Hirschfel, L. A. (1994). Is the acquisition of social categories based on domain-specific competence or on knowledge transfer? In L. A. Hirschfel & S. A. Gelman (Eds.), *Mapping the mind: Domain specificity in cognition and culture* (pp. 201–233). Cambridge University Press

Horn, A. (2013). *Las ideas infantiles sobre el derecho a la intimidad y las prácticas escolares* [Children's ideas about the right to privacy and school practices]. Dissertation, Master Degree (Education), Faculty of Philosophy and Letters, University of Buenos Aires, Argentina

Horn, A., & Castorina, J. A. (2010). Las ideas infantiles sobre la privacidad. Una construcción conceptual en contextos institucionales [Children's ideas about privacy. A conceptual construction in institutional contexts]. In J. A Castorina (Ed.) *Desarrollo del conocimiento social. Prácticas, discursos y teoría* [Development of social knowledge. Practices, discourses and theory] (pp. 191–214). Miño y Dávila.

Horn, A., Helman, M., Castorina, J. A., & Kurlat, M. (2013). Prácticas escolares e ideas infantiles sobre el derecho a la intimidad [School practices and children's ideas about privacy rights]. *Cadernos de Pesquisa, 43*(148), 198–219.

Hutchins E., & Goodwin C. (Eds.). (2011) *Embodied interaction. Language and body in the material world*. Cambridge University Press.

Krotz, E. (1988). Viajeros y antropólogos: aspectos históricos y epistemológicos de la producción de conocimientos antropológicos [Travellers and anthropologists: Historical and epistemological aspects of the production of anthropological knowledge]. *Nueva Antropología, 9*(33), 17–52.

Lave, J. (2001). La práctica del aprendizaje [The practice of learning]. In Chaiklin, S. & Lave, J. (Eds.), *Estudiar las prácticas. Perspectivas sobre la actividad y contexto* [Understanding practice: Perspectives on activity and context] (pp. 15–44). Amorrortu [English edition: Lave, J. (1996). The practice of learning. In Chaiklin, S., & Lave, J. (Eds.), *Understanding practice: Perspectives on activity and context.* Cambridge University Press.

Lévi-Strauss, C. (1977). *Structural anthropology.* Routledge.

LeVine, R. (2007). Ethnographic studies of childhood: A historical overview. *American Anthropologist, 109*(2), 247–260.

Malinowski, B. (1922/2014). *Argonauts of the Western Pacific.* Routledge.

Nunes, A. (1999). *A sociedade das crianças A'uwë-Xavante. Por uma antropologia da criança* [The society of the A'uwë-Xavante children. Towards an anthropology of children]. Instituo de Innovaçao Educacional, Ministério da Educaçao.

Ortner, S. (1984). Theory in anthropology since the sixties. *Comparative Studies in Society and History, 26*(1), 126–166.

Piaget, J. (1997). *The moral judgment of the child.* Free Press Paperbacks.

Pires, F. (2010). O que as criancas podem fazer pela antropología? [What can children do for anthropology?]. *Horizontes Antropológicos, 34*(1), 137–157.

Potter, J. (2000). Post-cognitive psychology. *Culture & Psychology, 10*(1) 31–37.

Psaltis, C., & Zapiti, A. (2014). *Interaction, communication and development. Psychological development as a social process.* Routledge.

Psaltis C., Duveen, G., & Perret-Clermont, A. (2009). The social and the psychological: structure and context in intellectual development. *Human Development; 52*, 291–312.

Reynoso, C. (1991). *El surgimiento de la antropología posmoderna* [The emergence of postmodern anthropology]. Gedisa

Rockwell, E. (1995). De huellas, bardas y veredas: una historia cotidiana en la escuela [Of footprints, fences and pavements: An everyday school story]. In E. Rockwell (Ed.), *La escuela cotidiana* [Everyday school] (pp. 130–157). FCE.

Rockwell, E. (1996). La dinámica cultural en la escuela [The cultural dynamics in the school]. In A. Álvarez, (Ed.), *Hacia un currículum cultural. La vigencia de Vygotski en la educación* [Towards a cultural curriculum. Vygotski's relevance in education] (pp. 87–112) Infancia y Aprendizaje.

Rockwell, E. (2009). *La experiencia etnográfica. Historia y cultura en los procesos educativos* [The ethnographic experience. History and culture in educational processes]. Paidós.

Rogoff, B. (1995). Observing sociocultural activity on three planes: Participatory appropriation, guided participation, and apprenticeship.. In J. Werstch, & E. del Río, (Eds.), *Sociocultural studies of mind (Learning in doing: social, cognitive and computational perspectives)* (pp. 139–164). Cambridge University Press

Schubauer-Leoni, M. L., & Grossen, M. (1993). Negotiating the meaning of questions in didactic and experimental contracts. *European Journal of Psychology of Education, 8*, 451–471.

Schubauer-Leoni, M. L., Perret-Clermont, A. N. & Grossen, M. (1992). The construction of adult child intersubjectivity in psychological research and in school. In M. V. Cranach, W. Doise, & G. Mugny (Eds.), *Social representations and the social bases of knowledge* (Vol. 1, pp. 69–77). Hogrefe & Huber Publishers.

Toren, C. (1990). *Making sense of hierarchy. cognition as social process in Fiji.* London School of Economics.

Toren, C. (1993). Making history: The significance of childhood cognition for a comparative anthropology of mind. *Man 28*(3), 461–478.

Toren, C. (2006) *Mind, materiality and history.* Routledge.

Toren, C. (2012). Antropologia e Psicologia [Anthropology and psychology]. *Revista Brasileira de Ciencias Sociais, 27*(80), 21–36.

Unicef, (1989). *Convention on the rights of the child.*

Valsiner, J. (2014). Breaking the arrows of causality: The idea of catalysis in its making. In K. Cabell & J. Valsiner (Eds.), *The catalyzing mind. beyond models of causality* (pp. 17–32). Springer.

Wagoner, B. (2008). Developing "development" in theory and method. In E. Abbey & R. Diriwätcher (Eds.), *Innovating genesis: Microgenesis and the constructive mind in action* (pp. 39–61). Information Age Publishers.

Weisner, T., & Gallimore, R. (1977). My brother's keeper: child and sibling caretaking. *Current Anthropology, 18* (2), 169–180.

Whiting, B., & Whiting, J. (1979). *Children of six-cultures. A psycho-cultural analysis.* Harvard University Press.

Willis, P., & Trodman, M. (2000). Manifesto for ethnography. *Ethnography, 1*(1), 5–16.

Winegar, L. T., & Valsiner, J. (1992). Re-contextualizing context: Analysis of metadata and some further elaborations. In L. T. Winegar & J. Valsiner (Eds.), *Children's development within social context, Vol. 2. Research and methodology,* (pp. 249–266). Lawrence Erlbaum Associates

Wolf, E. (1982). *Europe and the people without history.* University of California Press.

CHAPTER 4

THE CONTRIBUTION OF SOCIAL REPRESENTATIONS THEORY TO THE STUDY OF MORAL DEVELOPMENT

José Antonio Castorina and Alicia Barreiro

INTRODUCTION

Philosophical assumptions, including those of different types of ethics, as well as their associated political and ideological stance, have oriented psychological research on the development of moral judgments, in both explicit and implicit manners. While they do not determine empirical results, they do condition the formulation of problems and the outlining of the moral domain to be studied, as well as methods and units of analysis. These assumptions provide necessary but not sufficient conditions, since the process of psychological research presents relatively independent epistemic features (Castorina, 2020). Furthermore, they may influence, for example, the defence or rejection of the universality of moral knowledge development; whether or not to consider everyday life in the interviews conducted during research, or in the explanatory model of development. It is possible to identify reciprocal connections between philosophical assumptions and the process of psychological research, in such a manner that difficulties and unforeseen data—even certain methodological changes—as well as theoretical controversies and contributions from other disciplines, may lead researchers to review these basic assumptions (Castorina, 2020; Valsiner, 2012).

To begin with, when it comes to the study of psychology of moral development, four levels may be considered to analyse the connection between philosophy and worldviews or ideologies. In empirical studies, these levels are usually interconnected and may be hard to distinguish clearly. In the first instance, the theses of ethics, developed throughout the history of philosophical thought, have oriented, both explicitly and implicitly, all psychological research of moral development, from the deontological theory of Kantian tradition and the virtue ethics of Aristotelian origin, to the English utiliarianism, Taylor's communitarianism or Habermas' discourse ethics. These versions have competed fiercely throughout the history of philosophy, without any of them being able to establish a predominant position. In psychological research, philosophical assumptions are particularly integrated into the methodology cycle, which includes constructed data, studied phenomena, the researcher's own intuition, and the theories and methods of the research programme (Valsiner, 2012). In other words, they constitute the hard core of any research programme concerning moral psychology (Barreiro & Castorina, 2012, 2014). While they do not determine the research's results, they do strongly condition the formulation of problems and the units of analysis. Psychologists have made use of the abovementioned philosophies, not always in an explicit manner, and it is valid to ask at least one question: in what way do they come into play during decision-making in psychological research? The research of Piaget (1932/1971), for example, was influenced by Kant's duty-based ethics, however, his religious commitment, the result of his participation in theological debates when he was younger, came into play. In such debates it made no sense to adopt virtue centered perspectives or utilitarian calculation. According to the Liberal Protestantism in which Piaget participated, God is immanent in the individual conscience and in one's relationships with his neighbor, dwelling in each individual as a thought, and enabling the free examination of his conscience. That way, the individual becomes autonomous, and responsible for his own actions. Piaget made few references to Kantian ethics as he associated them to the Protestant thought, which suggests morality is immanent in conscience, whereas to Kant moral judgments were related to universal principles (Faigenbaum et al., 2007). Furthermore, Kantian thought was especially well accepted by Kohlberg, also a follower of the ideas of Rawls, a contemporary renovator of the same philosophy, who had a broad impact on psychological research.

A second level of analysis covers the influence of psychological research on one's own philosophical ethics. The purpose is to connect the latter to the study of moral development, in order to 'recover' it and obtain a reformulation of its theses, thus granting them a greater indirect credibility, as in the case of Habermas (1985/1976). His basic philosophical thesis is that the basic structure of human experience is communicative interaction between individuals, but at the same time he demands a certain empirical justification for this thesis. This implies acknowledging a reconstructive methodology status—the search of universal condition of possibility—not only for his own idea of universal pragmatics, but also for the reprocessing of those psychological studies regarding the construction of cognitive and moral competencies. A speaker's pretensions of validity or justice are constructed upon universal ones, through both social transformations of consciousness and individual learning processes, inspired by Piaget. Unlike transcendental philosophical analyses, such as those of Kant and his followers, the study of the formation of such moral and cognitive competencies involves causal mechanisms and empirical conditions of their production. This way, a dialogue is established with empirical science, inspired by philosophy: the latter with its claim of universality, embodied in universal pragmatic assumptions, a priori conditions of all empirical moral judgment; the former, in this case moral psychology, mainly Kohlberg's—a reconstructive science seeking moral judgment's conditions of universality—occupies a prominent place in the studies of Habermas, his being an empirical research aiming to give credit to certain philosophical theses (Castorina & Pizzano, 2004). With an even more radical approach, certain naturalistic versions of moral psychology (Haidt, 2008) maintain that one's judgments are based upon emotional intuition, originated in phylogenetic evolution, although requiring cultural forms to be able to emerge during childhood. Exclusively evolutionary, neurobiological, and psychological studies are invoked to support this thesis, revealing a resolute shift in the characterization of morality, from a philosophical field to psychological-biological studies. (Barreiro, 2012a; Turiel, 2008). For example, some psychologists (Premak & Premak, 1994), do not even take into account the philosophical definition of morality, using instead daily life's common sense: 'how an individual treats others' (Faigenbaum et al., 2007). From this cognitive perspective, the interdisciplinary field of moral psychology is sufficient to understand the nature of moral judgment and why people behave 'well' or 'badly'.

It is possible to consider a third level of meta-theoretical analysis, consisting in identifying worldviews and epistemic frameworks (Becerra & Castorina, 2015; Castorina, 2002; Piaget & Garcia, 1982). These are made up by ontological and epistemic theses orienting the researcher's decision-making, whether or not he explicitly accepts or rejects them. Decisions such as, for example, whether to dialectically dissociate or articulate components of moral experience and their biological, intellectual or socio-historical conditions; or whether to neatly separate or dynamically connect universal rationality and context, or collective beliefs and individual thought. This broader epistemic framework includes moral positions, extending to the researcher's philosophical theses, which are transformed into a kind of 'academic common sense' of moral development researchers. In this sense, the epistemic framework's constituent assumptions underlie psychological theories of moral development and guide the interpretation of moral ideas in children. To do this, these assumptions interconnect with ethical and psychological theories. Universalist, formalistic and deontological theories of moral philosophy, for example, are compatible with developmental studies focused on the individual, whose moral judgments tend towards autonomy (Barreiro & Castorina, 2012). Thus, the outlining of the field of knowledge constituted by the logical sequence of the construction of moral ideas, in terms of an increase of reciprocity between perspectives, is, in the case of Kohlberg (1981), a progressive and immanent equilibration of coordinations that will be fulfilled, at least ideally, since certain social atmospheres are allowed to intervene. Moreover, the questions he formulates, the structure of his interviews, and his data analyses, solely aim at children arguing justice without taking into consideration their daily life experiences with it (Barreiro & Castorina, 2014). Naturally, there is no uniformity, and it is common for an author to mingle this very perspective with a rather dialectic one when it comes to other aspects of moral judgment. To Piaget, for example, action and moral thinking are dynamically articulated, as are individual and society (Faigenbaum et al., 2007). To be more clear: this split strategy dominates contextualistic psychology, which neatly separates situations of participation in communitarian moral practice from the individual activity of cognitive elaboration, and is compatible with certain versions of communitarian ethics (Shweder et al., 1987; Walker, 2000), which understand moral acting as based on the individuals' social nature, on projects for a 'good life' and community sentiment (Taylor, 2010). In addition, needless to say, this split framework has explicitly conditioned the neo-innatist studies of moral development (Haidt, 2008).

On a fourth level of analysis, closely related to both the first and third level, it is of vital importance to point out the moral philosophy of ordinary men and women, as a worldview represented in their moral decisions. The main point of research in moral psychology is the following: is it safe to assume that philosophers' ethics are directly embodied in the ideas of children and adolescents, as is observed paradigmatically in Kohlberg's work? That is, do the judgements of justice present in children and adolescents reflect any of the philosophies relevant in the history of ethical thought? It is possible to analyse moral ideas in terms of the appropriation, to a large extent, of a philosophy 'figuratively spilled' onto social actors. A worldview impacting on these actors, and not only on researchers in the sense of the second level of analysis. Specifically, we are referring to the mediation of social representations (hereinafter SRs), a part of common sense knowledge intervening in the life of social groups (Moscovici, 1961). These become hegemonic in a society, since they interpret either justice or punishment, and in turn are promoted and enabled by the philosophy of common sense. In this way, the individuals' moral development involves an active process of appropriation of SRs, which, in turn, suppose the existence of an ideology, and its 'always-possible' influence on their construction and distribution (Howarth, 2014). In other words, the philosophy of philosophers, predominant in a certain era, became the philosophy of common sense, according to Gramsci (2003, 2011), who, unlike Moscovici, considers that common sense is the philosophy of hegemonic sectors translated into concrete actions experienced by the dominated social sectors. A worldview that loses argumentative consistency. On the other hand, to Moscovici (1961), SRs making up common sense are specific and imply a justification system of human acts. Along the same lines, to Jodelet (1991), worldviews make up the SR's horizon. This is how everyday moral ideology is constructed, as a kind of epistemic framework related to several ethical currents, not identical to intellectuals or academics' moral philosophy, since it lacks systematic argumentation, presents incoherencies, and is expressed implicitly in social sectors, specifically in those subordinate social sectors appropriating it. In general, their social function is to legitimize power relations, one of the versions of ideology as a worldview, tending to the sustaining of social order (Castorina & Barreiro, 2006). In other words, despite the many meanings that can be attributed to the concept of justice, people use a specific meaning in their daily lives, regulating their communication and social interactions. This meaning depends on one's individual commitment to belong to a group, ideology, and ontology (Barreiro et al., 2014; Barreiro & Castorina, 2016).

Finally, the characterization of the four possible levels of analysis regarding the relation between philosophy and psychological research is not exhaustive, nor does it establish clear distinctions since, for example, the split epistemic framework or the relational framework—discussed further on—can preside not only psychological research, but also philosophical ethics themselves. The latter are part of worldviews, and have clearly been modified to give rise to the philosophies of ordinary men and women. These levels interconnect in the exploration of their presence in research upon moral judgment, turning provisional the following reflections.

First, we will specifically examine the SR approach in the study of moral development, addressing their relation with the four levels of analysis previously mentioned. Then, we will analyse how empirical research, combining developmental psychology with SR theory and making its philosophical assumptions explicit, leads to a reconsideration of the concept of 'moral development'. Thus, some of the theses that have been upheld in classical studies on moral development, such as the 'path towards equilibrium' (Piaget, 1932/1971; Kohlberg, 1981), are now questioned: the not studying of moral judgments in daily life situations or the abstract universality of the arguments requested from the subjects.

PHILOSOPHICAL CONCEPTIONS AND MORAL DEVELOPMENT

Within the context of the fourth level of analysis proposed, this work's fundamental thesis is that moral philosophy turned into 'common sense' plays an active role regarding moral SRs. The latter are part of the cultural system of meanings, and are appropriated by boys and girls throughout their development (Barreiro, 2012b, 2013a,b). In other words, their moral inferences are strongly influenced by the common sense shared by their societies or their groups of belonging at a given historical moment.

In order to clarify this position, we should recall that most of the classic psychologists of moral development (Piaget and Kohlberg) were influenced by Kant, and contemporary authors by neo-Kantianism. Turiel (2008), for example, distinguishes between conventional and moral rules, thus following Gewirth's (1978) approach. According to the latter, moral rules are categorically obligatory, and rejecting them results in contradiction. On the contrary, studies on moral judgment that link Piagetian psychology to SR theory (Barreiro & Castorina, 2012a, 2014; Leman & Duveen, 1996) take for granted, to some extent, the rejection of the Kantian Categorical Imperative, that is, they question a certain ethic, according to the first level of analysis proposed. Kant's maxim, according to which one must act in such a way that one's conduct can become the norm for all men under similar conditions, assumes only one culture, one religion, a global conformity, when in reality such conditions do not exist. This perspective exposes the weak side of the Enlightenment's moral project: its pretension of universality of values being above historical-cultural differences. SR theory, in turn, considers moral beliefs to be relative to social groups and to the historic context in which they are formulated (Emler et al., 2007).

Among other critical thinkers of today's universalist tradition, Gramsci (2003, 2011) claims that any appeal to the categorical imperative inevitably leads to an absolutization or generalization of historically given beliefs. Attempting an absolute foundation of morality is unacceptable; in any case, it is necessary to depart from historical analysis in order to sustain ethical freedom. According to Marx, society does not take on tasks whose solution requires not yet existing conditions. Therefore, this historical perspective implies the admission of a certain cultural relativity, which, in turn, involves critical acknowledgement of the existence of different moral principles in different cultural contexts. Hence, rather than a universal ethic, ethics related to different narratives, traditions, and cultures are defended: whether they are virtues, norms, utilitarianism or communitarianism. It is hard to make an ultimate decision regarding the sustainability of any of them, regardless of historical contexts.

On the other hand, the study on moral SRs' ontogenesis not only implies abandoning the categorical imperative, but also the persistent belief that it is possible to study children's judgments without taking into consideration the beliefs circulating in society regarding good and bad, responsibility or blame. In this sense, although SR theory regarding moral judgments does not attempt to verify a moral philosophy in the individuals' development, it does include philosophical stances, at the very least because it rejects deontological theses. Duveen and Leman (1996) revealed that while agreeing on the solution of moral problems, boys and girls do not only rely on the epistemic authority of autonomous judgments, as described by Piaget (1932/1971), but also on the status authority of SRs of gender.

When trying to agree on a problem, it proves to be more difficult when the boys are heteronomous and the girls autonomous, than the other way around.

Furthermore, it is vitally important that studies on moral judgments related to SRT reveal valid moral philosophies in social imaginary, or at least, as Gramsci would say, 'common sense' ideologies. SRs, with their own characteristics, form part of worldviews, which tend to reproduce existing power relations (Thompson, 1990). In other words, the latter are maintained or continued through the creative and even abusive use of symbolic forms, including SRs, in specific historical conditions. That is to say, as SRs embody and give meaning to social experience, they are mystified or naturalized, even when it comes to the access to power (Howarth, 2014). We insist, the ideological meaning of a hegemonic SR (Moscovici, 1988), that is, one that is stable over time and is agreed upon by a large part of society, lies in the legitimization of a social order, which appears as the formation of an SR expressing a particular meaning of polysemous moral concepts, such as justice (Barreiro, 2013a; Barreiro et al., 2014). By definition, ideologies tend to support power relations, and to do so, they suppress or render irrelevant possible SRs or some of their elements at the same time. However, not all SRs legitimize social order, emancipating SRs question this social order, by expressing social conflicts and disputes. (Moscovici, 1988). From the perspective of their social origin, SRs and ideologies are similar, both being collective productions. However, their difference lies in the extent of this production. While the latter are worldviews assumed by individuals and sustaining social order, SRs always refer to specific objects, such as justice or punishment. Furthermore, SRs ask for a creative approach of intersubjective communication, in the face of a social process or event requiring a meaning-construction process in order to understand it: a proper elaboration and not just a mere reiteration of the existing worldview, although the latter is the horizon on which outlines are drawn (Barreiro & Castorina, 2006, 2015; Jodelet, 1991).

In this way, ideologies or worldviews may be considered as the background of SRs, and, for that very reason, they have the peculiar function of enabling the connection of ideologies to a diversity of everyday situations. What is more, ideology does not appear after the SRs' creation, but rather, in a certain way, it shapes them (Castorina & Barreiro, 2015; Howarth, 2014). Along these lines, for example, the belief in a just world, stating that everyone gets what they deserve (Barreiro, 2013b; Lerner, 1980), based in turn on the meritocratic legitimization of the social order established through French Revolution, is the ideological background in which the retributive SR of justice—hegemonic in Argentine society—is rooted (Barreiro & Castorina, 2015). However, social psychologists have not often acknowledged the ideological background of SRs, let alone carefully examined how the former participates in the shaping of the latter.

In short, the philosophy of non-philosophers, the dominant sectors' worldview uncritically absorbed by individuals from various social and cultural environments, influences their moral development, considered as an appropriation of SRs. Hence, each social group or stratum shares a moral common sense or an everyday moral philosophy: a relatively incoherent concept, in accordance with their social position, without a systematic intellectual order, since, like religion, it cannot be reduced to coherence and unity of the argumentation. In addition, it is keen on more or less peremptory certainties, and could even be considered as eager to conserve things as they are, and reluctant to welcome changes. Finally, it is not rigid, but is constantly transformed into a rather chaotic aggregate, including philosophical opinions or scientific ideas (Nun, 2015).

EPISTEMIC FRAMEWORKS IN MORAL PSYCHOLOGY

Generally, ontological and epistemological assumptions influence the very psychologists researching moral judgments, as they give rise to their innatist, constructivist, sociohistoric or contextualistic stance, as mentioned regarding the third level of analysis. For instance, the explanations for development proposed by various authors, in terms of a single factor such as naturalistic cognitivism, or appealing only to social and contextual conditions (Emler, 1987; Shweder, 1990; Shweder et al., 1998); or the explanations invoked by researchers claiming a dualism between innate forms or predispositions and social content (Premak & Premak, 1994), or by a development based on phylogenetic intuitionism, split from later rational judgment made in the context of social practices (Haidt, 2001). All these positions are indebted, explicitly or not, to a split epistemic framework. Even constructivist currents (from Piaget and more radically Kohlberg onwards) only studied the cognitive processes implied in the construction of moral judgments. While acknowledging the relevance of social interactions, they dissociated them from cultural contexts. Therefore, it can be said that they have not overcome such an epistemic framework (hereinafter EF). Certain culturalist psychologies imply an extreme overestimation of the different cultures' ability to produce meanings, by conceiving them as a homogeneous whole, and postulating that they shape psychological processes, while, at the same time, they underestimate individual agency, thus expressing the same split framework (Markus et al., 1997; Wainryb, 2004).

From the perspective of the first two levels of analysis, research articulating developmental psychology and social psychology when exploring ontogenesis of the concept of justice (Barreiro, 2012b, 2013a,b; Barreiro et al., 2014), has not attempted to deploy empirical studies to indirectly verify a moral philosophy, or justify such studies like Habermas, nor has it put into action an academic philosophy, whether deontological, utilitarian, or communitarist, as is the case of most moral psychology studies. However, considering the third level of analysis, it can be said that such empirical research has made explicit the EF influencing it while exploring moral development, by postulating certain dialectical relations between individuals and SRs, expressed and inferred from the practices in which they participate. This is a 'situated' constructivism in the way individuals adopt their social identities, based on their appropriation of SRs (Lloyd & Duveen, 1990). It is worth mentioning that it is not only a matter of linking moral judgments with social interactions, as described by Piaget (1932/1971). In heteronomous interactions, the intervention of pre-existing SRs decides on what can be thought of as moral or immoral, as good or bad, correct or incorrect, etc. The SRs of the culture in which boys and girls live, limit how they see justice: without a doubt, Piagetian 'novelties' are constructed, as the subjects elaborate a differentiation and integration of their beliefs, an 'inferential dialectic'. However, such 'novelties' are only novel to the subjects, not to the culture they live in.

In short, the research programmes of SRT and *critical* constructivism (Castorina, 2005; Duveen, 1994) have addressed moral development: developmental psychology from an individual perspective, social psychology from a social perspective. Both share, as mentioned before, the same epistemological and ontological assumptions, related to the relational and interactive character of the components of moral experience, to its components existing only in their interpenetration, both in the SRs' genesis and in the formation of concepts. Furthermore, on a meta-theoretical basis, there is a common triangular and contextual perspective, both for the construction of SRs and for moral conceptualizations. On the one hand, SRs are part of the dynamic relation between subject-other-object, a dynamic semiotic triangle Ego-Alter-Object (representation/symbol). In this sense, the dialectic EF is determined and specified in terms of triadic relations between subject, object and other, influencing the ontogenesis of SRs in a social group (Moscovici, 1961). The study on the conceptual development involved in the SRs' appropriation supposes triangularity, now between subject-object and the SR, where the centre of interest is the relation of the subject with the object of knowledge, mediated by the SR. In other words, social interactions in which children participate are modulated by SRs.

This relational epistemic framework allows for the compatibility of constructivism and SRT in their differences, by enabling an articulation of research on cognitive development with the constraints of this process. Precisely, by postulating the intervention of collective beliefs associated with social practices in which the subjects participate. We insist, this EF is the meta-theory regarding moral psychologies, parting from the third level of analysis. Even so, research combining both approaches is still exceptional (Barreiro, 2013a,b; Leman & Duveen, 1996; Lloyd & Duveen, 1990; Psaltis & Duveen, 2006; Psaltis et al., 2009).

Furthermore, and from the fourth level of analysis, the features of an ideology or worldview originated by our society's dominant sectors are implemented. It constitutes the backbone of daily life moral experiences. In this sense, a previous work by this research team (Barreiro, 2012b, 2013a,b) has clearly revealed the coexistence of a constructive process and the appropriation of collective beliefs. For example, after presenting a narrative where the child protagonist violates a daily life norm, the interviewed boys, girls, and adolescents were asked to propose a punishment for him, after which they had to justify why this punishment was fair (Barreiro, 2012b). Results show that there are two types of reasons why the interviewees considered a punishment as the fairest: retributive, based on proportionality between punishment and damage produced in the past; utilitarian, based on the future usefulness of punishment, whether preventive, inasmuch as it prevents the transgression from being repeated, or re-socializing, inasmuch as it avoids recidivism by educating the transgressor; and mixed justifications, based on both retributive and utilitarian theses. Retributive and mixed justifications are found in all age groups included in the study, from 6 to 17 years old, and utilitarian justifications appear from 10 years onwards, the presence of mixed justifications being significantly higher in all of the considered age groups. In this way, the subjects mostly appeal to the same type of arguments to justify why a punishment is fair, regardless of their age. This reveals an individual reconstructive activity constrained by their living in a system of punishments whose mixed justification is internalized without reflection. From this perspective, culture is not an exteriority 'stimulating' or 'obstructing' the individual's knowledge construction processes, but rather it shapes them.

On the other hand, these findings indicate that, although constructivist psychology does not address the construction of social subjectivity, it is essential to take it into account, to recognize the subject, committed to his social identity depending on SRs, in the activity of conceptual elaboration (Lloyd & Duveen, 1990). It is necessary to open up psychological theory to the framework of the social subject in constructive activity, which is also consistent with the thesis of social interaction between subject and object in the construction of social knowledge, whether in regulated exchanges, in interactions with institutional dispositives, or in the appropriation of collective beliefs.

Furthermore, as we mentioned when characterizing the third level of analysis, meta-theories do not 'float' above empirical research in a platonic sense, but rather condition it, and may be modified by the vicissitudes of the production of knowledge on moral development. The explicit adoption of a relational EF, and the consequent compatibility between theories, enable a collaborative dialogue leading to modifications, both in SR theory and in developmental psychology. Furthermore, conceptual arguments put forward by psychologists are influenced by empirical research's renovation, and, above all, by the reflection made explicit by the intervening EF—be they relational or split assumptions—of research programmes. This way, it is possible to face the difficulties inevitably arising every time an attempt is made to link moral psychology with SR theory and common sense philosophy (Castorina, 2020).

IDEOLOGY, POWER, AND MORAL DEVELOPMENT

We now return to the perspective of the fourth level of analysis, the common sense philosophy identified in our studies on the appropriation of the belief in a just world, that is, that the world is a just place where each one gets what he deserves. Here, we found a process of the individuals' intellectual elaboration of that ideological belief (Barreiro, 2013b). In addition, this belief forms the background on which the retributive SRs of justice, hegemonic in boys, girls, adolescents, and adults of the Autonomous City of Buenos Aires, are outlined (Barreiro & Castorina, 2015). Also, it contributes to the denial of other possible meanings, such as those connected to the distribution of goods and social resources, that may lead to the questioning of the established social order (Barreiro, 2013a; Barreiro & Castorina, 2016; Barreiro et al., 2014). Clearly, the belief in a just world, as a worldview broader than SRs, partly explains the development of the individuals' perception of justice. These findings inevitably lead to the question of the connection between moral judgment, ideology, and power. However, most of the empirical research and theoretical elaborations carried out within the framework of SRT, focusing on its sociogenetic construction process, have not addressed the analysis of the intervention of power relations. Although SRT has the theoretical and methodological tools to analyse the construction processes of a specific meaning as the only one possible for polysemous objects, such as justice or punishment, which in turn contributes to the legitimacy of the status quo (Barreiro & Castorina, 2016), there are very few studies that have taken into account society's unequal distribution of power (Barreiro et al., 2017; Howarth, 2014; Jovchelovich, 2010).

This way, SRs can be used to support and defend a specific construction of social reality, although they may also be applied to resist against the hegemonic realities imposed by dominant groups. In today's social world, multiple versions of reality coexist, and knowledge systems are less homogeneous and stable. Hence, there are greater possibilities for criticism, argumentation and discussion on moral questions, as well as on other aspects of the social world. In other words, SRs, as 'symbolic forms', providing limits and structure to social experience, may be used to legitimize or naturalize social order and, in this sense, are ideological forms (Thompson, 1990). However, SRs may also express a rebellious attitude towards this order. We insist, the SRs' ideological quality implies their contribution to the individuals' consolidation of reality, defending themselves from other SRs representing different realities, and thus limiting the range of possible meanings during their sociogenetic process. It is precisely the dialectical movement between cooperation and conflict (consensus and dissent) that differentiates SRs from the collective representations studied by Durkheim (Moscovici, 1961). The meanings prevailing in this struggle between different SRs in the social arena form a positive SR, a signifying structure replacing the real object in everyday life. However, the possible meanings that are not included in the SR's conformation are transformed into *nothingness*, making up the positive SR's negative or dark side (Barreiro & Castorina, 2016). That is, the unrepresented, the parts not present in that signifying structure. This exclusion or repression of certain meanings from the representational field is not accidental. They are excluded for they might challenge the dominant ideological worldview and, therefore, threaten social groups. The absence of an SR regarding an object that is emotionally decisive for the group may even indicate its overwhelming affective presence in its members' daily life.

This dynamic process of conflictive relations between SRs was addressed by Moscovici (2001), who distinguished hegemonic SRs from polemic and emancipated SRs. Polemic SRs express different social stances on the same object, generally contradictory, while emancipated SRs express a divergent point of view with respect to the hegemonic SR, but coming from a group without the social power necessary to dispute its status of reality to the dominant SR. Distinguishing these SRs is enriching when considering moral development, since hegemonic SRs express a social group's dominant value and belief system, while polemic SRs sustain an explicit conflict with them, as may occur, for example, in a society where secular morality and religious morality are confronted. Emancipated moral SRs express a system of values different from the dominant ones, and are tolerated without conflicting with the hegemonic SRs, since the group embodying them does not have the necessary power to threaten the status quo. Undoubtedly, these power conflicts and tensions between SRs corresponding to different value systems supported by groups with different levels of power in society intervene in the shaping of psychologists' EFs and ordinary men's everyday philosophies.

A CONCLUSION: REFORMULATING PROBLEMS

The aforementioned researches on ontogenesis of SRs of justice have been conditioned, explicitly or implicitly, by the relational EF, in their problem formulation and choice of units of analysis. Also, they have taken into serious consideration the acknowledgement of the worldview forming the individuals' common sense. Now, based on these assumptions, SRT and developmental psychology have been combined to study the development of moral judgments, and the results lead us to reframe—briefly and tentatively—some of the classic theoretical problems of this field of study.

Regarding the nature of constructivism, this is clearly the critical revision, strongly questioning the version unfailingly connecting it to the elaboration of 'more advanced ideas', in a direction immanent in the deployment of what 'ought to be', inspired by Kantian ideas. Revised constructivism does not address the study of justice as the formation of what ought to be, focused on norms. This version seeks to explore the production of cognitive novelties from a perspective of the subject's elaboration, but in terms of the reconstruction of the SRs pre-existing in his society. Cognitive activity involves an increase in abstraction and a dialectical articulation of concepts, such as relativization or the dynamic unity between independent knowledge systems. Such is the case of the dynamic articulation between retribution and utilitarianism in the ontogenesis of SRs of justice, in the conceptualizations made by individuals when appropriating the moral common sense embodied in our society's hegemonic SR's (Barreiro, 2013a). Clearly, we defend the individual elaboration of new arguments, by reorganizing the meanings given to moral situations, but we take a distance from a purely epistemic or 'moral' subject in Kantian sense. We propose a psychosocial subject, participating in contextualized social practices (family, school or institutions), thus inferring and appropriating the SRs expressed in these practices. Therefore, it is crucial to reconsider the moral subject's features in their diversity, unthinkable without a dialectic relation with the other and with the object of knowledge. He is formed by this ternary and dynamic articulation, in which cognitive activity can only be considered in the context of beliefs and social interactions, framed in an ideological worldview.

Regarding the intervention of culture in moral development, this constructivist approach differs significantly from some versions of cultural psychology (Shweder, 1990), in which the significant diversity of values within this image of culture is not an issue. What is more, culture is interpreted —without differences in values, power and conflict—within the structuring of social phenomena. Instead, the theory of SRs introduces heterogeneity and diversity, due to the different positions and values of social groups, significantly enriching the concept of culture. Also, as seen before, this diversity does not preclude the subjective side of the SR's functioning, the cognitive activity we highlighted.

At this point, we propose a certain convergence with other contemporary constructivist lines of research, highly critical of the homogenizing approach, or of global cultural orientations such as moral codes (Wainryb, 2004). This approach can never comprehend the multiplicity of concerns and goals that are part of the individuals' social life, nor the way in which they process those concerns in specific contexts. It is necessary to acknowledge the complexity of the individuals' experience within society, making them produce meanings that reinterpret cultural ideologies. When considering SRs, this diversity also forces us to reject the thesis of moral development as a progressive advance of reason towards a point of arrival, distancing ourselves from the 'immanentism' of the Piagetian perspective.

On the contrary, moral ideas emerge during the appropriation process of collective beliefs regarding good and bad, right or wrong, etc. The results of our studies (Barreiro, 2012b, 2013b) indicate that it is possible to distinguish different thought logics within the same subjects. As we have seen, different moral perspectives may coexist in these subjects, without an evolutionary line mediating between them that would allow the establishment of states of lesser or greater validity. This coexistence of different SRs of justice can be interpreted from different philosophical stances (retributionism or utilitarianism) instead of a univocal development of rationality, emphasizing the production of ideas in contextual situations. But the identification of different ethics in people's daily lives does not exclude the possibility of speaking of an increase in intellectual thoroughness and consistency through dialectical inferences (Barreiro & Castorina, 2012; Castorina & Baquero, 2005), and in an exact manner: boys and girls separately consolidate utilitarianism and Kantian retributionist ethics when understanding justice, and later achieve their integration during adolescence (Barreiro, 2013a).

In this sense, when we refer to the connections between the levels of analysis proposed at the beginning of this work, one might think that in the subjects' judgments we can identify strong analogies with Kantian retributionist philosophies or utilitarianism, from our first level of analysis. However, we are referring to a transformation into common sense and its appropriation in the SRs' ontogenesis, corresponding to the fourth level. Subjects may uphold different morals, but in this case retributive justice, hegemonic in Argentine society, predominates (Barreiro et al., 2014). We insist, this does not imply a hierarchy between them, nor the definitive abandonment of one for the other. Like we said, from an perspective of argumentation we cannot find reasons to justify a hierarchy, from less to more validity, of the ethical currents developed by academic philosophers, at least not when critically considering the history of thought.

Now, can universality, strongly supported in deontological versions of moral judgment, be defended? Undoubtedly, morality of a Kohlbergian style, with its claim of universality, is unsustainable, among many other reasons, because its characterization depends on the conflicts related to what 'ought to be' when it comes to justice, enabling moral reasoning. This version is very limited and leaves out conceptions related to common sense, as well as other aspects of moral judgments that are not purely reflective (Flanagan, 1996).

In general, various universalist and contextualistic versions collide on the scene of today's moral psychology. In the former, either constructed modes of thought, as in Kohlberg's theory, are upheld, or biological primitive ones (Premark & Premak, 1996), determining the development of adult morality, although admitting a vast variety of moral contents, with no room for the individuals' reflection. We can even draw a parallel between universality of neural networks and those contents depending on a 'selection', confirming or rejecting the individuals' decisions in certain contextual conditions. On the other hand, stances such as that of Shweder (1990; Shweder et al., 1998, 1987) are relativistic: either it is the cultural context that provides the contents containing the elements to think about moral judgments, or judgments ultimately depend on the narrative context in which we are confronted with moral situations. This relativism evades any search for universal aspects that might eventually emerge from a dialogue between cultures or subcultures. However, there is another type of universalist approach: Turiel (2000) does not defend the universality of empty forms or innate contents, but rather proposes the universal—very early—choice of moral acts causing harm. 'What causes harm' may vary depending on beliefs and cultural contexts, but the fact that harm is rejected, does not change. Clearly, cultural context intervenes, as informational assumptions, originating in various social systems, such as the religious system. Thus, beliefs about the social world provide the conditions for subjects to examine an act's harm. In this sense, it is opposed to 'contextualism', which does not differentiate the individual from his context, nor does it address the study of the individuals' argumentative contribution.

As we have said, SRT is not a philosophical theory defending a relativistic version with actual philosophical arguments; it is a psychological theory that supposes a contextual moral version. It is compatible with theses contextualizing moral value, but does not comment on questions of universality in philosophical terms.

Undoubtedly, carrying out studies from a psychosocial perspective reveals the sociocultural diversity of moral beliefs, a relativity that is not necessarily relativism. We are assuming that an individual thinks within context, that social conditions of moral thought are inseparable from intellectual activity, and that the subject has 'a point of view' when adopting a moral perspective, the subjective dimension of the SRs' genesis, insisted on by Jodelet (2008). This means that, from the perspective of SRT, moral thought depends, to a large extent, on cultural tools, in this case SRs. This does not in itself imply that subjects understand through social meanings. There are certain levels of reflection, precisely because cognitive processes are also put into play in the adherence to or rejection of SRs, as well as the participation in the affirmation of alternative SRs. This is a necessary condition to achieve 'advances in moral thought', which does not mean reaching some level of a hypothetical development from lower to higher degree of 'moral conscience of duty', applying to any human group or subject (abstract universalism and hierarchy of moral conceptions). In this perspective, we refer to moral universality in terms of something 'inductively general or universal,' generalizing shared features.

Yet, with the contribution of the SRT, does it still make any sense to speak of universality in an explanation of moral development? Clearly, in the situated constructivism that we have assumed, it is not a question of a supposed 'universality', developed from studies of moral judgment in children of different cultures, nor do we postulate innate universal forms or intellectual operations shared by all subjects, and lined up in teleological order. However, the studies using both research programmes (revisited Piagetian psychology and SRT), propose cognitive mechanisms responsible for the SRs' ontogenesis, operating each time subjects reconstruct SRs through their appropriation. In this sense, there is a functional invariant, an inferential dialectic expressing the subjects' constructive activity.

On the other hand, from the perspective of psychosocial subjects, SRs have a subjective dimension (Jodelet, 2008): the claim of rights that *should be acknowledged by all*. All subjects studied by SRT aspire, in a subjective dimension, for their belief of justice to be acknowledged by others (Faigenbaum et al., 2007). Surely, postulating the existence of a diversity of beliefs and moral conceptions in the life of children, as we do, does not contradict the subject's expectations that what he believes to be his rights, values, or idea of justice, *should be* acknowledged by other subjects. This requires a reflection on one's beliefs, and a dialogue with others to achieve this acknowledgement, strongly depending on the achievement of autonomy. More specifically, it assumes that the subject understands the intentions of other subjects, as well as the diversity of perspectives or moral beliefs.

Again, studies on moral judgment combining developmental psychology and SRT, reveal the rejection of both the decontextualized universalism of deontological or naturalistic versions, and of the relativism of contextualist theses. Both interpretations suppose the dissociation between what is universal and the context in which moral judgments occur. On the contrary, the dialectical approach of the unity of opposites (relational EF) affirms a certain universality, whether as the invariance of the cognitive process, or as the moral subjects' expectations of acknowledgement, both only existing or being produced in specific everyday life situations: the Thesis of Situated Universality (Bang, 2008).

Finally: what concept of moral development is relevant when it comes to empirical research on SRT and conceptual discussion? Essentially, studies on everyday life moral judgments do not reveal an abandonment of one type of moral thought for another, but rather they are contextual modalities, depending on the different SRs existing in society. Parting from these studies there are reasons to reject the thesis of the development of moral ideas from lowest to highest validity in a linear manner and common to all subjects. Clearly, given the different logics of thought, there is no reason to believe that there is a development towards critical thought. Moral development is understood as the possibility of constructing one's own moral identity, in terms of becoming a social actor capable of living with peers. In order to do so, it is necessary to appropriate the beliefs and values legitimized by the group of belonging. From a psychosocial perspective, to reduce moral development only to its cognitive dimension is equivalent to psychologizing it, as it is separated from its social conditions. In other words, moral heteronomy is an inevitable and essential social phenomenon, in which it is possible to distinguish cognitive development processes that should be acknowledged. Hence, moral development refers to the process through which people acquire those arguments justifying this heteronomous morality.

In this line of thought, our studies on the appropriation of the ideological belief in a just world (Barreiro, 2013b) and the justifications of punishment (Barreiro, 2012b), reveal the need to consider certain characteristics of dialectical interaction with specific objects. In knowledge of the moral domain, and in others, it has become clear that the particularities of the individuals' relations with collective beliefs give rise to different appropriation processes, with different modes or degrees of constraint of cognitive activity, far from the linearity or teleology of moral development. Even the very possibility of a critical stance, condition for the conceptualisation of an object of knowledge, depends on the assuming or questioning of evaluative and emotional commitments in the situations in which the subject of moral judgment is involved: the aforementioned subjective dimension of SRs (Jodelet, 2008). But when the objects of knowledge—placed in a context of pre-existing meanings, of SRs and their ideological horizon—act on the subjects in a literal manner, as is the case of punishment, a reflective attitude becomes more difficult. In other words, there would be less possibilities of taking a distance from those commitments (Elias, 1956/2002), in order to examine the punishment and distort it. It is plausible to consider that such differences in the constructive process are linked to those social interactions in which moral objects are formed. Undoubtedly, this last statement is a conjecture deriving from the nature of the subjects' arguments; however, it requires empirical research to support it. Likewise, it is necessary to deepen the study of the—apparently invariant—mechanisms intervening in the conceptual reconstruction of the object of moral knowledge, carried out during the appropriation of collective beliefs.

REFERENCES

Bang, J. (2008). Building a new house out of old materials—And with sharpened tools. *Culture & Psychology, 14*(1), 45–56.

Barreiro, A. (2012a). El desarrollo del juicio moral. [The development of moral judgement]. In M. Carretero & J. A. Castorina. (Eds.), *Desarrollo cognitivo y educación II: Procesos de conocimiento y adquisiciones específicas* [Cognitive development and education II: Knowledge process and specific acquisitions] (pp. 199–220). Paidós.

Barreiro, A. (2012b). El desarrollo de las justificaciones del castigo: ¿Conceptualización individual o apropiación de conocimientos colectivos? [The development of punishment justifications: ¿individual conceptualization or collective knowledge appropriation] *Estudios de Psicología, 33*(1), 67–77.

Barreiro, A. (2013a). The ontogenesis of social representation of justice: Personal conceptualization and social constraints. *Papers on Social Representations, 22,* 13.1–13.26.

Barreiro, A. (2013b). The appropriation process of the belief in a just world. *Integrative Psychological and Behavioral Sciences, 47,* 431–449.

Barreiro, A., & Castorina, J. A. (2012). Desafíos a la versión clásica del desarrollo en las investigaciones sobre el juicio moral. [Challenges to the classic version on development from moral judgement studies]. *Infancia y Aprendizaje, 35*(4), 471–481.

Barreiro, A., & Castorina, J. A. (2014). La investigación psicológica del desarrollo de la justicia. ¿Racionalidad inmanente o polifasia cognitiva? [Psychological research on justice development. ¿Immanent rationality or cognitive polyphasia?]. In J. A. Castorina, & A. Barreiro (Eds.), *Representaciones sociales y prácticas en la psicogénesis del conocimiento social* [Social representations and practices in social knowledge psychogenesis] (pp. 73–90). Miño y Dávila.

Barreiro, A., & Castorina, J. A. (2015). La creencia en un mundo justo como trasfondo ideológico de la representación social de la justicia. [Belief in a just world as ideological background to social representation of justice]. *Revista Colombiana de Psicología, 24*(2), 331–345.

Barreiro, A., & Castorina, J. A. (2016). Nothingness as the dark side of social representations. In J. Bang & D. Winther-Lindqvist (Eds.), *Nothingness: Philosophical insights into psychology* (pp. 69–88). Transaction Publishers.

Barreiro, A., Castorina, J. A., & Van Alphen, F. (2017). Conflicting narratives about the Argentinean 'Conquest of the Desert': Social representations, cognitive polyphasia, and nothingness. In M. Carretero, S. Berger, & M. Grever (Eds.), *Palgrave handbook of research in historical culture and education* (pp. 373–389). Palgrave Macmillan.

Barreiro, A., Gaudio, G., Mayor, J., Santellán Fernandez, R., Sarti, D., & Sarti, M. (2014). Justice as social representation: Diffusion and differential positioning. *Revista de Psicología Social, 29*(2), 319–341.

Becerra, G., & Castorina, J. A. (2015). El condicionamiento del "marco epistémico" en distintos tipos de análisis constructivista. [The conditioning of the "epistemic framework" in different types of constructivist analysis] In J. V. Ahumada, A. N. Venturelli, & S. S. Chibeni (Eds.), *Filosofía e Historia de la Ciencia en el Cono Sur* [Philosophy and history of science in the southern cone] (pp. 101–107). Universidad Nacional de Córdoba.

Castorina, J. A. (2002). El impacto de la filosofía de la escisión en la psicología del desarrollo cognitivo [The impact of philosophical split in the psychology of cognitive development]. *Psykhe 11*(1) 25–57.

Castorina, J. A. (2005). La investigación psicológica de los conocimientos sociales. Los desafíos a la tradición constructivista [Social knowledge research. challenges to constructivist tradition]. In J. A. Castorina (Ed.), *Construcción conceptual y representaciones sociales* [Conceptual construction and social practices] (pp. 19–44). Buenos Aires: Miño y Dávila.

Castorina, J. A. (2020). The importance of woldviews of development psychology. *Human Arenas, 1*, 1–19.

Castorina, J. A., & Barreiro, A. (2006). Las representaciones sociales y su horizonte ideológico [Social representations and their ideological background]. *Boletín de Psicología, 84,* 7–25.

Castorina, J. A., & Pizzano, A. (2004). La psicología moral en la obra de Habermas. Una mirada crítica. [Moral psychology in Habermas' work. A critical view]. *Epistemología e Historia de la Ciencia, 10*(10), 132–139.

Duveen, G. (1994). Crianças enquanto atores sociais: Representaçôes Sociais em desenvolvimento. [Children as social actors: Social Representations in development]. In P. Guareschi & S. Jovchelovitch (Eds.), *Textos em Representaçôes Sociais* [Writings on social representations] (pp. 261–296). Vozes.

Elias, N. (1956/2002). *Compromiso y distanciamiento.* [Commitment and distancing] Ediciones Península.

Emler, N. (1987). Socio-moral development from the perspective of social representations. *Journal of the Theory of Social Behavior, 17*(4), 371–388.

Emler, N., Tarry, H., & James, A. (2007). Posconventional moral rasoning and reputation. *Journal of Research in Personality, 41*(1), 76–89.

Faigenbaum, G., Castorina, J. A., Helman, M., & Clemente, F. (2007). El enfoque piagetiano en la investigación moral: alternativas frente al naturalismo y el relativismo. [The Piagetian approach in moral research: Alternatives to naturalism and relativism]. In J. A. Castorina (Ed.), *Cultura y conocimientos sociales. Desafíos a la psicología del desarrollo* [Culture and social knowledge. Challenges to Developmental Psychology] (pp. 89–116). Aique.

Flanagan, O. (1996). *La psychologie morale et éthique.* [Moral Psychology and Ethics] PUF.

Gewirth, A. (1978). *Reason and morality.* University of Chicago Press.

Gramsci, A. (2011). *Antologia.* [Antology]. Siglo XXI.

Gramsci, A. (2003). *Cartas de la cárcel 1926–1937.* [Letter from prison 1926–1937]. BUAP-Ediciones Era-Fondazione Istituto Gramsci.

Habermas, J. (1985/1976). *La reconstrucción del materialismo histórico.* [Reconstruction of Historical Materialism]. Taurus.

Haidt, J. (2001). The emotional dog and its rational tail: A social intuitionist approach to moral judgement. *Psychological Review, 108*(4), 814–834.
Haidt, J. (2008). Morality. *Perspectives on Psychological Science, 3*(1), 65–72.
Howarth, C. (2004). A social representation is not a quiet thing: Exploring the critical potential of social representations theory. *British Journal of Social Psychology, 45*(1), 65–86.
Howarth, C. (2014). Connecting social representation, identity and ideology: Reflections on a London 'riot'. *Papers on Social Representations, 23,* 4.1–4-30.
Jodelet, D. (1991). L' idéologie dans l'étude des representations sociales [The ideology in the study of the social representations]. In V. Aebischer, J. P. Deconchy, & E. M. Lipiansky (Eds.), *Ideologies et representations sociales* [Ideology and Social Representations] (pp. 15–33). Cousset Suisse.
Jodelet, D. (2008). El movimiento de retorno al sujeto y el enfoque de las representaciones [The back-to-subject movement and the social representations approach]. *Cultura y Representaciones Sociales, 3*(5). 32–62.
Jovchelovich, S. (2010) From social cognition to the cognition of social life, *Papers on Social Representations, 19,* 3.1–3.10.
Kohlberg, L. (1981). *Essays on moral development: The philosophy of moral development* (Vol I). Harper & Row.
Leman, P. J., & Duveen, G. (1996). Developmental differences in children's understanding of espistemic authority. *European Journal of Social Psychology, 26*(5), 683–702.
Lerner, M. J. (1980). *The belief in a just world: a fundamental delusion.* Plenum.
Lloyd, B., & Duveen, G. (1990). A semiotic analysis of the development of social representations of gender. In G. Duveen & B. Lloyd (Eds.), *Social representations and the development of knowledge* (pp. 27–46). Cambridge University Press.
Markus, H. R., Mullally, P., & Kitayama, S. (1997). Selfways, diversity in modes of cultural participation. In U. Neisser & D. Jopling (Eds.), *The conceptual self in context: Culture, experience, self understanding* (pp. 13–61). Cambridge University Press.
Moscovici, S. (1961). *La psychanalyse son image et son public.* [The Psychoanalysis, its image and its public]. PUF.
Moscovici, S. (2001) Social Representations. Explorations in Social Psychology. New York: New York University Press
Nun, P (2015) *El sentido común y la política.* [Common sense and politics]. Fondo de Cultura Económica.
Piaget, J. (1932/1971). *El Criterio Moral en el Niño* [*The moral judgement of the child*]. Fontanella.
Piaget, J., & García, R. (1982). *Psicogénesis e Historia de la Ciencia* [Psychogenesis and history of science]. Siglo XXI.
Premak, D., & Premak, A. J. (1994) Moral beliefs: Form vs. content. In L. Hirschfeld & S. A. Gelman (Eds.). *Mapping the mind* (pp. 149–168). Gedisa.
Psaltis, C., & Duveen, G. (2006). Social relations and cognitive development: The influence of conversation type and representation of gender. *European Journal of Social Psychology, 36,* 407–430.
Psaltis, C., Duveen, G., & Perret-Clermont, A.-N. (2009). The social and the psychological: Structure and context in intellectual development. *Human Development, 52*(5), 291–312.

Shweder, R. A. (1990). Cultural psychology—what is it? In J. W. Stigler, R. A Shweder, & G. Herdt (Eds.), *Cultural psychology. Essays on comparative human development* (pp. 1–43). Cambridge University Press.

Shweder, R. A., Goodnow, J., Hatano, G., Levine, R., Markus, A., & Miller, P. (1998) The cultural psychology of development: One mind, many mentalities. In W. Damon & R. M. Lerner (Eds.), *Handbook of child psychology. Fifth Edition, Vol 1: Theoretical models of human development* (pp. 865–937). John Lonley & Sons Inc.

Shweder, R. A., Mahapatra, M., & Miller, J. (1987). Culture and moral development. In J. Kagan & S. Lamb (Eds.), *The emergence of morality in young children* (pp. 1–83). University of Chicago Press.

Taylor, Ch. (2010) *El multiculturalismo y la política del reconocimiento.* [Multiculturalism and politcs of recognition recognition]. Fondo de Cultura Económica.

Thompson, J. B. (1990). *Ideology and modern culture.* Stanford University Press.

Turiel, E. (2000). *The culture of morality: Social development, context and conflict.* Cambridge University Press.

Turiel, E. (2008). The development of children's orientations toward moral, social and personal orders: More than a sequence in development, *Human Development, 51*, 21–39.

Valsiner, J. (2012). La dialéctica en el estudio del desarrollo [Dialectics in the study of development]. In J. A. Castorina & M. Carretero (Eds.), *Desarrollo Cognitivo y Educación. Los orígenes del conocimiento* [Cognitive development and education. The origin of knowledge] (pp. 137–164). Paidós.

Wainryb, C. (2004). The study of diversity in human development: Culture, urgencies, and perils. *Human Development*, 47, 131–137.

Walker, A. (2000). Choosing biases, using power and practicing resistance: Moral development in a world without certainty. *Human Development 43*(3), 135–156.

CHAPTER 5

DIALECTICAL INFERENCES IN THE ONTOGENESIS OF SOCIAL REPRESENTATIONS[1]

Alicia Barreiro and José Antonio Castorina

INTRODUCTION

Within the framework of Social Representations (hereafter SR) theory, ontogenesis corresponds to a level of analysis in the construction of SR. According to Duveen and Lloyd (Duveen, 2001; Duveen & Lloyd, 1990) SR can be described as genetic structures, since their formation implies developmental processes in which it is possible to distinguish three different analytical levels: sociogenesis, microgenesis, and ontogenesis. Specifically, the ontogenetic level is concerned

---

[1] A previous version of this chapter was published in Barreiro, A. & Castorina, J. A. (2017). Dialectical inferences in the ontogenesis of Social Representations. *Theory & Psychology, 27*(1), 34–49. doi: 10.1177/0959354316681863. Also, it was previously published in Spanish in Barreiro, A. y Castorina, J. C. (2018). Procesos constructivos en la apropiación de las representaciones sociales. En A. Barreiro. (Ed). *Representaciones sociales, prejuicio y relaciones con los otros. La construcción del conocimiento social y moral* (pp. 55–72). Buenos Aires: UNIPE. ISBN: 978-987-3805-29-5.

with the study of "a process through which individuals re-construct social representations and in doing so they elaborate particular social identities" (Duveen & Lloyd, 1990, p. 7). Children are born in a world that is already constituted by SR, shared by their parents and other adults. This way, in becoming social actors they acquire their social group's SR. Nonetheless, this process is not limited to childhood, but takes place whenever individuals become part of different groups and appropriate the SR constituted within them.

In postulating that developmental psychology and the theory of SR are two sides of the same discipline, Moscovici (1990, 2001) also contributed to the analysis of the ontogenetic process of SR. On the one hand, he established that SR derive from social interactions and provided reasons why it is impossible to explain them through individual psychology. On the other hand, he linked social beliefs with individual experience, going against the intellectual stream that dissociates the individual from society. However, he did not specifically look into the process by which individuals make SR their own. This is probably due to his emphasis on differentiating SR from the individual representations studied by cognitive psychology. Therefore, Moscovici's (1990) emphasis on the specific focus of both social psychology and developmental psychology may have influenced the present lack of empirical research dedicated to the study of the ontogenesis of SR. In agreement with his approach, the social nature of the composition of human consciousness should be studied by comprehending the individual internalization of the social experience. It is possible to distinguish different moments in this process, as well as specific operations through which different consciences are articulated between each other and with the culture as a whole. Notwithstanding, for Moscovici (1990) this analysis lies beyond the focus of social psychology, given that it remains an object of study for developmental psychology.

Following these seminal ideas, Duveen (1994) points out that the challenge for social psychologists is precisely to adopt a genetic approach when tackling SR; while for developmental psychologists the challenge lies in explaining how children become social actors. In other words, both disciplines study the same phenomenon, but the former does this on a positional or collective level of analysis, while the latter adopts a viewpoint centered in intraindividual psychological processes (Doise, 1982).

Our inquiry will deal with the ontogenesis of SR assuming the compatibility between developmental psychology and social psychology, based on common ontological and epistemological principles (Castorina, 2010; Duveen, 2001, 2007; Leman, 2010; Psaltis et al., 2009; Psaltis & Zapiti, 2014). These principles consist, fundamentally, in assuming that the studied psychosocial phenomena are constitutively linked to culture. That is, we assume a revised Piagetian perspective, which affirms that meaning is constructed and expressed in practice with others, that subjects actively understand the world they are a part of, and that individuals are constitutively related to society (Castorina, 2010; Kitchener, 2009; Martí, 2012; Overton, 2006a; Psaltis & Zapiti, 2014).

We will therefore not be dealing with "two sides of a single discipline" (Moscovici, 1990), but rather with an explicit collaboration between two different disciplines, with their own methodologies and theories. Although SR are the object of study of social psychology, their ontogenesis implies psychological processes traditionally analyzed by developmental psychology. Thus, it requires that the process of assimilation by individuals be studied in interdisciplinary collaboration. Even though the research would be enriched by complementing both disciplines' perspectives, this kind of approach is scarcely found (e.g., Barreiro, 2013a,b; Leman & Duveen, 1996; Lloyd & Duveen, 1990; Psaltis & Duveen, 2006; Psaltis et al., 2009). Therefore, there have not been great advances in explaining the development processes involved in the appropriation of SR.

The study of the ontogenesis of SR assumes placing the development of representational forms in the limelight, as subjects elaborating and modifying their cognitive structures throughout the process by which they appropriate SR. In this sense, specifically in Piaget's later work (1974, 1980), developmental psychology has devised an empirically based theory about the dialectical inferences involved in the construction of new meaning through the individual's activity with objects of knowledge. The present chapter proposes that considering dialectical inferences as cognitive instruments might explain the mechanisms responsible for the transformations of SR during their appropriation. Here it is important to clarify that we suggest using dialectical inferences differently than is originally done in Piagetian psychology. That is, in this chapter they will be employed to explain the process by which individuals reconstruct the fields of meaning of SR as they are appropriated during ontogenesis.

Therefore, this chapter's aim is to analyze the potential of the category of *dialectical inferences* (Piaget, 1980) as a tool, when considering the psychological processes implied in the ontogenesis of SR. We will first present a reading of dialectics as an inferential process within the construction of new meaning or concepts by individuals. We will then analyze the studies on the ontogenetic processes of SR, interpreting their findings by appealing to dialectical inferences. Finally, we will provide a critical analysis of the possibilities and difficulties that arise in the research on the ontogenesis of SR, as well as their implications for future research.

DIALECTICAL INFERENCES IN THE CONSTRUCTION OF NEW MEANINGS

In the first place, when talking about dialectics one refers to an extensive history of philosophical thought: from China and Classical Greece, passing through modern philosophy with Hegel and Marx, up to contemporary debates on its features, scope, limits, and universality or contextual adaptation to the processes being studied (Jameson, 2010). Despite the considerable differences between historical periods and thinkers, it is possible to give a general outline of dialectics in terms of a minimal meaning the various versions have in common. They all share the dynamism and movement of a system, induced by tensions—in many cases, oppositions—in its internal relationships. A dialectical change occurs where the interactions intervene decisively in changing the system. For example, in Piaget's (1980) theory, these interactions would take place between action schemas or between action schemas and objects, which would then lead to transformations in the individual's concepts. Likewise, in Marx's (1894/1971) theory the interaction between the use value and exchange value allows for transformations in capitalism. In a general sense, dialectics therefore refers to the process of self-movement in the system in question, which allows for the construction of novel events (Castorina & Baquero, 2005).

In Piaget's (1980) theory, dialectics acquires a new specific meaning as it is used to refer strictly to the constructive inferential process of the emergence of novelties in logical thought systems. The construction of new meanings assumes that previously existing ones are included in the new one constructed by this movement. Thus, a spiralling process of meaning construction takes place. The consolidation of new meanings is triggered by the natural contradictions produced by problems the subject is not yet able to solve. These contradictions, as defined by Piaget (1974, 1980), are cognitive conflicts resulting from inconsistencies between the schemas or concepts available to the subject and employed to understand some object of knowledge. These conflicts express moments of significant imbalance in the development of the individual's system of knowledge. However, they constitute only an instant of the broader equilibration process of knowledge systems, because the mere existence of these conflicts does not necessarily lead to overcoming them. Cognitive development is actually produced when the conflicts are overcome (Piaget, 1975). Therefore, cognitive conflict in itself is not the true engine of the development of knowledge but constitutes merely the possibility of this development occurring. In other words, the reorganization of systems of knowledge presupposes the existence of imbalances provoked by conflicts. It is because of them that processes of re-equilibration are activated, compensating affirmations with negations by means of reflective abstractions and generalizations (Piaget, 1975, 1977, 1978). In this way, contradictions are a part of a more general process that involves constructive mechanisms producing cognitive novelty. Such constructive mechanisms are what Piaget (1980) considered to be truly dialectical. This is why, from this point of view, it is possible to deal with the inferential process leading to the construction of novelties, without having to refer to the contradictions that take place in a previous logical step.

Piaget (1980) thereby reconsidered dialectics in terms of a—non-deductive—inference leading either from one conceptual system to another more advanced system, irreducible to the former, or to a conclusion from premises that do not include it. Thus, Piaget defended the alternation between deductive inferences, characteristic of thought on its structural level, and dialectical inferences that allow for interpreting the dynamics of cognitive development when explaining how knowledge is derived by individuals from other knowledge as they interact with objects of knowledge. This way, Piaget (1980) considers dialectics as the inferential facet in the equilibration of cognitive systems.

Thanks to this process, which allows passing from one system of meanings to another that surpasses and includes it, it is possible to conceive the emergence of cognitive novelties. Although Piaget (1980) described five modes of dialectical inferences, here we will only describe those we consider to be pertinent for the analysis of the available research on the ontogenesis of SR: the process of undifferentiation, differentiation and integration of systems of meanings; the articulation of systems of meanings that previously existed independently; and the relativization of properties that at first were considered by the subjects to be absolute[2]. Additionally, it is worth mentioning that one constructive process of meaning can be examined from more than one dialectical mode, as we shall see, given that each of them refers to a different analytical perspective on a single process.

A crucial inference for the development of new meanings is the shift from the initial undifferentiation (with respect to a degree of knowledge) of the properties attributed to an object, to their differentiation and ultimate integration. To study the way this mode of dialectical inference works, Piaget (1980) recalls the well-known experiment on the articulation of spatial projections, where a child is placed in front of a model of three mountains and is asked what they would look like from various angles or spatial projections. Younger children imagine that on the opposite side from where they are, the mountain chain looks just like how they see it from their present location, that is, the mental viewpoints they adopt remain undifferentiated. They get to differentiate the possible perspectives only gradually, until they construct an operational system of thought that admits all possible perspectives. For instance, the inversion of right and left or front and back as they turn 180 degrees around the mountains. Thus, the children can simultaneously consider the reciprocity of the relationships at stake, that is, of the spatial projections. It is an inferential process that goes from the undifferentiation of the projections to their differentiation and integration of the viewpoints. The elaboration of these inferences depends on the mechanisms of reflective abstraction and generalization, broadly developed in Piaget's later work (1977, 1978), but in line with this paper's argument will only be mentioned.

The dialectical movement of undifferentiation, differentiation, and integration that characterize this type of dialectical inference is not only found in the formation of general or operational systems of knowledge studied by Piaget. It is also found in the genesis of strictly conceptual systems specific to fields of knowledge that interest psychologists and educators today (Castorina & Faigenbaum, 2002; Martí, 2005). In the field of social knowledge, for example, the levels of conceptualization in the shaping of early childhood ideas on political authority have been reconstructed (Castorina & Aisenberg, 1989). In this developmental process, first

---

[2] Neither the modes of subject–object interaction, nor the circle from preactive to retroactive relations between concepts will be considered here.

the early child's hypothesis that the president is a moral benefactor, dedicated to carrying out what is best for the country and to intervene in times of emergency, was identified. In the version of an intermediate stage, the president becomes an institutional benefactor: he or she does society good through rules while supervising the activity of others, with the power of final decision over the laws. Finally, for the few children who offer more complex arguments, the president does not *have* to do good because of a virtue that is his or her own, but as a result of the contract that binds society. Also, for them the president's activity is regulated by social norms and moral principles. In brief, this conceptual construction on political authority begins in a state of undifferentiation between morality and politics, which then gives way to an intermediary stage where political and moral activity are differentiated. This differentiation is expressed in that the children endow the president with the function of regulating the laws. Finally, there is a movement of integration as the subjects come to think that certain moral principles are required to elaborate laws, and that there are also norms regulating the president. A president who, at the same time, is obeyed by people given that he or she is caring for the greater good.

Another mode of dialectical inferences studied by Piaget (1980) is the articulation of elements or systems formerly separated or independent of each other. For example, Piaget (1980) observed this was the case with mathematical operations such as adding and subtracting in an experiment where he asked children to balance groups of tokens with unequal quantities (e.g., 3, 5, and 7 elements). The participants began by taking two elements away from the group of five and adding them to the group of three, and then vice-versa, which brought them back to the imbalance between the groups. When children act this way, they only bear in mind addition and overlook subtraction. They later begin to articulate addition with subtraction, but only when they are able to use reserve elements, available outside the groups in question. The children are finally able to solve the problem, that is, able to equal the collections of elements compensating for the differences, when coming to terms with the idea that adding is relative to subtracting. One implies the other; $+n$ and $-n$ are simultaneous. This constitutes something akin to a unit of opposites, in so far as two opposed operations refer to each other and are executed in coordination in order to obtain the result.

This articulation of previously independent systems is a type of dialectical inference and can also be identified in the construction of specific fields of knowledge. For example, in the results obtained by Carey (1999) on the biological field of knowledge, it is evident that a conceptual reorganization of the children's ideas on a "living being" takes place, consisting of coordinating originally independent ideas. For 4-year-old children plants and animals are ontologically separate entities: the former are a natural kind without behavior, while the latter are a natural kind with behavior. Around 10 years of age, these entities coalesce by a process of inference that coordinates the independent entities into a common ontological unit: living beings.

Finally, by means of the dialectical inference mode of relativization, a property previously considered by a subject to be absolute or isolated from others becomes a part of a system of interdependencies. In the Piaget's (1974) experiments on seriation, differences in size between objects are first considered by children as absolute, "the large ones and the small ones." Yet, years later they are conceived in relative terms, as parts of a system, a seriation where any object is at the same time larger and smaller than others. In general terms it could be stated that the construction of new concepts is to a great extent a matter of broadening the notion's referent, along with the relativization of its properties. In the case of the aforementioned study on political authority, the president possessed the inherent moral attribute of doing what was right by everyone. Whereas on the third level of conceptual construction, it becomes clear there is a shift from a substantialist version to a relational version of these attributes. The president tends to act for the greater good, but according to the norms that regulate his or her functions, given by the relations within the political system.

It is worth noting that the features of the dialectics offered here are not the results of an a priori philosophy, but rather of a cautious experimental inquiry into the development of certain knowledge. Its credibility depends on its ability to generate new hypotheses that may account for cognitive novelties and their verification (Castorina, 2010). In summary, the study of dialectical inferences has contributed to pinpointing how one conceptual system is transformed into another, inferring novelties by means of relativizations and reorganizations.

THE ONTOGENESIS OF THE SOCIAL REPRESENTATIONS OF GENDER

As outlined in the introduction, the ontogenesis of SR refers to the process by which individuals—not just children—appropriate the cultural knowledge available in the group they belong to when becoming social actors (Duveen & De Rosa, 1992). In this vein, the empirical work by Lloyd and Duveen (1990) describes the ontogenesis of the SR of gender. The authors understand gender as a semiotic system, where the terms *masculine* and *feminine* are associated with values, ideas, and specific practices. In other words, those categories frame sets of objects and personal trends specific to each gender. This way, when someone says that a doll is a feminine toy and a car is a masculine toy, attributions are made based on the social significance of these objects and not on their physical characteristics. Lloyd and Duveen (1990) point out that babies are born in a social world structured by adults, where gender representations pre-exist them. During the first six months of life, they do not yet assimilate gender meanings, therefore they are signifiers for adults, because of their biological characteristics. It follows that although certain toys may have a different meaning for adults; babies show the same interest towards any of them.

With the appearance of the semiotic function children expand their activity in controlling and regulating gender expressions, in such a way that the externalized identity (bestowed by adults) proper to the sensorimotor stage starts to be internalized at the age of two. According to Lloyd and Duveen's (1990) findings, in order to take on social gender markings children must be able to differentiate signifier from signified (signs and symbols). This requires progress in terms of the undifferentiation that characterizes sensorimotor activity (signals). In order to take on gender identity, the subject's cognitive development—described by Piagetian psychology (Piaget, 1959)—involves a process of differentiation that comes in tandem with the development of the semiotic function. Thus, boys of approximately two years of age choose to play with toys socially marked as masculine more than do girls, because it allows them to express a clearly differentiated identity. In contrast, girls know the social tags of objects but do not use them to express differentiated gender identity (Duveen, 2001). Therefore, boys' identities are not exclusively internal elaborations, but reconstructions of collectively constructed meanings. In this research it is not only evident that boys internalize SR, but also that during this process they construct particular identity standpoints in relation to those representations. Even in a single individual assuming his/her identity there are externalized identity elements (the signals) as well as internalized elements (the signs).

These findings clarify that the ontogenic process in children, unlike what happens in adults, calls for considering the development of the cognitive instruments implied in handling different signifiers (signals, symbols, and signs), that is, the constitutive elements of representation. Considering the development of semiotic processes in children allows for understanding the genesis of gender representation processes, through which the individual gains access to the gender significations agreed upon in the children's social group.

Lloyd and Duveen (Duveen, 2001; Lloyd & Duveen, 1990) employed categories borrowed from Piagetian psychology, such as construction, semiotic function, and sensorimotor signals. However, they did not take the categories from the Geneva School's functional research (Campbell, 2009) into account, as is the case with dialectical inferences. Particularly when interpreting their results on the ontogenesis of gender SR, we could call upon the dialectical mode of undifferentiation, differentiation, and integration. Before developing the semiotic function, children cannot differentiate between the self and the world, because they have not yet formed a sense of agency or a social identity. Here a possible interpretation is that there is a sensorimotor undifferentiation between signifier and signified. That is, there is no representation of an absent object, but rather there is a bond where one is part of the other. At first, when babies spend more time playing with certain objects this would not be due to identifying them with a gender representation, but instead the behavior would be encouraged by the adult's representations. Next, accessing the semiotic function allows children to differentiate between signifier and signified. That is, objects would begin to represent gender for the children —for instance guns become toys for boys and not for girls. Finally, the achieved differentiations come together in a gender identity, or this identity is constituted by a unit of multiple semiotic differentiations. At this point "being a boy" for boys would equal assuming the set of signifiers socially marked as characteristic of that gender. When we speak of a process constituted by dialectical inferences, we mean that the transition from exterior identity (attributed by adults) to assumed identity (or internalized) would be a transformation of gender meanings. Those are at first indistinguishable from the signifiers, then become distinct and for the eyes of children constitute social gender markings, and are finally integrated when the complete set of social markings becomes an assumed identity. This way the SR of gender would be activated in children as their identity.

THE ONTOGENESIS OF THE SOCIAL REPRESENTATION OF JUSTICE

Aside from Lloyd and Duveen's (1990) research, we know of only one other research project dedicated specifically to the study of the ontogenesis of SR. This study was carried out by Barreiro (2013a), who analyzed the individual reconstructive activity within the ontogenetic process of the SR of justice. Contrary to Lloyd and Duveen's (1990) work, its approach hinges on psychological analysis, however, acknowledging that this phenomenon is shaped by the individual's social position, and suggesting that different levels of analysis within social psychology (Doise, 1982) should be articulated. Barreiro (2013) points out that developmental psychology has a longstanding tradition in the study of the psychogenetic process of the notion of justice, ever since Piaget's (1932) research on children's moral judgements (Damon, 1990; Kohlberg, 1981). From this point of view, distributive justice is considered as the most rational of moral notions, given that it is based on a main property of operational thinking: reciprocity. Moral development is thereby conceived as an uninterrupted process of increasing balance towards operational rationality. Thus, the work on the notion of justice in the Piagetian research tradition was based on the hypothesis of an isomorphism between the development of operational thinking and the conceptions of justice, without taking into account the common sense used by people in their ordinary lives (Moscovici, 2001; Wagner & Hayes, 2005).

In this vein Barreiro (2013) emphasizes that the notion of justice does not have an unambiguous meaning, even in debates on moral philosophy. Therefore, different ways of understanding justice coexist in line with different ideologies and social interests (e.g., socialism, feminism, and liberalism). And so, it is that different social groups call upon justice to legitimize their interests and criticize power relations in confrontations with other social groups (Campbell, 2001). In spite of the plurality of possible meanings, recent studies show that both Buenos Aires inhabitants and Argentina's most read newspaper represent justice in a hegemonic (Duveen, 2007; Moscovici, 1988) retributive manner (Barreiro, 2013; Barreiro et al., 2014). The country's most important newspaper mentions justice mainly in institutional terms with a negative assessment. It demands more severe sanctions to combat the increase in delinquency, placing the population in a continuous state of so-called "insecurity" (Barreiro et al., 2014). The same representation can be found in youths and adolescents, who associate the term "justice" with laws, punishment, delinquency, judges, and impunity (Barreiro et al., 2014; Morais Shimizu & Stefano Menin, 2004).

To inquire into the ontogenesis of this hegemonic SR of justice, a developmental approach was used by interviewing boys and girls as well as adolescents from different socioeconomic backgrounds in Buenos Aires (Barreiro, 2013a). During the interview, the participants were asked to construct narratives about how justice formed part of their daily lives. Three basic representations of justice were identified: retributive, utilitarian, and distributive. The retributive representation refers to justice in terms of punishment or reward proportional to the actions carried out. In the utilitarian representation, justice is understood in terms of "bringing happiness to people," where "good" is a synonym for happiness. In the distributive representation justice is a form of distribution based on norms equally applied to everyone implicated in a situation, without favoritism or preference. The results show that the utilitarian representation of justice is present in all age groups. Also, the appearance of retributive representations increases with the participants' age and the distributive representation features poorly throughout all age groups compared to the other two representations.

In the course of cognitive development these three basic representations, which at first emerge as independent argumentative systems, merge to form a dialectical movement from independency to articulation, and also relativization. This gives way to four different representations: utilitarian representation in a distributive situation; distributive representation in a retributive situation; utilitarian representation in a retributive situation; utilitarian representation in a situation of retributive distribution (Barreiro, 2013a). Upon integrating with utilitarian representation, retributive representation attains the highest frequency in the age group of 10 to 17 years. For most of the adolescents who participated in this study justice is what allows people to live happily and the way to achieve this is through punishment.

Thus, the representations that were formerly independent of each other are integrated and their properties start to depend on one another. At the same time, they constitute an example of conceptual relativization, in that the properties that characterize them are defined by their relationships with the remaining elements in the system that integrates them. In the case of SR of justice, both retributive and distributive justice become a method for utilitarian justice. They are, in other words, turned into a strategy for achieving happiness for the greatest number of people. This is how the construction of new meanings in the field of justice as an object of representation, follows the path from initial independence of its characteristics and properties to integration into a more complex representation. This dynamic of meanings allows for explaining the developmental process that lets people achieve a broader and more abstract understanding of the SR of justice constructed by their social group.

Therefore, the ontogenesis of SR of justice as described by Barreiro (2013a) involves a meaning construction process, principally manifest in a process of dialectical integration and relativization of the representations (Piaget, 1980). It could be argued that the interdependent representations express the development of novelties, in the sense that the construction of a new form of representing justice includes and transcends the three basic representations (utilitarian, retributive, and distributive). As we have said, the more complex representations not only provide a definition of justice (e.g., justice is making people live happily), but also a method of achieving it (e.g., administering punishment or rewards according to personal merit). In another vein, these interdependent representations refer to a broader field of phenomena. Subjects think about the way social or institutional systems involving different individual and social roles work, beyond their direct personal experience. The latter is precisely what smaller children base their representations on. The fact that none of the representations of justice are abandoned during development indicates a strong continuity of the collective meaning in the individual conceptualization processes. Moreover, the process of construction of meaning, in this case of integrated representations, can be considered as the result of a genuine inference. That, for instance, goes from isolated representations of retributive and utilitarian justice to a new representational unit that includes and transcends them.

Furthermore, it is likely that the process of interdependence and relativization during the ontogenesis of the SR of justice may occur simultaneously with cognitive decentration. This is the process that allows subjects to include different social and personal perspectives in their representations of justice. Hence, the growing complexity expressed within the moral sphere, as in other areas of social thought, allows passing from the concrete characterization of personal experience to the more abstract thought about aspects of a social system (e.g., Barreiro, 2012, 2013b; Castorina & Lenzi, 2000; Delval & Kohen, 2012; Duveen, 2013; Faigenbaum, 2005; Kohlberg, 1981; Nucci & Gingo, 2012; Piaget, 1924). This cognitive process takes place during the ontogenesis of SR, allowing children to reconstruct them by means of their own intellectual activity. It is important to note that the retributive representation of justice does not correspond to any development stage of thought in particular, since it is present in all age groups (Barreiro, 2013). Actually, retributive representation becomes viable through persistent participation in specific interactions and discussions that highlight this particular meaning, limiting the construction of other possible meanings.

To summarize, the conceptualization process in the ontogenesis of SR of justice implies the construction of novelties, framed by collective constraints (inherent to SR) and cognitive constraints (what subjects can achieve depending on their development). These constraints condition the construction of specific meanings of the social object, limiting the construction of alternative meanings. There would be novelty only for the individual actors of the ontogenesis, not for the group to which they belong, where SR are already installed.

THE INDIVIDUAL'S RECONSTRUCTIVE ACTIVITY IN THE ONTOGENESIS OF SOCIAL REPRESENTATIONS

We have presented two studies dealing with the ontogenesis of SR (Barreiro, 2013a; Lloyd & Duveen, 1990) and have seen that in both cases developmental psychology has provided interpretations that allowed a more precise description of the process. In order to describe the process of appropriation of SR it is necessary to make explicit how psychological mechanisms render this possible. Here it should be clarified that social psychology has not dealt with individual psychological mechanisms, due to how it approaches its problems. However, upon inquiring about the individual's appropriation of SR, involving the process by which individuals constitute their identity and structure the social world from birth, social psychology stars to veer towards developmental psychology. In any case, a situation of great interest arises here, as it leads to reflecting on how these two disciplines could cooperate, each from their own perspective, when dealing with a common issue.

As has been shown above, developmental psychology will be resource in advancing our understanding of the ontogenesis of SR, while SR have become restrictive conditions for studying the process of individual construction of social notions (Castorina, 2010; Psaltis et al., 2009). This collaboration is possible because both research programs share the same relational epistemological framework (Overton, 2006b). The dialogue between disciplines is made possible by their compatibility, based on shared ontological and epistemological philosophical assumptions. We can then assert that there is a relational epistemic framework, brought about by the dialectical interaction of the terms at hand. In the case of developmental psychology this dialectical perspective is expressed in the relation between individual and society or subject and object (which is at the same time restricted by SR). In the case of SR theory, dialectical interaction is expressed in the relation between individual and society in the frame of the subject/alter/object triad (Castorina, 2013).

In Lloyd and Duveen's (1990) research on the ontogenesis of gender SR, the developmental psychological resource is Piaget's theory of the formation of sensorimotor and semiotic instruments, as a precondition for the process of knowledge construction. Accordingly, the authors consider the constitutive processes of the semiotic function. These are general in nature, as they are involved in the construction of any kind of knowledge (whether logical, mathematical, or social). These instruments give way to the genesis of truly representational knowledge, based on differentiating signifier from signified (whether these are images, linguistic signs, or symbols). In this sense Lloyd and Duveen (1990) present the differentiation and integration processes implicated in the psychogenesis of the semiotic function, as they help in acquiring gender meanings. This is supported by the formation of the differentiation between signifier and signified.

Cognitive development thereby allows for ontogenesis, because the development of the semiotic function is an indispensable condition for children to assume their gender identity. However, the authors have not been dedicated to clarifying the dynamics or process by which SR are reconstructed when the social object marked by adults is assimilated. Even though the authors recognize those processes of differentiation and integration in their empirical data, they have not characterized them explicitly. In this vein it is worth recalling that resorting to dialectical inferences corresponds to a level of Piagetian theory that is not considered by Duveen. This would nonetheless provide a more precise explanation of the process of ontogenesis of SR, as it emphasizes the individual's psychological dynamics through which the subjects actively reconstruct SR when they assimilate them.

Meanwhile, Barreiro (2013a) explicitly uses the processes of dialectical inference to explain the reconstruction of meanings in the ontogenesis of SR of justice. Through working with interviews, in the discourse of adolescents it could be identified as interdependence of representations into the subjects' narratives. That is, articulating fields of meaning to acquire an understanding that subsumes retribution to utilitarianism as a means to an end. In so doing the previously differentiated significations become relative to each other. The analysis in this investigation is concerned with the personal process of elaborating arguments contained in the narratives, thus providing access to the transformation of the SR during their ontogenesis. Nevertheless, having limited the analysis to the subjects' discourse excludes the social ways of enacting SR in everyday interactions with others (Jodelet, 1991; Zittoun et al., 2003). That is, in patterns of interaction or habits that express meaning. Furthermore, the discursive approach does not contemplate the existence of unreflective elements of SR that lie beyond the scope of discourse (Flament et al., 2006).

One can say regarding Lloyd and Duveen's (1990) research that not having considered the personal perspective on gender it has not taken into account a structural aspect of the appropriation of any symbolic resource, including SR. In recent years, Jodelet (2008) has enriched SR theory by offering a particular approach to the issue of subjectivity. She understands the relation between SR and subjectivation, among others, on the level of the production of knowledge and meaning. By doing so the subjective dimension is included in the study of SR, in addition to social interaction and trans-subjectivity. In the present chapter, we refer to subjectivity in terms of an inquiry on the dynamics subjects undergo in assimilating SR and reconstructing them. Jodelet (2008) proposes, in other words, to consider SR in their subjective dimension, referred to as the intervention of cognizant and emotional processes susceptible to discursive expression. This dimension covers the singular aspects with the experiences proper to each individual's history, but it also includes certain general processes constituting the individual construction of a collective belief. It is in this sense that this work is proposing a dialectics of meanings.

To sum up, focusing on the dynamics of meanings and the cognitive processes by which subjects actively construct and reconstruct entails delving into the mechanisms involved. This chapter has tried to show the potential explanations provided by appealing to the processes of dialectical inferences in order to account for the individual's reconstructive activity during the process of assimilation of SR. This resource allows us to precisely capture the transformations of collective meanings throughout the process in which subjects actively assimilate them. Specifically, it allows for approaching a kind of cognitive activity involved in the processes of the psychological activation of SR (Duveen & Lloyd, 1990). Future research will have to corroborate our interpretative hypotheses empirically, as well as it needs to continue studying other cognitive mechanisms that might be involved in the ontogenesis of SR, such as abstraction, generalization, thematization, or analogical thought.

REFERENCES

Barreiro, A. (2012). El desarrollo de las justificaciones del castigo: ¿conceptualización individual o apropiación de conocimientos colectivos? [The development punishment justifications: Individual conceptualization or collective knowledge appropiattion?] *Estudios de Psicología, 33*(1), 67–77.

Barreiro, A. (2013). The appropriation process of the belief in a just world. *Integrative Psychological and Behavioral Sciences, 47,* 431–449.

Barreiro, A. (2013a). The ontogenesis of social representation of justice: Personal conceptualizations and social constraints. *Papers on Social Representations, 22,* 13.1–13.26.

Barreiro, A., Gaudio, G., Mayor, J., Santellán Fernandez, R., Sarti, D., & Sarti, M. (2014). Justice as social representation: Diffusion and differential positioning. *Revista de Psicología Social/ International Journal of Social Psychology, 29*(2), 319–345.

Campbell, R. L. (2009). Constructive processes: Abstraction, generalization, dialectics. In U. Müller, J. M. Carpendale, & L. Smith (Eds.), *The Cambridge companion to Piaget* (pp. 150– 170). Cambridge University Press.

Campbell, T. (2001). *Justice*. Palgrave Macmillan.

Carey, S. (1999). Sources of conceptual change. In E. K. Scholnick, K. Nelson, S. A. Gelman, & P. H. Miller (Eds.), *Conceptual development: Piaget's legacy* (pp. 293–326). Erlbaum.

Castorina, J. A. (2010). The ontogenesis of social representations: A dialectic perspective. *Papers on Social Representations, 19,* 1–19.

Castorina, J. A. (2013). La Psicología del desarrollo y la Teoría de las representaciones sociales. La defensa de una relación de compatibilidad [Developmental psychology and Social Representations Theory: Defending compatibility]. *Schème, 4*(3), 112–135.

Castorina, J. A., & Aisenberg, B. (1989). Psicogénesis de las ideas infantiles sobre la autoridad presidencial: un estudio exploratorio [Children's ideas about presidential authority psychogenesis: an exploratory study]. In J. A. Castorina, B. Aisenberg, C. Dibar Uribe, G. Palau, & D. Colinvaux (Eds.), *Problemas en Psicología Genética* [Problems in genetic psychology] (pp. 63–153). Miño y Dávila.

Castorina, J. A., & Baquero, R. (2005). *Dialéctica y psicología del desarrollo* [Dialectics in Developmental Psychology]. Buenos Aires: Amorrortu.

Castorina, J. A., & Faigenbaum, G. (2002). The epistemological meaning of constraints in the development of domain knowledge. *Theory & Psychology, 12,* 315–334.

Castorina, J. A., & Lenzi, A. M. (2000). Las ideas iniciales de los niños sobre la autoridad escolar. Una indagación psicogenética [Children's initial ideas about school authority. A psychogenetic inquiry]. In J. A. Castorina & A. M. Lenzi (Eds.), *La formación de los conocimientos sociales en los niños. Investigaciones psicológicas y perspectivas educativas* [The formation of social knowledge in children. Psychological investigations and educational perspectives] (pp. 19–40). Gedisa.

Damon, W. (1990). *The moral child: Nurturing children's natural moral growth*. Macmillan.

Delval, J., & Kohen, R. (2012). La comprensión de nociones sociales [Understanding social notions]. In M. Carretero & J. A. Castorina (Eds.), *Desarrollo cognitivo y educación II: Procesos del conocimiento y contenidos específicos* [Cognitive development and education II: Knowledge processes and specific contents] (pp. 171–198). Paidós.

Doise, W. (1982). *L'explication en psychologie sociale*. [Explanation in social psychology]. PUF.

Duveen, G. (1994). Crianças enquanto atores sociais: As Representações Sociais em desenvolvi- mento [Children as social actors: Social Representations in development]. In P. Guareschi & S. Jovchelovitch (Eds.), *Textos em Representações Sociais* [Texts on social representations] (pp. 261–296). Vozes.

Duveen, G. (Ed.). (2001). Introduction: The power of ideas. In S. Moscovici (Ed.), *Social representations: Explorations in social psychology* (pp. 1–17). New York University Press.

Duveen, G. (2007). Culture and social representations. In J. Valsiner & A. Rosa (Eds.), *The Cambridge handbook of sociocultural psychology* (pp. 543–559). Cambridge University Press.

Duveen, G. (2013). Social life and the epistemic subject. In S. Moscovici, S. Jovchelovitch, & B. Wagoner (Eds.), *Development as a social process: Contributions of Gerard Duveen* (pp. 67–89). Routledge.

Duveen, G., & De Rosa, A. (1992). Social representations and the genesis of social knowledge. *Ongoing Production on Social Representations—Productions Vives sur les Repésentations Sociales, 1*(2–3), 94–108.

Duveen, G., & Lloyd, B. (1990). Introduction. In G. Duveen & B. Lloyd (Eds.), *Social representations and the development of knowledge* (pp. 1–10). Cambridge University Press.

Faigenbaum, G. (2005). *Children's economic experience: Exchange, reciprocity, and value*. Libros en Red.

Flament, C., Guimelli, C., & Abric, J. C. (2006). Effets de masquage dans l'expression d'une représentation sociale [Masking effects in the expression of a social representation]. *Les Cahiers Internationaux de Psychologie Sociale, 69*, 15–31.

Jameson, F. (2010). *Valences of the dialectic*. Verso.

Jodelet, D. (1991). *Madness and social representations*. University of California Press.

Jodelet, D. (2008). El movimiento de retorno al sujeto y el enfoque de las representaciones sociales [Back to the subject movement and the social representations approach]. *Cultura y Representaciones Sociales, 3*(5), 32–63.

Kitchener, R. F. (2009). On the concept(s) of the social in Piaget. In U. Müller, J. M. Carpendale, & L. Smith (Eds.), *The Cambridge companion to Piaget* (pp. 110–131). Cambridge University Press.

Kohlberg, L. (1981). *Essays on moral development: The philosophy of moral development*. Harper & Row.
Leman, P. (2010). Social psychology and developmental psychology: Conversation or collaboration? *Papers on Social Representations, 19*, 1–8.
Leman, P. J., & Duveen, G. (1996). Developmental differences in children's understanding of epistemic authority. *European Journal of Social Psychology, 26*(5), 683–702.
Lloyd, B., & Duveen, G. (1990). A semiotic analysis of the development of social representations of gender. In G. Duveen & B. Lloyd (Eds.), *Social representations and the development of knowledge* (pp. 27–46). Cambridge University Press.
Martí, E. (2005). *Desarrollo, cultura y educación* [Development, culture and education]. Amorrortu.
Martí, E. (2012). Thinking with signs: From symbolic actions to external systems of representation. In E. Martí & C. Rodriguez (Eds.), *After Piaget* (pp. 151–170). Transaction.
Marx, K. (1894/1971). *El capital* [Capital]. Fondo de Cultura Económica.
Morais Shimizu, A., & Stefano Menin, M. (2004). Representaciones sociales de ley, justicia, e injusticia: un estudio con jóvenes argentinos y brasileños utilizando la técnica de evocación libre de palabras [Social representations of law, justice, and injustice: A study with young Argentines and Brazilians using word-free association technique]. *Revista Latinoamericana de Psicología, 36*(3), 431–444.
Moscovici, S. (1988). Notes towards a description of social representations. *European Journal of Social Psychology, 18*(3), 211–250.
Moscovici, S. (1990). Social psychology and developmental psychology: Extending the conversation. In G. Duveen & B. Lloyd (Eds.), *Social representations and the development of knowledge* (pp. 164–185). Cambridge University Press.
Moscovici, S. (2001). Why theory of social representations? In K. Deauz & G. Philogène (Eds.), *Representations of the social* (pp. 8–35). Blackwell.
Nucci, L. P., & Gingo, M. (2012). The development of moral reasoning. In U. Goswami (Ed.), *Childhood cognitive development* (pp. 446–472). Wiley-Blackwell.
Overton, W. (2006a). A relational and embodied perspective on resolving psychology's antinomies. In J. I. Carpendale & U. Muller (Eds.), *Social interaction and the development of knowledge*. Erlbaum.
Overton, W. (2006b). Theoretical models of human development. In M. Lerner & W. Damon (Eds.), *Handbook of child psychology* (pp. 18–88). John Wiley & Sons.
Piaget, J. (1924). *Le jugement et le raisonnement chez l'enfant* [Judgement and reasoning of the child]. Delachaux & Niestlé.
Piaget, J. (1932). *Le jugement moral chez l'enfant*. [The moral judgement of the child] Presses Universitaires de France.
Piaget, J. (1959). *La formation du symbole chez l'infant: imitation, jeu et rêve*. [Play, dreams and imitation in childhood]. Delachaux & Niestlé.
Piaget, J. (1974). *Reccherches sur la contradiction. Études d' Epistemologie génétique, XXXI et XXXII* [Research on the contradiction. Genetic epistemology studies, XXXI and XXXII]. Presses Universitaires de France.
Piaget, J. (1975). *L'equilibration des structures cognitives. Problème central du développement. Etudes d'Epistemologie génétique XXXIII* [The equilibration of cognitive structures]. Presses Universitaires de France.

Piaget, J. (1977). *Recherches sur l'abstraction réfléchissant* [Research on reflexive abstraction]. Presses Universitaires de France.
Piaget, J. (1978). *Recherches sur la généralisation.* [Research on generalization]. Presses Universitaires de France.
Piaget, J. (1980). *Les formes élémentaires de la dialectique.* [The elemental forms of dialectic]. Gallimard.
Psaltis, C., & Duveen, G. (2006). Social relations and cognitive development: The influence of conversation type and representation of gender. *European Journal of Social Psychology, 36,* 407–430.
Psaltis, C., Duveen, G., & Perret-Clermont, A. N. (2009). The social and the psychological: Structure and context in intellectual development. *Human Development, 52,* 291–312.
Psaltis, C., & Zapiti, A. (2014). *Interaction, communication and development: Psychological development as a social process.* Routledge.
Wagner, W., & Hayes, N. (2005). *Everyday discourse and common sense: The theory of social representations.* Palgrave Macmillan.
Zittoun, T., Duveen, G., Gillespie, A., Ivinson, G., & Psaltis, C. (2003). The use of symbolic resources in developmental transitions. *Culture & Psychology, 9*(4), 415–448.

CHAPTER 6

REPRESENTATION AND SILENCING OF SOCIAL MEANINGS IN CARTOGRAPHY

The Case of the Conquest of the Desert

Cristian Parellada, José Antonio Castorina, and Alicia Barreiro

A map shows certain things and hides others. Maps cover and uncover, shape and deform. If a cartographer tells you he is neutral, do not trust him. If he tells you he is neutral, you know which side he is on. A map always takes sides. Why was the most important man in Versailles, after the king, his cartographer? Why was Mervetius burned? Ortelius from Antwerp, Mercator from Rupelmonde, they were all dangerous, and they all lived in danger (…). So many catastrophes began on a map! Good times for the cartographer, difficult times for humanity.[1]

—Juan Mayorga, El cartógrafo (2017)

[1] Translated by the authors from the Spanish edition

INTRODUCTION

According to Harley (1988), in the field of the history of cartography, the expression 'cartographic silences' refers to the suppression of information when transmitted onto maps, whether intentionally or unintentionally. To this author "silence and utterance are not alternatives but constituent parts of map language, each necessary for the understanding of the other" (p. 58). He believes silence is sometimes a determining part of cartographic discourse, since through its analysis it is possible to reveal not only what is shown on the map, but also what is hidden. Among the different types of silences, he describes the unintentional silences as a set of social meanings that determine 'within a culture, the appearance or disappearance of statements on maps' (p. 65). In other words, to Harley (1988), unintentional silences are those omissions in cartographic representations that do not respond to technical factors or state secrets, but rather, may be explained based on certain scientific, political, and social knowledge, shared by the community in which the map originated. Thus, to the author, both types of knowledge configure the framework within which cartographic knowledge is constructed.

On the other hand, it has been argued that spatial representations built within different social groups influence the way a map is read and conceived by the subjects (Parellada & Castorina, 2019). The purpose of this work is to promote a dialogue, through the analysis of historical maps, between some of the types of cartographic silences described by Harley, and the social construction of 'nothingness' during the sociogenetic process of social representations (hereinafter SRs). As stated by Barreiro and Castorina (2016), this construction refers to those meanings that are not affirmatively represented in an SR, but that, nevertheless, are part of its structure. From this perspective, they identified three different modalities in which the presence of nothingness can be found in the SR's construction process. In the first modality, a meaning that is functional to the dominant groups' interests becomes hegemonic, and other possible meanings are hidden, for being contradictory to the group's interests. The second modality identified by the authors, considers that during the meanings' construction process, some parts of the elements are omitted and become 'nothingness'. Finally, in the third modality, the object's existence is denied completely.

In what follows, we will reflect on this categorization's potential, in order to study the construction process of cartographic images and the students' comprehension when representing the space in which certain historical processes occurred. In order to do so, we first develop Brian Harley's (1988) ideas upon political and social discourse as constructors of silences in cartographic representations. Secondly, we will relate silences on the maps with the conception of 'nothingness' in the construction process of social representations. Thirdly, we will reveal how the elites, ruling at the time the Argentine national territory was shaped, contributed to the legitimacy of the development of the 'Conquest of the Desert', by producing several empty spaces on the official map, thereby inducing the population's idea that Patagonia was a 'vacant' territory (Lois, 2018). Then, we will analyse the way in which these cartographic representations and silences still remain in force today, both in textbooks' historical maps, and in the way subjects draw the national territory when producing a cartographic narrative. Finally, we will come back to these considerations in order to analyse possible implications for the teaching of history, aiming to give a voice to and allow for the visibility of those sectors silenced in the official story of the past.

Political and Social Discourses of Maps, According to Brian Harley

In the field of the history of cartography, various researches have been carried out in the last decades, with the purpose to analyse the economic, social, political, and cultural context in which cartographic images have been produced (Edney, 2007; Jacob, 2006). These studies reflect on the type of spatial representations offered by maps, and on the set of shared meanings within a community, involved in the production, consumption, and circulation of cartographic images. This new interest in maps differs from a traditional perspective that considers them as merely technical, neutral, and transparent products representing reality (Lois, 2009).

This new approach focuses on the production conditions, the context, and the social, academic, and technical mediations affecting the maps' elaboration. It is, in a certain way, heir to Brian Harley's theoretical. He specifically insisted, inspired by the works of Foucault (1966/2005) and Derrida (1976), on assuming that maps occupy a strategic place as resources of authority, and express a perspective related to the dominant groups' ideology, since they contribute to the legitimisation of a society's power relations. Some authors state that these arguments enabled to study maps from a theoretical approach, opening a dialogue between the history of cartography and other social sciences (Edney, 2005; Jacob, 2006), with the purpose of interpreting the maps. The social meanings present in the maps are transmitted and shape the way subjects construct spatial representations. Thus, they consist of formal or technical aspects, characteristic of the development of cartographic science, and of meanings that, in a non-reflexive way, are attributed to the representations embodied in them, and that condition both what is shown and what is hidden, as well as what and how this is observed.

On the other hand, Harley (1988) believes that maps affect the way in which subjects represent space, both through omissions and through the characteristics they describe and emphasise. To the author, these omissions are related to two types of power. On the one hand, that exercised by a social elite, with the purpose of deliberately manipulating a cartographic image in the mapping process. On the other hand, a more subtle, unintentional type, in which a society's values and representations, or those of a hegemonic social group, are present and structure the image represented on the map.

Unintentional silences are present on maps and are expressed through the cartographer's unintended manipulations. Specifically unintentional silences are defined as '"active performances" in terms of their social and political impact and their effects on consciousness' (Harley, 1988, p. 59). Such silences imply a series of shared meanings acquired and internalized by the cartographer as member of a social group. In this sense, the empty spaces on the maps are understood as yet another aspect of cartographic images to take into account, since they are part of the cultural codes underlying all forms of knowledge. The category of 'unintentional silences on maps' is related to the Foucauldian concept of *episteme*. It is through the concept of episteme that Harley (1988) questions and analyses these cartographic silences, which participate in defining what information is included and what aspects are excluded, according to the context and the political and cultural values influencing the production of maps, which, in turn, contribute to the reproduction of these values. As an example, he analyses certain European maps from the late 16th and early 17th century, on which peasant populations, rural workers, and the cities' economically less favored sectors were not visualized (Harley, 1988).

In short, instead of being the more or less arbitrary decision of the cartographer or whoever commissioned the representation, unintentional silences are a remnant of the way in which the world is conceived, typical of a given historical and social moment. In other words, they are constructions of meanings regarding space, visualized on maps, and often define the conditions under which the discourse regarding the world, as well as the cartographer's perspective as a society member, is sustained. Thus, often, blank spaces are not just a lack of knowledge, or simply leftover spaces, but rather absences in the construction of social knowledge on space. This empty or blank cartographic space can be linked, as we will see, to the statements about the social construction of 'nothingness' by Barreiro and Castorina (2016), since these empty spaces generally imply real erasures on which other representations are founded and sustained.

Silences on Maps, Between Emptiness and Nothingness

In much of Western tradition—especially Anglo-Saxon—the concepts of 'nothingness' and 'emptiness' express the absence of content, and therefore, their irrelevance, being associated with the ontological thesis of empirical philosophy, according to which the non-observable does not exist (Bang, 2009; Barreiro & Castorina, 2016). Therefore, an empty space and its representation on the map as a blank space or *cartographic blanks* (Lois, 2018) relate to the absence of entities, equating 'emptiness' with 'nothingness'. This apparent synonymy between the two concepts is even found in the *Merriam-Webster Dictionary* (2020), where 'empty' is defined, among other meanings, as 'not occupied or inhabited' or 'marked by the absence of human life, activity, or comfort'; while 'nothingness' is understood as 'the quality or state of being nothing: such as nonexistence' or 'emptiness' (*Merriam-Webster Dictionary*, 2020). As can be seen, both meanings emphasise the lack of content, hence, nothingness would be a perfect emptiness. From this perspective, nothingness clearly means an imposition of the non-existing, and it is far from being regarded as a social construct, rather it would be an objective feature of the space in question. However, when thinking of specific spaces that might be considered empty, we immediately notice that they are not spaces devoid of any object. In them we see the absence of certain elements, but at the same time the presence of others. This way, emptiness, or the presence of nothingness, becomes not an absolute attribute, but rather a relational issue. From this perspective, the concept of empty space is defined by what an individual or social group expects to find in it (Campbell et al., 2019). Thus, emptiness is a matter of perspective, a highly subjective, for social phenomenon, depending to a large extent on the intentions, meanings, and expectations of the observer.

In this sense, a space referenced as empty on a map, is not a purely objective state. It is partly the product of the cartographer's intentions or a group's representation regarding this place. History of cartography shows that these spaces mapped as empty are loaded with meanings. Some of them remain hidden, and help to sustain what is shown and said in the representation (Harley, 1988). For example, the maps analyzed by Harley represented only the spaces inhabited by aristocrats, not visualizing the peasant villages. The cartographer conceived space according to a social group's values and meanings, among other things. However, for the inhabitants of these lands, they were full of meanings and elements related to their daily practices. What is more, the era's conceptions about society's poorest classes and their relation to land ownership are present, in a hidden way, since their properties are not referenced.

For their part, Barreiro and Castorina (2016), situate nothingness in the construction process of SRs—which are not addressed in this work, but are compatible with the aforementioned cartographic silences—and it is a necessary condition, at least for the production of certain social beliefs. The authors, following Bang (2009), understand nothingness as the presence of an absence, unconsciously constructed from an individual's perspective in a social group. In other words, the construction of nothingness refers to a process carried out by social groups without premeditation. This way, some SRs, or parts of the objects represented in them, are silenced because they would contradict the legitimized social order. Hence, the need to suppress or silence them, as their recognition or visibility might conflict with the dominant groups' hegemonic ideology. This aspect, unknown or, at most, treated as marginal in the empirical tradition, has been revised in recent years in the field of cultural psychology research (Bang & Winther-Lindqvist, 2016).

We believe that studying the presence of "absence" in the social construction process of spaces does not imply disregarding the physical space and its characteristics, or cartographic science, but rather emphasises its complexity. In this sense, it seems consistent to state that unintentional silences on maps are part of the cartographic image's construction process, as shown by Harley (1988), and to assert, at the same time, that this is a process of figuration and expression of SRs. Next, we will show, through our own research in the field of cartographic history, how some of the blank spaces of the map of the Argentine Republic were constructed in relation to certain representations of the ruling elites regarding indigenous people, at the end of the 19th century, and how they contributed to the legitimisation of the historical process known as "Conquest of the Desert" (1878–1885).

Blanks in the Representation of the 'Desert' at the End of the 19th Century

In the context of Argentine history, the expression 'Conquest of the desert' refers to a series of military campaigns undertaken by the Argentine Army between 1878 and 1885, with the purpose of incorporating Patagonia and Chaco lands into state control. In those years, these lands were inhabited by diverse indigenous populations (Bayer, 2010). The historical process of the 'Conquest of the Desert' is similar to the expansion of the USA from the Atlantic to the Pacific Ocean. In this sense, Brudney (2019) uses the concept of manifest destiny in order to analyse similarities between the two historical processes. The author concludes that both expansionist projects were sustained through parallel discourses on race, religion, and civilisation.

Specifically, in Argentina the presence of the concept *desert* is not accidental, and, in this work's context, we should recall the conclusions drawn by various researchers reflecting on this issue (Navarro Floria, 2002; Palti, 2009; Torre, 2011). These authors coincide that at the end of the 19th century, the ruling elite believed the desert was another name for 'barbarism', or was related to it, while the space under state control was territory inhabited by civilisation. Thus, according to the ruling elites' political enterprise, the desert was associated with the 'wild', and was the name for the lands that the indigenous population, being 'wild', did not value or work in order to contribute to the nation's development. The civilizing saga of the desert consisted of a policy of several steps: first the discursive emptying, considering those territories as vacant and inhospitable; second, the actual emptying, by murdering the populations inhabiting it, and, third, once the conquest was achieved, the making up of a story about the territory, establishing it as a fertile space and prosperous for the nation (Lagos & Ratto, 2011; Lois, 2018; Ratto, 2014). In short, the desert was named and constructed from the ruling elite's imaginary of those years: a specific geographical place not occupied by the 'white' population, wasted for capitalist production, and that had to be conquered for the good of the national state's development.

The representation of the lands inhabited by indigenous people was the product of a social construction in accordance with meanings that certain social sectors sought to consolidate; both in discourse and in maps, not only through the actual presence of certain representations, but also through the invisibility of others. Hence, this construction of meanings is related to power, since the imaginary looking to be transmitted, legitimized a state policy whose purpose was to incorporate these lands into central control. The lands occupied by these populations were understood as empty spaces, while at the same time, the different communities inhabiting Patagonia and the Northwest were hidden on the cartographic representations (Lois, 2018). These lands began to appear on the maps as blank spaces, clearly delimited by lines representing the border with neighboring countries, although these frontiers were not yet consolidated. Their inhabitants were referred to with the generic noun 'Indians', concealing the diversity of populations and the various political and commercial treaties between the Argentine state and several communities, signed in previous years (Lagos & Ratto, 2011).

In the case of Patagonia, we can see on the following map, drawn by Martin de Moussy in 1873 (Figure 6.1), that within the representation of Patagonia, different communities of 'Indians' are mentioned, inhabiting these lands.

In addition, we would like to emphasise that at the time, this cartographer enjoyed a notable prestige within the government of the Argentine Confederation. Such was his recognition among the ruling elite that, on September 9, 1865, he was appointed delegate of the commission that was in charge of preparing the World Exposition to be held in Paris in 1867. Although the explicit presence of different indigenous communities is shown on the map, we can also read that 'the only inhabited points of Patagonia are Carmen, on the Río Negro, and the Chilean colony Punta Arenas, in the Brunswich peninsula, at the southern end of the continent'. Clearly, the cartographer referred to the existence of inhabited points based on his conception of territorial occupation by 'Christian, white people'. However, there is coexistence, without apparent contradiction, of the legend of non-existence of inhabited points, on the one hand, and the explicit mention of indigenous populations, on the other.

A few years later, in 1875, under the presidency of Nicolás Avellaneda, the national government entrusted the preparation of a new map of the Argentine Republic (Figure 6.2) to cartographers Arthur von Seelstrang and Alfred Tourmente, on the occasion of Argentina's participation in the Philadelphia World Exposition, which would take place the following year.

In the previous image, we can see how most of the knowledge on the settlements of the groups of 'Indians' included in Moussy's map, has been 'erased', and how Patagonia became a blank space, clearly delimited by borders, and named *Territorio de la Patagonia* [Territory of Patagonia]. This act of erasing is even more relevant when comparing the date the map was made (1875) with the beginning of the 'Conquest of the Desert' (1878). This means that three years before the military campaign to conquer those territories began, the map already included Patagonia within the national territory's outlines, as a blank space, an emptiness to fill, although the state was not yet effectively controlling these lands.

The emergence of a new cartographic outline allowing for the incorporation of Patagonia into the national territory was legitimized by technical knowledge and by the era's meanings considering this region as a desert. Furthermore, the maps of Patagonia produced up to that point, even that of de Moussy, began to be considered as inaccurate by the ruling elite. For some members of this sector of the population, these maps had to be replaced because 'they were drawn at a time

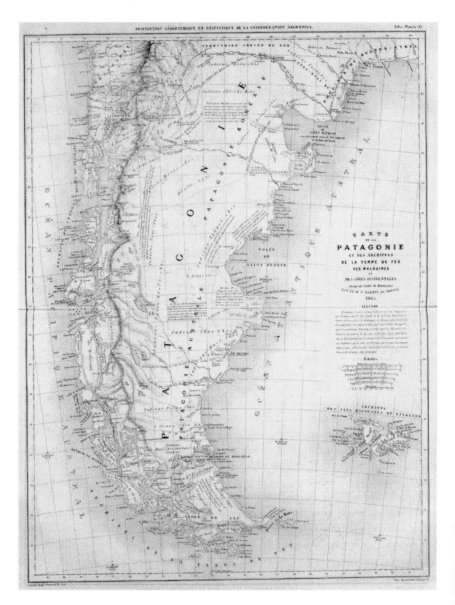

FIGURE 6.1. Map of Patagonia and Tierra del Fuego archipelagos, Malvinas and the western coasts De Moussy (1865/2005). Available at https://www.davidrumsey.com/luna/servlet/detail/RUMSEY~8~1~20539~510065:Carte-de-la-Patagonie-et-des-archip

Representation and Silencing of Social Meanings in Cartography • 117

FIGURE 6.2. Map of Argentine (1875) De Moussy (1867). Available at https://gallica.bnf.fr/ark:/12148/btv1b530253461

when our country was an immense unexplored desert' (Zeballos, 1882, as cited in Lois, 2018, p. 143). Hence, new ones should be made, reflecting reality as it was. Imagining these spaces as empty converts them, in turn, into places waiting to be occupied. They represented a land of opportunities to immigrants, to settle there and put the land to work, at the service of the national state's economic development. Upon the constructed emptiness, this space is visualized as land fertile for progress; in other words, the territorial emptying implied 'the indigenous people's deterritorialization and a Eurocentric reterritorialization' (Braticevic, 2017, p. 217). While the territory was integrated into Argentina and became a place of prosperity, its population, not coinciding with the ruling elite's project of a nation, was denied and exterminated.

The new cartographic image matched the era's discourse and contributed to promoting in the population the necessary legitimacy to carry out the military campaigns for the territory's appropriation (Lois, 2014). Now, if those lands belonged to Argentina, then their inhabitants could be considered as Argentines, with the purpose of affirming they were within state territory. In those years, and with a complete lack of naivety, issues related to indigenous people began to be considered as internal conflicts (Lagos & Ratto, 2011), and a concept closely associated with that of 'emptiness' emerged: *the internal border*. The line separating the indigenous communities from the Argentine territory, considering them as 'exterior' to the territory, turned into borders within a consolidated state. In this regard, Benedetti and Salizzi (2014) state that the concept of internal border, related to the ideas of desert and barbarism, allows us to understand how the very concept of border is related to socially assigned meanings in the production and dissemination of territorial imaginaries.

At the same time, the space, devalued and called 'desert' when inhabited by indigenous people, was offered to immigrants for their economic development. The cartographic representation accompanied the construction process of these lands' meaning, from a desert to a non-desert, fertile and productive for capitalist production (Lois, 2018). This meaning of the desert as a space of economic potential is inseparable from the silencing of other meanings: the lack of integration of the indigenous communities to the desired project of a nation and their exclusion in the construction of a national identity. These meanings are substituted by others that agree with an operational political and ideological project, pursuing certain ends in the future. Installed meanings regarding the space as a desert and the belonging of Patagonia to the Argentine state, have the particularity of indicating an absence. They refer to emptiness as a spatial category and define it based on the place it occupies from the ruling elite's perspective. In sum, the invisibilization of the indigenous population was vital, not only for the expansion of the national territory but also for the construction of a national identity.

The absence we reveal on this occasion has its own peculiarities, but it can be related to Barreiro and Castorina's notions (2016) on the omission of certain meanings and their becoming 'nothingness' when suppressed in the SR construction process. In this way, we may consider an analysis of the SRs' construction based on the 'presence of absence' of the occupied lands, as well as the appropriation of these territories. The emptiness on the map 'rather than to be filled, appeared with the purpose of delegitimizing previously existing knowledge and, at the same time, announcing a knowledge programme. That is why a blank space, rather than emptiness, is an act of emptying' (Lois, 2018, p. 128). This act of emptying Patagonia cannot be considered as a mere silencing, but rather as being part of the meaning's very production process.

THE PERSISTENCE OF SILENCES IN SCHOOL TEXTBOOKS

The territory was a central element in the construction process of the Argentine national identity (Hollman & Lois, 2015). This shows, for example, in law N° 22963 of the Charter that enables the state, through the 'Instituto Geográfico Nacional' (IGN) [National Geographic Institute], to regulate Argentina's cartographic representations, reproduced by different means. The official version regarding the state's establishment insists that Patagonia has belonged to Argentina since before the beginning of the 'Conquest of the Desert' (Lacoste, 2003). In this official story, national territory is presented as an entity that has not changed over the years, almost as an immutable essence (Carretero, 2018).

The aforementioned concept of internal border, in relation to this conception of national territory transmitted in the official story, made it possible to refer to Patagonia as a space belonging to the national state. At the same time, the recognition of the indigenous population as these lands' original inhabitants was concealed (Benedetti & Salizzi, 2014). What is more, according to this official version, since these lands belonged to Argentina, they could be used—after they had been recovered—according to the criteria and at the convenience of the ruling elites, in favor of the nation's development, without the need to grant any rights to the indigenous population. For example, in 1867, a bill was debated in National Congress to extend the border that separated the state from the indigenous population. One of the debate's axes was article 2 of the bill. In the original text, the 'indigenous tribes' were guaranteed the right of territorial possession (Congreso Nacional, Cámara de Senadores, 1867, p. 117). But, when this point was debated, the article's text was revised and the concession removed. The predominant argument for this modification was that these lands belonged to Argentina, and that it was not possible to make a pact with the indigenous population as it was with the rest of the foreign nations. Also, senator Anselmo Rojo said that 'the Pampa Indians should fall to their knees before the Argentine nationality (…). They then will be like all the Republic's inhabitants, under the guarantees common to all the inhabitants. There is no reason to grant them possession rights' (Congreso Nacional, Cámara de Senadores, 1867, p. 134). Once the occupation was achieved, and no right over those territories was granted to the indigenous population, a set of political decisions was made, ranging from handing over lands to those groups financing the military campaigns, to the promotion of colonies in order to favor immigration.

Also, in those years other voices could be heard, in which the inhabitants' rights over the lands to be conquered were acknowledged. For example, in the same debate on article 2 of the bill to expand the border line, carried out in 1867, it was senator Madariaga's opinion that Argentina was about to occupy this territory: 'We are going to authoritatively occupy that territory, and it can be said that this article establishes that the indigenous people who accede to the conditions of civilisation, and voluntarily submit to the nation's authority, shall then be granted the right to possess the lands they occupy' (Congreso Nacional, Cámara de Senadores, 1867, p. 135).

Also, in those years, the inhabitants of Patagonia began to be considered as Argentinians under the argument that the territory was Argentine. To deny that they were Argentinians, according to their place of birth, would imply questioning the sovereignty over the territory (Lagos & Ratto, 2011). This argument also contributed to the legitimacy of the territorial expansion process, and to the state's disregard of the autonomy of the populations inhabiting these lands. With them, they would agree on treaties and conventions but, according to the rulers' point of view, these did not have international status since the indigenous populations were not regarded in the same way as other foreign nations (Navarro Floria, 2002). Next, we will reveal how these historically formed meanings are still present today in school textbooks and on maps accompanying the narrative of the 'Conquest of the Desert', silencing other voices according to which those lands did not belong to the Argentine state and were occupied by force. This apparent contradiction between the consideration that the inhabitants of Patagonia were Argentinians and, at the same time, they 'should fall to their knees before the Argentine nationality', as Senator Rojo said, was present in those years and was reproduced without any qualms (Navarro Floria, 2002).

Most historical maps regarding the *Conquest of the Desert*, reproduced in school textbooks, represent the moving of the *internal borders* during the 19th century (Pacciani & Poggi, 2014). These refer to the national territory's current boundaries, and the moving of the borders appears to have occurred within a territory that was always part of Argentina (Figure 6.3). Also, when analyzing the narrative accompanying these maps, the 'Conquest of the Desert' is presented as a historical process decided by the then President Nicolás Avellaneda, who, 'decided to take measures in order to occupy and secure the lands dominated by the indigenous population, to achieve, thus, the **complete integration of the Argentine territory**' (Celotto et al., 2013, p. 28. Emphasis in original).

As can be seen, the above map is drawn on the basis of the current map and closely resembles the territorial representation of Argentina made by Seeltrans and Tourmente. Carretero (2018) argues that this overlapping between present and past in historical maps reproduced in textbooks is a product of an essentialist and timeless representation of national territory, shaped at the end of the 19th century. Its presence in textbooks in the form of historical maps, the concept of internal borders, and the consideration that it contributed to the integration of na-

Representation and Silencing of Social Meanings in Cartography • 121

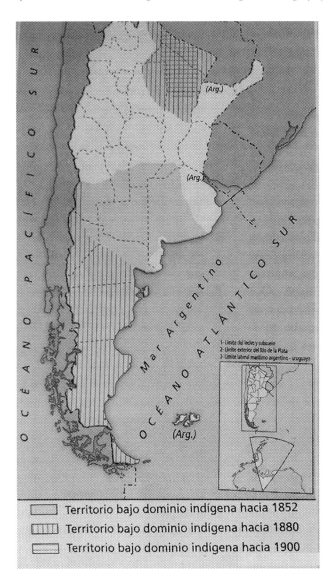

FIGURE 6.3. Moving of Internal Borders During the Second Half of the 19th Century (Celotto et al., 2013) Territory under indigenous control by 1852 (solid yellow) . Territory under indigenous control by 1880 (vertical lines). Territory under indigenous control by 1900 Moving of the internal borders during the second half of the 19th century (horizontal lines).

tional territory, remain in force. Thus, the belief was promoted that the 'Conquest of the Desert' did not involve territorial expansion, but rather was a reassurance of state authority over this space. In this regard, it can be assumed that in the current narrative a certain core of meanings constructed in the late 19th century persists, according to which Patagonia is presented as part of the Argentinean national territory, 'occupied' by indigenous population and needing to be secured through a military campaign.

In short, some textbooks, when treating the 'Conquest of the Desert', do not question or critically analyse whether the lands of Patagonia belong to the Argentine national state. Since the external boundaries are not under discussion, neither in the narrative nor on the historical maps accompanying it, what remains is a confrontation between two groups of Argentines. The reason is simple: the border with the indigenous population does not appear as a boundary of the Argentine national state, which are shown as clearly defined. In addition, the historical maps accompanying this narrative confirm this interpretation, showing that these lands—according to the ruling elite in the late 19th century—belonged to Argentina (Parellada, 2019). In our view, the concept of internal borders and the essentialist representation of national territory on historical maps operate by silencing, in textbooks, the possibility to incorporate other voices and meanings of that era concerning the territory's ownership.

SUBJECTS PRODUCING SILENCES ON MAPS

The way subjects conceive territorial space is not only the product of their cognitive interaction with the world or with the maps presented to them, but, to a large extent, it is produced by the appropriation of the meanings circulating in a group, activating an SR. Subjects know large spaces, such as national territory, through maps, being those the instruments mediating the relation between individual and represented area (Uttal, 2000). The territory makes sense according to the individuals' historical, cultural and social background. In other words, the subjects' socio-spatial representations are 'anchored' in different social thought systems (de Alba et al., 2020). In this sense, the individual's belonging to and identification with certain social groups play an important role in the subjects' construction of meanings regarding space.

From the perspective of SR theory, research was carried out on how this approach may be useful for the study of territory and the way in which subjects represent it (De Alba, 2007, 2011, 2014; Milgram & Jodelet, 1976). This perspective specifically considers maps and narratives revolving around territory to be ways in which SRs can materialize. Also, research revealed how these representations concerning territory vary according to different social groups, and how they may coexist in a city or space. In this sense, the study of the maps produced by subjects—whether or not in school context—on national territory in the past, is of psychosocial and educational relevance. In this way, research reveals how subjects appropriate the representations drawn on the maps, by making cognitive reconstructions. In this regard, assuming 'nothingness' is a constituent part of the elaboration of certain SRs, it is likely that they are present in the subjects' representations of territorial space. These arise as a product of the active appropriation of the SRs transmitted in the official narrative. In other words, we assume that the historical maps taught at schools are constructed in relation with certain historical discourses. Thus, they are shaped by much of the official meanings regarding the national past.

Next, we will show some results of our previous research (Parellada et al., 2020) in which we studied how subjects represent the national territory, independent as from July 9th, 1816, and whether or not they consider Patagonia as belonging to Argentina since before the 'Conquest of the Desert' began. While these researches were not conducted from the SR approach, we believe their results may be interpreted on the basis of the relations mentioned in this chapter. Specifically, in our works, we found that most of the subjects who were asked to draw the national territory independent as from July 9, 1816, drew a map representing the current borders of Argentina. In other words, these subjects considered Patagonia as part of the territory that had become independent, as if these lands had always belonged to Argentina, hiding territorial expansion in their cartographic representations. Thus, just as Harley (1988) reflected upon the cartographers' productions, we may assume that these silences on the interviewed subjects' maps are 'unintentional silences', as they are reproduced in an unreflective manner, but they orient and condition what is referenced.

According to these results, the ways subjects represent national territory may be, at the same time, brought into dialogue with what was found in this team's previous research, also on the topic of the 'Conquest of the Desert' (Barreiro et al., 2016, 2017; Sarti & Barreiro, 2014, 2018). The latter show that subjects, in their stories, exclude the state's role in the military process, shifting the responsibility to the Spanish conquerors. In this sense, our findings allow us to consider that, when the Argentine state is acknowledged as being responsible, and the executor of the 'Conquest of the Desert', one of the strategies to deny the indigenous population the rights over the annexed land they previously inhabited, is stating that these lands were part of Argentina. In other words, the indigenous population's rights over these lands and how they conceive them are suppressed.

Also, our results show that in many of the subjects' stories, the arguments were similar to those given at the end of the 19th century to justify territorial expansion; this allows us to consider the impression of certain SRs, hegemonic for a long time, on their interpretation of the belonging of Patagonia to Argentina. The interviewees stated that the territory of Patagonia was Argentine but 'was occupied by indigenous people' (Parellada, 2019, p. 246), or that the indigenous population could be considered as Argentines because they were in Argentine territory, which was 'already delimited' (Parellada, 2019, p. 247). From these findings we can infer that the subjects construct their stories around the belief that the territory was Argentine since before the conquest, and that the indigenous population was Argentine for inhabiting it, that is, from an essentialist representation of the nation that also implies its territory (Carretero & Kriger, 2011). We consider that this belief conceals the dynamic, historical, and political character of the conformation of Argentina's current territory, and the atrocities committed against the indigenous populations inhabiting this space. They were those lands' original owners, and the state deprived them of their belongings and of any recognition of rights over them. Thus, coinciding with the appropriation of pre-existing SRs regarding the *'Conquest of the Desert'* (Barreiro et al., 2016, 2017), and of the indigenous population (Barreiro et al., 2019, 2020), we can see, both in relation to the elaboration of maps and in the produced narratives regarding the belonging of this territory, the presence of an emptiness or 'nothingness' related to the suppression of other SRs or elements of the represented objects. The result is a legitimation of the dominion of the elite carrying out this process of territorial expansion, and of its conception regarding the conquered lands.

A CRITICAL PERSPECTIVE OF HISTORICAL MAPS IN THE TEACHING OF HISTORY

In this work we have pointed out certain meanings concerning national territory, constructed by the ruling elite, at a certain historical and social moment, in order to legitimize the conquest of spaces not belonging to the national state. These meanings were forged on the basis of the construction of an imaginary of Patagonia as an empty space. For the lands of Patagonia, the imaginary of a territory belonging or attributed to the Argentine state was constructed, inhospitable and with little use for production with capitalist purposes. However, this is contradicted by other cartographic representations, expressing other meanings—from the same period—highlighting the presence of indigenous settlements in those lands, and the recognition of that space as being outside of national territory.

Territorial expansion and the subsequent creation of meanings concerning the lands conquered by the Argentine state, as a space of economic potential for future immigrants, are consistent with the geographical silences still operative when speaking of the 'desert' and the 'internal border' with the indigenous population. From the perspective of the ruling elites, those lands were constructed as an empty space with the sole purpose of conquering them. Today, these meanings are still in force, both in textbooks and in the subjects' representation of the territory. A question arises: how can we make these hidden meanings visible in the field of history teaching, thus avoiding interpretations that reproduce the hegemonic discourse?

In the first place, we believe it is necessary to make the social conditions operating during cartographic production visible in the educational field, as shown in the history of cartography. In addition, we believe this needs to be complemented with the study of the present SRs, not only in the materialization of the cartographic image, but also in the way subjects interpret historical maps and represent national territory.

Secondly, a collaborative dialogue between critical approaches in cartographic history (Harley, 1988) and SR theory may be a promising programme for future empirical research on cartographic silences. In this sense, this work proposes that some of the maps' omissions, analyzed by the history of cartography, are compatible with the social construction of 'nothingness' in the process of SR's sociogenesis (Barreiro & Castorina, 2016).

Thirdly, and from the perspective of teaching and learning processes of historical maps, we need a critical vision that allows questioning the different knowledge circulating in schools. The active elaboration of arguments by the students, the search for better information, the confrontation of different approaches, or the comparison with the indigenous population's knowledge concerning this space, are necessary didactic conditions when it comes to teaching the maps' function in history and the discourses constructed upon them. We wish to emphasise that the proposal to make emerge what has been silenced, includes the hearing and actively including of other voices in history education. It is important for students to get in touch with the arguments with which the indigenous population defended, and still defends, its territories, and with those arguments sustained by the ruling elite's political actors opposing the conquest of those lands. We believe this task cannot be fulfilled with a mere nominal inclusion of the recognised groups, it is necessary to give them a voice and situate them as historical actors resisting the territorial conquest and the consequent genocide of indigenous populations. In this way, in confrontation or convergence, in agreement or discussion, these voices will be part of the students' intellectual work, questioning approaches and having a wide arsenal of ideas and social experiences available when thinking about their history.

Finally, we believe history teaching and the interpretation of historical maps are always approached from a political and ideological position (Parellada & Castorina, 2019). The presence of nothingness, both in cartographers and in students, unconsciously involves the intervention of SRs in individual activity within the framework of an ideological outline. The latter does not only legitimize a political and hegemonic order, but also conditions the groups' future actions while justifying those of the present. The presence of a hegemonic perspective on the 'Conquest of the Desert' hides the historical process's complexity and reveals the national state's supremacy. Questioning this perspective implies adding the indigenous people's meanings of space to the didactic game, an unofficial version of history, and assuming the necessary participation of the students' thought, interacting with both the teacher and the objects of knowledge. In order to achieve a genuine deconstruction and reconstruction of the historical school maps, and of how we think about the national space in the past, it is essential that teachers enable those questions that allow for students to get closer to a certain visibility of denied usurpation and domination, and question the official historical narrative.

REFERENCES

Bang, J. (2009). Nothingness and the human umwelt. A cultural-ecological approach to meaning. *Integrative Psychological and Behavioral Science, 43*, 374–392.

Bang, J., & Winther-Lindqvist, D. A. (Eds.) (2016). *Nothingness Philosophical Insights into Psychology.* New Jersey: Transaction Publishers.

Barreiro, A., & Castorina, J. A. (2016). Nothingness as the dark side of social representations. In J. Bang & D. A. Winther-Lindqvist (Eds.), *Nothingness philosophical insights into psychology* (pp. 69–88). Transaction Publishers.

Barreiro, A., Ungaretti, J., & Etchezar, E. (2019). Representaciones sociales y prejuicio hacia los indígenas en Argentina [Social representations and prejudice against indigenous people in Argentina]. *Revista de Psicología, 37*(2), 529–558.

Barreiro, A., Ungaretti, J., Etchezar, E., & Wainryb, C. (2020). They are not truly indigenous people? Social representations and prejudice against indigenous people in Argentina. *Papers on Social Representations, 29*(1), 6.1–6.24.

Barreiro, A., Wainryb, C., & Carretero, M. (2016). Narratives about the past and cognitive polyphasia: Remembering the Argentine conquest of the desert. *Peace and Conflict: Journal of Peace Psychology, 22*(1), 44–51.

Barreiro, A., Wainryb, C., & Carretero, M. (2017). Power struggles in the remembering of historical intergroup conflict: hegemonic and counter-narratives about the Argentine "Conquest of the Desert." In C. Psaltis, M. Carretero, & S. Cehajic-Clancy (Eds.), *History teaching and conflict transformation: Social psychological theories, history teaching and reconciliation* (pp. 125–145). Palgrave Macmillan.

Bayer, O. (Ed.) (2010). *Historia de la crueldad argentina. Julio A. Roca y el genocidio de los Pueblos Originarios* [History of Argentinean cruelty. Julio A. Roca and the genocide of native people]. El Tugurio.

Benedetti, A., & Salizzi, E. (2014). Fronteras en la construcción del territorio argentino [Borders in the Construction of Argentinean Territory]. *Cuadernos de Geografía, Revista Colombiana de Geografía, 23*(2), 121–138.

Braticevic, S. (2017). Frontera, frente y formación social de fronteras. Aproximación a los diferentes conceptos a partir del avance productivo reciente en el Norte Argentino [Border, front and social formation of borders. Approach to the different concepts based on the recent productive advance in the north of Argentina]. In S. Braticevic, C. Tommei, & A. Rascovan (Eds.), *Nación, límites, frente e interfaces. Algunos aportes sobre la cuestión de las fronteras* [Nation, boundaries, front and interfaces. Some contributions on the question of borders] (pp. 209–229). M&A Diseño y Comunicación S.R.L.

Brudney, E. (2019). Manifest destiny, the frontier, and "El Indio" in Argentina's conquista del desierto. *Journal of Global South Studies, 36*(1), 116–144.

Campbell, C., Giovine, A., & Keating, J. (2019). Introduction: Confronting emptiness in history. In C. Campbell, A. Giovine, & J. Keating (Eds.), *Empty spaces. Perspectives on emptiness in modern history* (pp. 1–13). University of London Press.

Carretero, M. (2018). Historical consciousness and representations of national territories. What Trump's and Berlin walls have in common? In A. Clark & C. Peck (Eds.), *Contemplating historical consciousness: Notes from the field* (pp. 76–88). Bergham Books.

Carretero, M., & Kriger, M. (2011). Historical representations and conflicts about indigenous people as national identities. *Culture & Psychology, 17*(2), 177–195.

Celotto, A. (Ed.) (2013). *Ciencias sociales 6 bonaerense* [Social Sciences 6. Bonaerense]. Santillana.

Congreso Nacional, Cámara de Senadores de la Nación Argentina. (1867). *Sesión de 1867* [Session in 1867]. Imprenta del Orden.

de Alba, M. (2007). Mapas imaginarios del Centro Histórico de la Ciudad de México: de la experiencia al imaginario urbano [Imaginary maps of the historic center of Mexico City: From experience to urban imaginary]. In A. Arruda & M. de Alba (Eds.), *Espacios imaginarios y representaciones sociales. Aportes desde Latinoamérica* [Spaces imaginaries and social representations. Contributions from Latin America] (pp. 285–319). Anthropos.

de Alba, M. (2014). Imaginary maps and urban memory: Elements for the study of territorial identity. *Papers on Social Representations, 23*, 16.1–16.22.

de Alba, M. (2011). Social representations of urban Spaces: A comment on mental maps of Paris. *Papers on Social Representations, 20*, 29.1–29.14.

De Alba, M., Herrera, L., & Loubier, J. C. (2020). Social representations of México City historic center: Heritage and controversial memories. *Papers on Social Representations, 29*(1), 7.1–7.25.

De Moussy, M. (1865/2005). *Descripción geográfica y estadística de la Confederación Argentina* [Geographic and statistical description of Argentine confederation]. Academi Nacional de la Historia.

De Moussy, M. (1867). *Carte de la patagonie et des Archipels de la Terre de Feu, des Malouines et des cotes occidentales jusqu'au Golfe de Reloncavi* [Map of Patagonia and the Archipelagos of Tierra del Fuego, Falklands and Western Coasts of Reloncavi Gulf]. 1: 3.750.000. https://www.davidrumsey.com/luna/servlet/detail/RUMSEY~8~1~20539~510065:Carte-de-la-Patagonie-et-des-archip

Derrida, J. (1976). *Of grammatology*. Johns Hopkins University Press.

de Seelstrang, A., & Tourmente, A. (Cartógrafos.) (1875). *Mapa de la República Argentina* [Map of the Argentine Republic]. 1: 5.000.000. https://gallica.bnf.fr/ark:/12148/btv1b530253461

Edney, M. (2005). Brian Harley's career and intellectual legacy. *Cartographica. The international Journal for Geographic Information and Geovisualization, 40*(1–2), 1–17.

Edney, M. (2007). Mapping empires, mapping bodies: Reflections on the use and abuse of cartography. *Treballs de la societat catalane de geografía, 63*, 83–104.

Empty. (2020). *Merriam-Webster Dictionary*. https://www.merriam-webster.com/dictionary/emptiness

Foucault, M. (1966/2005). *The order of things. An archaeology of the human sciences*. Routledge Classics.

Harley, J. B. (1988). Silences and secrecy: The hidden agenda of cartography in early modern. *Europe, Imago Mundi: The International Journal for the History of Cartography, 40*(1), 57–76.

Hollman, V., & Lois, C. (2015). *Geo-grafías. Imágenes e instrucción visual en la geografía visual* [Geo-graphies. Pictures and visual instruction in visual geography]. Paidos.

Jacob, C. (2006). *The sovereign map. Theoretical approaches in cartography throughout history*. The University of Chicago Press.

Lacoste, P. (2003). *La imagen del otro en las relaciones de Argentina y Chile (1534–2000)* [The image of the other in the relationship between Argentina and Chile (1534–2000)]. Fondo de Cultura Económica.

Lagos, M., & Ratto, S. (2011). El concepto de "frontera interior": de la política a la historiografía [The concept of "internal border": From politics to historiography]. *Entrepasados, 36*, 51–71.

Lois, C. (2009). Imagen cartográfica e imaginarios geográficos. Los lugares y las formas de los mapas en nuestra cultura visual [Cartographical image and geographical imaginary. places and shapes of maps in our visual culture]. *Geocrítica, Scripta Nova. Revista electrónica de geografía y ciencias sociales, XIII*(298). Available at http://www.ub.edu/geocrit/sn/sn-298.htm

Lois, C. (2014). *Mapas para la Nación. Episodios en la historia de la Cartografía Argentina* [Maps for the nation: Episodes in the history of Argentine cartography]. Editorial Biblos.

Lois, C. (2018). *Terrae incognitae. Modos de pensar y mapear geografías desconocidas* [Terrae incognitae. Ways of thinking and mapping unknown geographies]. Eudeba.

Mayorga, J. (2017). *El cartógrafo* [The cartographer]. Uña Rota.

Merriam-Webster. (2020). *Merriam-Webster's collegiate dictionary*. Merriam-Webster Inc.

Milgram, S., & Jodelet, D. (1976). Psychological maps of Paris. In H. M. Proshansky, W. Ittelson, & L. G. Rivlin (Eds.), *Environmental psychology: People and their physical settings* (pp. 104–124). Holt, Rinehart & Winston.

Navarro Floria, P. (2002). El desierto y la cuestión del territorio en el discurso político argentino sobre la frontera Sur [The desert and the question of territory in the Argentine political discourse on the southern border]. *Revista Complutense de Historia de América, 28*, 139–168.

Nothingness. (2020). *Merriam-Webster Dictionary*. https://www.merriam-webster.com/dictionary/nothingness

Pacciani, B., & Poggi, M. (2014). La historia enseñada: La mal llamada "conquista del desierto" en los libros escolares en la Argentina, desde 1880 a la actualidad [History taught: The misnamed "conquest of the desert" in Argentinean textbooks, from 1880 to the present]. In J. Prats, I. Barca, & R. López Facal (Eds.), *Historia e Identidades Culturales* [History and Cultural Identities] (pp. 590–599). Universidad do Minho.

Palti, E. (2009). *El momento romántico. Nación, historia y lenguajes políticos en la Argentina del siglo XIX* [The romantic moment: Nation, history, and political languages in nineteenth-century Argentina]. Eudeba.

Parellada, C. (2019). *Representaciones del territorio nacional y narrativas históricas. Implicaciones para la enseñanza de la historia* (tesis doctoral). Facultad de Psicología, Universidad Nacional de La Plata [Representations of National Territory and Historical Narratives: Implications for Teaching History; Doctoral dissertation, National University of La Plata, Argentina]. http://sedici.unlp.edu.ar/handle/10915/80106

Parellada, C., & Castorina, J. A. (2019). Una propuesta de diálogo entre la psicología del desarrollo y la cartografía crítica [A proposal for a dialogue between developmental psychology and critical cartography]. *Cadernos de Pesquisa, 49*(171), 244–263.

Parellada, C., Carretero, M., & Rodríguez-Moneo, M. (2020). Historical borders and maps as symbolic supporters of master narratives. *Theory & Psychology, 30*(6), 1–17.

Ratto, S. (2014). Visiones del chaco y de su población en el siglo XIX [Images of the Chaco and its population in the 19th century]. *Revista de ciencias sociales, segunda época, 26*, 49–66.

Sarti, M., & Barreiro, A. (2014). Juicios morales y memoria colectiva: narrativas de jóvenes sobre la "Conquista del Desierto" [Moral judgments and collective memory: student´s narratives about the "Conquest of the Desert"]. In J. A. Castorina & A. Barreiro (Eds.), *Representaciones Sociales y prácticas en la psicogénesis del conocimiento social* (pp. 125–138). Miño y Dávila.

Sarti, M., & Barreiro, A. (2018). Identidad nacional en las narrativas sobre un proceso histórico moralmente cuestionable [National identity in the historical narratives of a morally questionable historical process]. *Cultura y Educación, 30*(3), 433–459.

Torre, C. (2011). *El otro desierto de la nación argentina. Antología de narrativa expedicionaria* [The other desert of the Argentine nation. Expeditionary narrative anthology]. Quilmes, Argentina: Universidad Nacional de Quilmes.

Uttal, D. (2000). Seeing the big picture: Map use and the development of spatial cognition. *Development Science, 3*(3), 247–286.

CHAPTER 7

COGNITIVE POLYPHASIA, SOCIAL REPRESENTATIONS AND POLITICAL PARTICIPATION IN ADOLESCENTS

Daniela Bruno and Alicia Barreiro

INTRODUCTION[1]

In the last few decades, the changes in the way of conceptualizing the civic has given rise to new ways of thinking about political participation that go beyond voting behavior and engagement in political parties (Flanagan, 2003; Flanagan et al., 2011; Haste, 2017; Syvertsen, et al., 2011). In this vein, there is an ongoing discussion about political participation in Political Psychology and Social Sciences, in which the diverse types of political commitments have been named and described in different ways (Castillo, 2008; Muxel, 2008; Parés, 2014; Torney-Purta et al., 2001). The classical studies on this topic were dedicated to investi-

---

[1] This work was originally published in Bruno & Barreiro (2021) Cognitive polyphasia, social representations and political participation in adolescents. *Integrative Psychological and Behavioral Sciences.* https://doi.org/10.1007/s12124-020-09521-8.

gating the conventional political participation that consists of traditional forms of behavior, such as voting or participating in political campaigns and political parties (Almond & Verba, 1963; Campbell et al., 1960).

In the frame of the social and political revolts of the 1960s and 1970s there was a reconceptualization of political participation (Haste, 2017). The researchers began to recognize some types of unconventional political participation that were not new, but opposed to those that were traditionally considered in Social Sciences as practices of political participation (Barnes et al., 1979; Haste, 2017; Milbrath, 1981; Sabucedo, 1988). Before the 1960s, most of this kind of behaviors were considered peripheral activities and disruptive of the social order (Haste, 2017). Nowadays, the so called "unconventional political practices" include legal (e.g., demonstrations, strikes) and even illegal practices (e.g., occupation of buildings, violent protests) whether they seek to question institutions or to maintain the status quo (Barnes et al., 1979; Sabucedo, 1988). In this way, the unconventional forms of political participation entail a wide variety of communication resources to make voices heard. Therefore, this kind of participation include the importance that people give to causes of public interest as a goal in their personal lives, that is, citizen participation to help their country or community to improve society as a whole (Flanagan et al., 2007a, 2007b; Haste, 2017). Moreover, activism gains relevance in this new way of thinking about political practices in understanding the reasons to act in the face of specific social problems and not only regarding to partisanship in the democratic process (Haste, 2017).

According to various studies, young people prefer to engage in unconventional forms of political participation rather than conventional ones (e.g., Castillo, 2008; Eurobarometer, 2007; Euyoupart, 2005; Muxel, 2008; Parés, 2014; Stacchiola, 2016; Torney-Purta & Barber, 2011; Vázquez & Vommaro, 2008). The higher participation of young people in such practices might be due to the fact that they are more flexible, autonomous and they offer adolescents the possibility of their actions obtaining more immediate and visible results than the conventional ones, that taking place in organizations with a more hierarchical structure (Castillo, 2008; Muxel, 2008). An example of a very common unconventional political participation for Argentinean youths, but illegal, is the occupation of the school space, organizing direct forms of participation by means of assemblies (Beltrán & Falconi, 2011). In the most important Argentine cities there has been a reactivation of students' movements at the high school level of education (Beltrán & Falconi, 2011; Núñez, 2010, 2013), interweaving local political phenomena with school practices (Nuñez, 2010). Students 'claims for better schooling conditions have been made through occupation of the school space which, being a public setting, constitutes a political scenario. Adolescents' involvement in such experiences would enable the development of active citizen participation in the public-social setting, by making demands upon the State (Beltrán & Falconi, 2011; Nuñez, 2010, 2013). Another very common example of this unconventional participation all around the word, but of the legal type, is to be part of an NGO (non-governmental organization) in which the adolescents feel respected, they feel their voices are heard and considered in the decision-making processes (Flanagan, 2003; Flanagan et al., 2007b; Flanagan & Levine, 2010). However, despite their active engagement in such practices, young people think of politics as an activity inherently related to conventional forms of political participation, to which they have a very negative evaluation (Eurobarometer, 2007; Euyoupart, 2005; Inglehart et al., 2014; Programa de las Naciones Unidas para el Desarrollo, 2010; Torney-Purta & Richardson, 2004).

Specifically, in Argentine context, Brussino et al. (2008) studied the forms of political participation of young people aged between 18 and 30 (Barnes et al., 1979; Sabucedo, 1988). Their results indicate the existence of three types of practices: party-union; community and expressive. The first one involves the canalization of society's demands through political parties and trade unions. The second group of practices includes the claims of the neighbors and the presentation of neighborhood proposals to politicians. The third one includes going to the media to present claims or proposals and participating in demonstrations (Brussino et al., 2008). In addition, the authors found that older subjects with a higher educational level are more prone to engage in party-union participation. On the other hand, younger subjects with a lower educational level tend to engage in community and expressive participation practices (Brussino et al., 2008).

POLITICAL PARTICIPATION AND COGNITIVE POLYPHASIA

The various ways of describing and studying political participation and the discussions about them in the frame of different scientific disciplines as Political Psychology and Social Sciences show the polysemic nature of the concept (Anduiza & Bosch, 2012; Barnes et al., 1979; Delfino & Zubieta, 2010; Haste, 2017; Milbrath, 1981; Sabucedo, 1988; Verba et al., 1978). The different types of political participation, as social practices, express social representation (hereinafter SR). This is of paramount importance considering the constitutive relationship between SRs and social practices since they are beliefs that constitute social behavior (Jodelet, 2011; Wagner, 2015). From this theoretical perspective, SRs express themselves in social practices and communicate through them (Wagner, 2015). They are a practical knowledge that links the subject with the object of knowledge as follows: on the one hand, because they emerge from the experiences of interaction; on the other hand, because social practices are a condition of SR, because the requirement to assume new situations by the subject leads to their construction; finally, because they are used by individuals to act on other members of their social group and to adjust their behavior in social life (Jodelet, 1989/1991).

SRs are meaningful structures which provide a shared code to enable communication among the members of a group about the phenomena of daily life and how they understand them (Marková, 2012; Moscovici, 2001). Such common sense knowledge that people use to guide their daily interactions is based on a consensus about what they regard as reality, which allows them to categorize the world and to communicate with others (Moscovici, 2001; Wagner & Hayes, 2011). Thus, SRs symbolically constitute the social environment for individuals, they allow people to act on it and to interpret and predict the behavior of others (Jodelet, 2011). In the theory of SRs, when talking about an individual, it refers to a subject that cannot be thought independently of his or her social group located in a specific cultural and historical context (Castorina & Barreiro, 2006). The social group is the basis from which the individual understands and interacts with the world through his or her system of representations elaborated in the communication process (Wagner & Hayes, 2011).

According to the theory of SR it is possible for different meanings of the same social object to coexist since people develop multiple identities –within the framework of different social groups– and they inhabit multiple contexts. Representational fields contain multiple ways of thinking which coexist in the same social group, and even in the same individual in a state of *cognitive polyphasia* (Jovchelovitch & Priego-Hernandez, 2015; Moscovici, 1961/1979; Wagner & Hayes, 2011). Cognitive polyphasia states express the relationships between SRs, identity and culture, and confirm the internal plurality of human socio-cognitive systems (Jovchelovitch & Priego-Hernandez, 2015). Such states may vary according to the communicative dynamics established in relation to the recognition or rejection processes of the different meanings of an object (Jovchelovitch, & Priego-Hernandez, J., 2015). There are situations in which, when the discourse is unique and coercive, it rejects the different representations consolidating a single perspective. However, in other situations, the existence of multiple perspectives is recognized, what Jovchelovitch & Priego-Hernandez (2015) define as polyvocality.

It is possible to distinguish three types of cognitive polyphasia: *selective prevalence*, *hybridization* and *displacement* (Jovchelovitch & Priego-Hernandez, 2015). The first one referred to different knowledge systems that stay together and they are retrieved separately in different points of time/space retaining their content, logic and emotional burden. It involves the recognition of multiple kinds of knowledge, which are used alternately depending on the situations, contexts and which aspects of the phenomenon are considered. As a result, knowledge is preserved in interdependent relations and tension, is maintained and stabilized through practices which make it functional and useful for daily life. The second type of cognitive polyphasia, hybridization, involves the existence of multiple systems of knowledge which are used simultaneously, and which blend into a single mixed representational field. Thus, SRs not only combine or are applied simultaneously, but they are merged and create a new form of knowledge. The third modality, displacement, refers to a system of knowledge which prevails over other parallel systems, leading to the rejection of alternative representations.

SOCIAL REPRESENTATIONS OF POLITICS IN LATIN AMÉRICA

Studies conducted in Latin America on the SR of politics show that young people think of it in an institutional sense, as an activity based on the procedures inherent to the democratic political regime, with a negative evaluation of it (Bruno & Barreiro, 2014; Cárdenas et al., 2007; González Pérez, 2006; RechWachelke & Hammes, 2009; Villarroel & De Armas, 2005). Such SR entails a way of understanding politics that is closely related to conventional forms of political participation. In addition, such studies show that this SR would be considered *hegemonic* (Bruno & Barreiro, 2014; Cárdenas et al., 2007). Hegemonic SRs are coercive, uniform, stable in time and shared by the most part of the society (Moscovici, 1988). In fact, affiliation to a social group is evidenced through the acceptance and preservation of its hegemonic representations (Ben-Asher, 2003). This kind of SRs implicitly prevail in different symbolic and affective practices of people's daily lives, since they are ideational and value structures deeply rooted in such practices (Lo Monaco & Guimelli, 2011; Moscovici, 1988).

In addition to the hegemonic SR, Moscovici (1988) raises the existence of SR *polemic* and *emancipated*. Polemic SRs emerge as a result of social controversies or conflicts and they are generally expressed as a dialogue with an imaginary interlocutor They arise from antagonistic relationships in the context of a struggle between groups and they involve mutually excluding views of an object. Emancipated SRs are the result of the exchange of knowledge and ideas of subgroups which have some kind of contact between them. In this case, each subgroup creates their own version of the object and shares it with the others. It should be pointed out that the systems of meaning of polemic and emancipated SR, unlike the hegemonic ones (which systems of meaning are closed and resistant to change), are more prone to discussion, reflection and debates because different social groups take positions within the symbolic world of a society that need to be defended in order to guarantee their legitimacy (Duveen, 2007).

In line with the findings mentioned before regarding Latina-American youth, our previous research (Bruno & Barreiro, 2014) showed that such hegemonic SR appears to be present among Argentine young people, since they think of politics in institutional terms, taking a narrow view. They regard it as an activity related to government. Further, they relate it to representative democracy and their mechanisms of functioning. This mode of functioning is considered "corrupt" and thus young people have a negative evaluation of politics which is, in addition, associated to some political leaders who have been Presidents of the Nation. Such study was conducted within the framework of the central core theory of SR (Abric, 2001; Moliner & Abric, 2015). As stated by this school of thought, SRs are constituted by a central core and a set of peripheral elements (Abric, 2001; Moliner & Abric, 2015). The central core is composed by the meanings that organize the representation, that is, the most shared and stable elements, constitutive of its identity. Peripheral elements are more flexible, they transform and protect the central core from changes, they are the defense system of representation (Abric, 2001; Moliner & Abric, 2015). According to our previous study (Bruno & Barreiro, 2014), there were no differences in adolescents' SR of politics structure, according to sociodemographic variables (gender and socioeconomic level), because the meanings located in the different zones of the SR structure were similar. However, in the SR contrast zone -defined as a peripherical zone which may contain meanings proper to a minority group (Sarrica, 2007)—certain meanings were expressed which may link politics with social and popular participation, in the context of different conflicts and proposals that involve equality and people's rights. Then, we point out that these findings might suggest the presence of a polemic SR (Moscovici, 1988), which should be more deeply analyzed in further studies.

Therefore, the present study takes our previous work (Bruno & Barreiro, 2014) on the SR of politics as a starting point in order to explore the possible existence of representations different from the hegemonic one by using a different data collection technique. In the aforementioned study we implemented the word association technique (Wagner & Hayes, 2011) which provides access to the most automatic, spontaneous and impulsive response. From the information obtained, we performed prototypical analysis to describe the structure of the SR. In contrast, in this study we use an interview for data collection, which makes it possible to explore the arguments and reasons why subjects adopt a certain perspective in relation to the object (in this case, politics), as well as to introduce new questions in order to delve more deeply into the responses they provide (Barreiro, 2013a,b). In addition, to go forward in the study of the different SR of politics will help to provide an understanding of the relationship between action and beliefs expressed in the young people's rejection of conventional forms of political participation and their engagement in unconventional political practices, even though they do not consider them as such.

HOW DO ADOLESCENTS THINK ABOUT POLITICS IN THEIR DAILY LIFE?

To study go further in the comprehension of adolescents' SR of politics we performed a qualitative study with 32 adolescents aged between 16 and 18 who lived in the Autonomous City of Buenos Aires. 50% of the sample were men and the other 50% were women. The sample was selected using the procedure known as theoretical sampling (Corbin & Strauss, 2008). It consists in simultaneously performing data collection and analysis, conducted the necessary interviews until to achieve the saturation of information, that is, a point at which the inclusion of new cases does not provide additional information for the development of analytical categories.

The instrument used for data collection was a semi-structured interview, based on Piaget's clinical method (Delval, 2001; Piaget, 1984). The main characteristic of this type of interviews is that, although they are guided based on certain tasks and basic questions, the discursive exchange takes place according to a dialectic process of interaction between the interviewer's hypotheses and the interviewee's answers. The interviewer poses new questions or expands on the existing ones in order to understand the meanings underlying the responses provided by the interviewees (Barreiro, 2013a,b). According to which participants were asked to provide a narrative of their experiences with politics following these instructions: "*Please tell me about a time when you had an experience that has to do with politics.*" A narrative was demanded for two main reasons. First, narrative thinking is one of the privileged ways in which subjects organize their daily experiences (Bruner, 2001) and, therefore, asking them to provide a narrative would be a way to get close to the way in which politics is present in their daily life and to have indirect access to their practices in relation to it. The second reason is that the way the task is presented makes it different from those interviews seeking to obtain conceptual knowledge about an object, as traditionally found in Piagetian works. In contrast, participants are here asked to talk about what is evoked by that object to them, similarly to the word association technique, typically used in SR research (Barreiro, 2013a). Once the interviewees finished narrating the situation they were asked to talk about, the interviewer posed the following question to them: "*What does this story you are telling me have to do with politics?*" Then, they were further asked: "*What does politics means to you?*" This question sought to explore the meanings that the interviewees give to politics. In all cases they were requested to justify their answers.

Participants' narratives and their responses to the other questions asked during the interviews were analyzed using Strauss and Corbin's (1990) constant comparative method. Therefore, a systematic comparison was performed regarding similarities, differences and recurrences in the narratives and arguments presented by the subjects that showed their views on politics and what kind of social practices they relate it to. According to this analytical method one of the ways of naming the identified categories is to use denomination of scientific concepts that resemble the collected information. As a result, three categories were built, reflecting different ways of understanding politics: a) *conventional*, b) *unconventional* and c) *oscillating* (conventional and unconventional). A description of each of them is presented below together with extracts from the interviews to illustrate them.

A. Conventional: In this category the answers of the interviewees express meanings in which politics consists of an activity performed by the government and other forms of traditional political participation (Milbrath, 1981; Sabucedo, 1988; Verba et al., 1978). As can be seen in Diego's answers:

> Diego (17 years-old): [Request for a narrative about a situation related to politics][2] *Well, I voted last year, it was my first time and I was nervous (…).*

---

[2] The following criterion was used for the transcription of the interview extracts: the interviewer's words are written in square brackets [ ]; the interviewee's words are written in italics. Whenever a fragment of the interview has been omitted, (…) is written and when the omitted fragment belongs only to the interviewee's words, *(…)* is written.

> [What does this story you are telling me have to do with politics?] *Well, I don't know, the fact that you elect someone as representative or senator and that this may affect the measures adopted in the country. (...)* [What does politics means to you?] *To me, politics is the way in which the country is run, the president, representatives, senators with their collaborators or with those who support them, it is the way it is organized (...).*

Diego reflects that politics is related to conventional forms of political participation, in particular, voting in elections and the political representatives and the government are the responsible for organizing and running the country.

B. Unconventional: This category includes those answers which express certain meanings about politics that relate it to forms of political participation going beyond the traditional mechanisms of representative democracy (Barnes et al., 1979; Brussino et al., 2008; Delfino & Zubieta, 2010). In this sense, politics would constitute a familiar and attainable object, unlike the answers included in the conventional category as can be seen in Agustina's answers:

> Agustina (17 years-old): [Request for a narrative about a situation related to politics] *Actually, it is something I have always been very interested in, since my second year I have been part of the students' union (...) I have also been to many demonstrations, and students' strikes and protests. (...)* [What does this story you are telling me have to do with politics?] *Well, because it means participation and also being a citizen, it is exercising this on a daily basis, it is like fighting for something for everyone (...)* [What does politics means to you?] *I think it's what I told you before, participation (...) I know that I do politics, everybody does politics.*

Agustina's answers express meanings of politics linked to unconventional forms of political participation (demonstration, protests) which differ from conventional forms of participation. According to this interviewee, politics means participating through everyday activities, regarding participation as the exercise of citizenship.

C. c) Oscillating: This category was named *oscillating* based on previous works (Barreiro, 2009, 2013b) where the participants' responses showed a passage or "oscillation" from one representation to another, depending on the discursive context of the interview. Thus, when requesting participants to elaborate a narrative about their experiences with politics, they narrated a situation about politics which might be categorized as unconventional, but then, when requesting a more conceptual type of definition by asking "What does politics means to you?" their answers fell into the conventional category:

> Julieta (17 years-old): [Request for a narrative about a situation related to politics] *When I was in first year, the heaters were out of order and*

our teachers decided to go on strike and occupy the school (...) So, we blocked the street. We demonstrated peacefully. [What does this story you are telling me have to do with politics?] *In my opinion, all of this is related to the State, I mean Macri and Cristina, who are those in charge of helping us financially to repair the heaters, of giving us the money to repair them.* [What does politics means to you?] *Ehm... everyone who represents us, our representatives. Delegates, representatives. And going up to the President. I believe that Cristina gave me the most*: scholarships, Buenos Aires citizenship, and so many things she gives us; she helps us financially, especially students, which I find excellent because otherwise I would have to get a job.

Julieta's answers reflect unconventional forms of political participation (school occupations, demonstrations, street blocking) and certain meanings related to the conventional category when the interviewee says that politics is the State and political figures like the former Presidents Macri and Cristina are the ones in charge of repairing the heaters that were out of order in the school.

Regarding the distribution of the categories two large groups were identified: oscillating, accounting for 44% of the participants, and conventional with the 41%. The unconventional category accounts for a lower percentage of 15%.

CONTRIBUTIONS TO THE PSYCHOLOGICAL DISCUSSION ON YOUNGS' RELATION WITH POLITICS

The results obtained by the analysis of the narratives and responses of the adolescents during the interviews yielded two large categories: conventional and an unconventional political practices. The conventional SR seems to be in line with previous studies which identified the hegemonic SR of politics based on a strong consensus common to different social groups from different Latin American countries (e.g., Bruno & Barreiro, 2014; Cárdenas et al., 2007). Such studies indicate that, in general, young people consider politics as a public activity performed by politicians and linked to conventional forms of political participation. However, it should be noted that in the study presented in this chapter we identified answers which might indicate the existence of an SR that links politics with unconventional forms of political participation. This unconventional SR is consistent with the previous work by Bruno and Barreiro (2014), who proposed the possible existence of a polemic SR, which expresses meanings which challenge the conventional hegemonic SR.

Although this unconventional SR of politics present in a minority of the participants in its "pure" form—independently from the conventional SR—it is present in a larger group of subjects interviewed together with the conventional one, constituting the category named as oscillating. We think the answers where conventional and unconventional SR were both alternatively expressed show the existence of state of cognitive polyphasia of the type that Jovchelovitch and Priego-Hernandez (2015) call selective prevalence. This form consists in different knowledge systems that stay together, and they are retrieved separately in different points of time/space retaining their content. It also involves the recognition of multiple kinds of knowledge, which are used alternately depending on the contexts and which aspects of the phenomenon are considered. In this way, this type of cognitive polyphasia could be expressed in oscillating answer because of the way that the interviews were conducted, since the interviewees answer from the perspective of one SR or the other, depending on the type of question being asked. In other words, the discursive context of the interview that moved from asking narratives based on daily life experiences to conceptual definitions of politics may results in one representation prevailing over another depending on the type of thought convened by each of them.

Furthermore, the findings presented in this chapter allow us to affirm the potential contribution of the concept of SR to better understand the way in which young people think of politics and the practices related to it. However, it would be necessary to observe the practices of adolescents in future studies, since SRs are created within everyday social practices (Jodelet, 1986, 2011; Marková, 2012; Moscovici, 1988) and they are forms of practical knowledge which is used to interpret the social world (Jodelet, 2011). In this sense, the data collection instrument used in this study was discursive and it become necessary to go farther this level of analysis. Also, for future research it would be challenging to analyze the sociogenesis and ontogenesis of the SR identified (Duveen & Lloyd, 1990/2003) in this study to go deeper in the understanding the historical processes that gave rise to them and to better understand the process by which adolescents reconstruct them during their socialization.

Finally, it is also important to conduct further research which includes more heterogeneous samples and other geographical contexts (beyond the Autonomous City of Buenos Aires) in order to test whether the conventional hegemonic SR prevails in other social groups or if it is possible to identify different SRs of politics apart from the two identified in this study.

REFERENCES

Abric, J. C. (2001). *Prácticas sociales y representaciones.* [Social practices and representations]. Coyoacán.

Almond, G., & Verba, S. (1963). *The civic culture: Political attitudes and democracy in five nations.* Princeton University Press.

Anduiza, E., & Bosch, A. (2012). *Comportamiento político y electoral.* [Political and voting behavior]. Ariel.

Barnes, S. H., Kaase, M., Allerbeck, K. R., Farah, B. G., Heunks, F., Inglehart, R., Jennings, M. K., Klingemann, H. D, Marsh, A. & Rosenmayr, L. (1979). Political action: Mass participation in five western democracies. Sage Publications.

Barreiro, A. (2009). La Creencia en la Justicia Inmanente Piagetiana: Un Momento en el Proceso de Apropiación de la Creencia Ideológica en un Mundo Justo. [Piagetian belief in immanent justice: A moment in the appropriation of ideological belief in a just world]. *Psykhe (Santiago), 18*(1), 73–84.

Barreiro, A. (2013a). The ontogenesis of social representation of justice: Personal conceptualization and social constraints. *Papers on Social Representations, 22,* 13.1–13.26. Recuperado de http://psr.iscte-iul.pt/index.php/PSR/issue/view/25.

Barreiro, A. (2013b). The appropriation process of the belief in a just world. *Integrative Psychological and Behavioral Science, 47,* 431–449.

Beltrán, M., & Falconi, O. (2011). La toma de escuelas secundarias en la Ciudad de Córdoba: condiciones de escolarización, participación política estudiantil y ampliación del diálogo social. [The occupation of secondary school premises in the City of Cordoba: Schooling conditions, student political participation and expansion of social dialogue]. *Propuesta Educativa, 35*(20), 27–40.

Ben-Asher, S. (2003). Hegemonic, emancipated and polemic social representations: Parental dialogue regarding Israeli naval commandos training in polluted water. *Papers on Social Representations, 12,* 6.1–6.12.

Bruner, J. (2001). *Realidad mental y mundos posibles. Los actos de la imaginación que dan sentido a la experiencia.* [Mental reality and possible worlds. The acts of imagination that give meaning to the experience]. Gedisa.

Bruno, D. S., & Barreiro, A. (2014). La política como representación social. [Politics as social representation]. *Psicología Política, 48,* 69–80.

Bruno, D., & Barreiro, A. (2021). Cognitive polyphasia, Social representations and political participation in adolescents. *Integrative Psychological and Behavioral Sciences, 55*(1), 18–29. https://doi.org/10.1007/s12124-020-09521-8

Brussino, S., Rabbia H., & Sorribas, P. (2008). Una Propuesta de Categorización de la Participación Política de Jóvenes Cordobeses. [A proposal for the categorization of youth political participation in the city of Cordoba]. *Revista Psicología Politica, Associação Brasileira de Psicologia Política (ABPP) Sao Paulo, 8*(16), 285–304.

Campbell, A., Converse, P., Miller, W., & Stokes, D. (1960). *The American voter.* University of Chicago Press.

Cárdenas, M., Parra, L., Picón, J., Pineda, H., & Rojas, R. (2007). Las representaciones sociales de la política y la democracia. [The social representations of politics and democracy]. *Última Década, 15*(26), 53–78. https://ultimadecada.uchile.cl/index.php/UD/issue/view/5375.

Castillo, A. M. J. (2008). Trayectorias de Participación Política de la juventud europea: ¿efectos de cohorte o efectos de ciclo vital?. [Political participation trajectories of the European youth: Cohort effects or life cycle effects?]. *Revista de Estudios de Juventud, 81,* 68–94.

Castorina, J. A., & Barreiro, A. (2006). Las representaciones sociales y su horizonte ideológico. Una relación problemática. [Social representations and their ideological horizon. A problematic relationship]. *Boletín de Psicología, 86,* 7–25.

Corbin, J., & Strauss, A. (2008). *Basics of qualitative research: Techniques and procedures for developing grounded theory* (3rd ed.). Sage Publications.

Delfino, G. I., & Zubieta, E. M. (2010). Participación política: concepto y modalidades. [Political participation: Concept and modalities]. *Anuario de investigaciones, 17,* 211–220.

Delval, J. (2001). *Descubrir el pensamiento de los niños: introducción a la práctica del método clínico.* [Discovering children's thinking: introduction to the practice of the clinical method]. Paidós.

Duveen, G. (2007). Culture and social representations. In J. Valsiner & A. Rosa (Eds.), *The Cambridge handbook of sociocultural psychology* (pp. 543–559). Cambridge University Press.

Duveen, G., & Lloyd, B. (1990 /2003). Las representaciones sociales como una perspectiva de la psicología social. [Social representations as a perspective of social psychology]. En J. A. Castorina (Comp.). *Representaciones sociales. Problemas teóricos y conocimientos infantiles.* [Social representations. Theoretical problems and children's knowledge] (pp. 29–40). Gedisa.

Eurobarometer. (2007). *Youth survey among people aged between 15–30, in the European Union. Flash Eurobarometer series 202.* European Commission: Gallup Organization Survey.

Euyoupart. (2005). *Political participation of young people in Europe—Development of indicators for comparative research in the European Union, deliverable 17: Final comparative report.* Institute for Social Research and Analysis (SORA).

Flanagan, C. (2003). Developmental roots of political engagement. *PS: Political Science & Politics, 36*(2), 257–261.

Flanagan, C. A., Cumsille, P., Gill, S., & Gallay, L. S. (2007a). School and community climates and civic commitments: Patterns for ethnic minority and majority students. *Journal of Educational Psychology, 99*(2), 421–431.

Flanagan, C. A., & Levine, P. (2010). Civic engagement and the transition to adulthood. *The Future of Children, 20*(1), 159–179.

Flanagan, C. A., Martinez, M. L., Cumsille, P., & Ngomane, T. (2011). Youth civic development: Theorizing a domain with evidence from different cultural contexts. *New Directions for Child and Adolescent Development, 134*, 95–109.

Flanagan, C. A., Syvertsen, A., & Wray-Lake, L. (2007b). Youth political activism: Sources of public hope in the context of globalization. In R. K. Silbereisen & R. M. Lerner (Eds.), *Approaches to positive youth development* (pp. 243–256). SAGE Publications.

González Pérez, M. A. (2006). *Pensando la Política: Representación Social y Cultura Política en Jóvenes Mexicanos.* [Thinking about politics: Social representation and political culture in young Mexicans]. Plaza y Valdez.

Haste, H. (2017). *Nueva ciudadanía y educación. Identidad, cultura y participación.* [New citizenship and education. Identity, culture and participation]. Paidós.

Inglehart, R., C. Haerpfer, A. Moreno, C. Welzel, K. Kizilova, J. Diez-Medrano, M. Lagos, P. Norris, E. Ponarin & B. Puranen et al. (Eds.). (2014). *World values survey: Round six.* JD Systems Institute. https://www.worldvaluessurvey.org/WVSDocumentationWV6.jsp

Jodelet, D. (1986). La representación social: fenómenos, concepto y teoría. [Social representation: Phenomena, concept and theory]. In S. Moscovici (Ed.), *Psicología social II: pensamiento y vida social* [Social psychology II: thought and social life] (pp. 469–493). Paidós.

Jodelet, D. (1989/1991). *Madness and social representations.* University of California Press.

Jodelet, D. (2011). Aportes del enfoque de las representaciones sociales al campo de la educación. [Contributions of the social representation approach to the field of education]. *Espacios en Blanco, Serie Indagaciones, 21*(1), 133–154.

Jovchelovitch, S., & Priego-Hernandez, J. (2015). Cognitive polyphasia, knowledge encounters and public spheres. In G. Sammut, E. Andreouli, G. Gaskell, & J. Valsiner (Eds.), *The Cambridge handbook of social representations* (pp. 163–178). Cambridge University Press.

Lo Monaco, G., & Guimelli, C. (2011). Hegemonic and polemical beliefs: Culture and consumption in the social representation of wine. *Spanish Journal of Psychology, 14*(1), 237–250.

Marková, I. (2012). Social representations as an anthropology of culture. In J. Valsiner (Ed.), *The Oxford handbook of culture and psychology* (pp. 487–509). Oxford University Press.

Milbrath, L. W. (1981). Political participation. In S. L. Long (Ed.), *The handbook of political behavior.* (pp. 197–240). Springer. https://doi.org/10.1007/978-1-4684-3878-9_4

Moliner, P., & Abric, J. C. (2015). Central core theory. In G. Sammut, E. Andreouli, G. Gaskell & J. Valsiner (Eds.), *The Cambridge handbook of social representations* (pp. 83–95). Cambridge University Press.

Moscovici, S. (1961/1979). *El psicoanálisis, su imagen y su público*. [Psychoanalysis, its image and its audience]. Huemul.

Moscovici, S. (1988). Notes towards a description of social representations. *European Journal of Social Psychology, 18*(3), 211–250.

Moscovici, S. (2001). *Social representations. Explorations in social psychology*. University Press Washington Square.

Muxel, A. (2008). Continuidades y rupturas de la experiencia política juvenil. [Continuities and ruptures of youth political experience]. *Revista de Estudios de Juventud, 81*, 31–44.

Nuñez, P. (2010). Escenarios sociales y participación política juvenil. Un repaso de los estudios sobre comportamientos políticos desde la transición democrática hasta Cromagnon. [Social scenarios and youth political participation. A review of the studies on political behavior from the democratic transition to Cromagnon]. *Revista SAAP, 4*(1), 49–83.

Núñez, P. (2013). *La política en la escuela: jóvenes, justicia y derechos en el espacio escolar*. [Politics at school: Youth, justice and rights in the school setting]. Buenos Aires: La Crujía.

Parés, M. (2014). La participación política de los jóvenes ante el cambio de época: estado de la cuestión. [Political participation of young people in the change of era: State of the art]. *Revista Metamorfosis: Revista del Centro Reina Sofía sobre Adolescencia y Juventud, 0*, 65–85.

Piaget, J. (1984). *La representación del mundo en el niño*. [The child's conception of the world]. Morata.

Programa de las Naciones Unidas para el Desarrollo. (2010). *Informe Nuestra Democracia*. [*Report our democracy*]. Fondo Cultura Económica.

RechWachelke, J. F., & Hammes, I. C. (2009). Representaçõessociais sobre política segundo posicionamento político na campanha eleitoral de 2006. [Social representa-

tions on politics according to political position in the 2006 electoral campaign]. *Psicologia em Estudo, 14*(3), 519–528.
Sabucedo, J. M. (1988). Participación Política. [Political participation]. In J. Seoane & A. Rodríguez (Eds.), *Psicología Política* [Political psychology] (pp. 165–194). Pirámide.
Sarrica, M. (2007). War and peace as social representations: Cues of structural stability. *Peace and Conflict: Journal of Peace Psychology, 13*(3), 251–272.
Stacchiola, O. (2016). Prácticas culturales y construcción de identidades juveniles en la Argentina actual. [Cultural practices and construction of youth identities in Argentina today]. *Trabajo y sociedad. Sociología del Trabajo—Estudios Culturales- Narrativas Sociológicas y literarias, 26,* 299–308.
Strauss, A., & Corbin, J. (1990). *Basics of qualitative research: Grounded theory procedures and techniques.* Sage Publications.
Syvertsen, A., Wray-Lake, L., Flanagan, C., Osgood, D., & Briddell, L. (2011). Thirty-year trends in U.S. adolescents' civic engagement: A story of changing participation and educational differences. *Journal of Research on Adolescence, 21,* 586–594.
Torney-Purta, J., & Barber, C. (2011). Fostering young people's support for participatory human rights through their developmental niches. *American Journal of Orthopsychiatry, 81*(4), 473–481.
Torney-Purta, J., Lehmann, R., Oswald, H., & Schulz, W. (2001). *Citizenship and education in twenty-eight countries: Civic knowledge at age fourteen.* IEA.
Torney-Purta, J., & Richardson, W. K. (2004). Anticipated political engagement among adolescents in Australia, England, Norway and the United States. In J. Demaine (Ed.), *Citizenship and political education today* (pp. 41–58). Palgrave /Macmillan.
Vázquez, M., & Vommaro, P. (2008). La participación juvenil en los movimientos sociales autónomos. El caso de los Movimientos de Trabajadores Desocupados (MTDs). [Youth participation in autonomous social movements. The case of the Unemployed Workers' Movements (MTDs)]. *Revista Latinoamericana de Ciencias Sociales Niñez y Juventud, 6*(2), 485–522.
Verba, S., Nie, N., & on Kim J. (1978). *Participation and political equality: A seven-nation comparison.* Cambridge University Press.
Villarroel, G., & De Armas, E. (2005). Desprecio por la política: aproximación a las representaciones sociales de estudiantes venezolanos. [Contempt for politics: an approach to the social representations of Venezuelan students] *Revista Politeia, 28*(34–35), 11–18.
Wagner, W. (2015). Representation in action. In G. Sammut, E. Andreouli, G. Gaskell, & J. Valsiner (Eds.), *The Cambridge handbook of social representations* (pp. 12–28). Cambridge University Press.
Wagner, W., & Hayes, N. (2011). *El discurso de lo cotidiano y el sentido común. La teoría de las representaciones sociales.* [Everyday discourse and common sense. The theory of social representations]. Anthropos.
World Values Survey. (2010–2014). *World values Survey.* Association wave 6. Madrid: Aggregate File Producer Asep/JDS.

CHAPTER 8

THE GOVERNMENT, THE PRESIDENT, AND THE POLICE

Politics According to Children Living in a Squatted House[1*]

Paula Nurit Shabel

INTRODUCTION

The implementation of the neoliberal regime in our country meant an unprecedented advance of capital over labour in today's Argentina. This resulted in wealth concentrating in few hands, and the consequent impoverishment of the life of the working class in general (Fernández Álvarez, 2015), and of childhood in particular (Carli, 2009). The reason for this is "a growing lack of protection for families, undermining their capacities to provide basic conditions of development for girls, boys and adolescents" (CEPAL & UNICEF, 2005, p. 27).

[1*] This work is a revision of the article '"Please don't take us out of here." Constructions of Knowledge on the State According to Children Living in a Squatted house, published in Papeles de trabajo.

Faced with this impoverishment of life, popular sectors got organized in order to resist and forge new political and social alternatives. Working and—more and more—unemployed families began to take to the streets with all their members, to fight for work and food, thus generating a strong appearance of women and children in the fields of struggle (Padawer et al., 2009; Santillán, 2009). The new context of neoliberal precariousness also modified the fight against adjustment, shifting its place from the factory to towns and neighborhoods. This resulted in a territorial character of the dispute, and boys and girls began to gain visibility as protagonists of political vicissitudes, as they participated in the marches and the "puebladas" [massive demonstrations] together with their families.

In this process, protest actions became part of the subjects' daily life in their organisations, establishing new ways of relating to the state and to other organisations, multiplying throughout the whole country (Manzano, 2013). The *Movimiento Territorial de Liberación* (MTL) [Territorial Liberation Movement] is one of the organisations that emerged in June 2001 from the daily resistance practices of families within popular movements. With roots in the Communist Party and related to unionism, the movement was created to fight for "bread, work, and decent housing, education and health for everyone" (Founding Act of the MTL, in Poli, 2007, p. 56).

Particularly in the city of Buenos Aires, the movement squats, defends and builds houses for its families, as the principle strategy of struggle and survival facing the housing crisis affecting the Argentine capital since the 1990s (Carman, 2005). Through the MTL, various housing and work cooperatives have emerged in this territory, always emphasizing their autonomy in relation to the state, although without breaking off relations with it. In this territory the MTL has about ten squatted houses, calling them *hospedajes transitorios*[2] [transitory lodging]. This means that, although the houses are squatted, there is a certain margin of legality, achieved through the movement's pressure exerted on the City Government, agreeing on the price of a modest rent and the payment of utilities, thus avoiding evictions. Each *transitory lodging* has its own particular agreement, depending on the size, the number of families living there, and the general conditions of the property, which is, with variations, in all cases precarious. The agreements are always short-term, and although some of the houses have been in this situation for more than ten years, there is always a high possibility for the negotiations to end, hence, the danger of eviction is permanent.

The fieldwork analyzed here was carried out between 2014 and 2018, in one of the houses squatted by the MTL, located in the Almagro neighborhood, in the city centre. Boys and girls, as well as adults, call the place *La casa de Humahuaca* [the house of Humahuaca], or simply *the house* [la casa]. It has more than thirty occupied rooms, and there are more than fifty boys and girls. In this presentation we

---

[2] Stated in italics are the concepts extracted directly from the discourses of the subjects living in the squatted house, both boys, girls, and adults.

will limit the age range to between 8 and 15 years old, since most of the subjects with whom we interacted in the field are between these ages, and it is here that we drew significant conclusions. About twenty boys and girls belong to this group, with whom we worked to construct the following analysis.

The house of the MTL is a three-story building, occupying almost half a block. It is a private property that functioned as a public school until the City Government closed it in the 90s. The building remained unoccupied until 2004, when it was squatted by the Movement and each classroom was turned into a tiny family room, inhabited by no less than four people. In each of these rooms, the MTL built an even tinier bathroom, and on each floor they set up a gas cooker, with several burners to be shared among the ten women belonging to the families occupying each level. We especially mention the women, since they are the ones usually in charge of the meals and of cleaning each room, which is why they are in the common spaces more often.

These spaces are usually uninhabited for most of the day, except for the hours when the mothers cook and wash. This fact points out one of the characteristics of the ethnography presented here, since the adult voices are mostly these women's, men being practically absent in their narratives (but not in practices), given that they spend most of their time inside the rooms, when not working outside of the house. Regarding the general employment situation, the vast majority of adults in *the house* oscillate between unemployment and underemployment, completed with plans and scholarships for the children, although this is never enough to pay for everything. There are frequently disputes on this issue, and the possibility of a collective eviction due to non-payment is a reality they live with on a daily basis.

The house is organized as a cooperative, also acting as management. The latter is made up of three or four of *the house's* inhabitants, chosen by their companions through voting or consensus in the weekly or fortnightly meetings. In general, these cooperative members rotate every three or four months, since no one is overly excited about fixing broken things, mediating conflicts between families and, much less, collecting money to pay for utilities and monthly rent, as agreed with the local government.

Meanwhile, the children spend most of their time playing together in the hallways. One can arrive at *the house* at any time, except during school hours, and hear the shouting of children playing everywhere around the house. Sometimes these groups are separated by gender, but at other times boys and girls play together. The most popular activities are the computer, ball games, chasing games (generally called *mancha* [tag] or *zombis* [zombies]), and doing schoolwork together. *The house* ground floor has two rooms, used for meetings and for the daily afternoon snack provided by the Movement to the boys and girls living at *the house*. The building also has a *tendedero* [place with clotheslines], shared by the entire *house* to hang their clothes, and generally used by children as a playground.

It is in this context that we wondered how the boys and girls between 8 and 15 years old, living in one of the Movement's houses, construct knowledge about politics, condensed in the concepts of president, government, and police, from their daily life practices. To get closer to a possible answer, we will first address some theoretical and methodological discussions about children's knowledge construction processes within the framework of this prolonged ethnographic research. Then, we will concentrate on a precise analysis of the records and interviews in light of our research question, and finally, we will close with some conclusions and future lines of work.

KNOWLEDGE CONSTRUCTION AS AN ETHNOGRAPHIC PROBLEM

In order to examine what children know about politics from their daily life practices in the MTL house, we have focused on the latest anthropological productions that, in dialogue with Piagetian and Vygotskian developmental psychology, address this question from an ethnographic approach (García Palacios, 2012; Lave, 1988; Shabel, 2018; Toren, 1999).

These researches, as well as those of psychologist Rabello de Castro (2002), maintain that the meaning of all of our thought's categories is always historical, and is constantly evolving, individually and socially. Also, these authors' works reveal that context is constituent of cognitive processes on a variety of scales, including relations with present subjects and objects, but also those connecting with past history and other spaces, taking into account the political-economic structures operating in each situation. Both the world's materiality and the histories of the subjects participating in an activity, condition the course of the knowledge produced there, without ever determining it.

In this sense, the authors state that the meanings we give to things are never completely given, but always contain an emergent element, contributed by the subject in interaction with the object, thus considering children as active and reflective producers of their own reality. In this way, they refute the idea that children's thought is a mere copy of adult knowledge, or that they only know what adults enable. The subject's experience in the world is the basis of all knowledge, thus, daily life experiences produce meanings about life assimilated by each child from his or her historical present. Thus, from this perspective, living and knowing are part of the same process.

This historical process of the construction of meaning upon the meaning that others have made or make, in a process that is individual and collective *at the same time*, is called "microhistory" by both Toren (1999) and García Palacios (2012), and it is what we try to trace through our own research, with regard to politics, condensed into concepts such as the government, the police, the movement, etc., without losing sight of the historical-cultural dimension of these categories. At this point, although acknowledging Piagetian tradition, these authors take a distance from his research programme, since they focus on the knowledge produced by the particular subjects with whom they work in the field, far from generic conditions of age—or even culture—and very close to the ethnographic perspective and the possible questions formulated within it, just as we intend to do here. We put this perspective in dialogue with the contributions of Lave (1988), who, related to Vygotsky's school of socio-historical psychology, has studied "the activity of the person-in-action in his environment" (Lave, 1988, p. 145), which allows us to analyse the construction of knowledge upon the daily activities in the squatted house.

The uniqueness of each subject in their inter-subjective relations turns each scenario into a possibility of multiple meanings, although never infinite or random. This singularity within each person or group's particular history, recovered by the aforementioned anthropologists, is what generates different meanings from identical objects in contexts shared with other people and groups, in their sociohistorical coordinates. That is why we value the studied concepts' microhistory, as it is from the production of these differences that the change or continuity of cognitive meanings arises (as well as cultural ones in the long term, and according to the force correlations).

Regarding the social object of politics, we can broadly agree that it always refers to the relations of power and dispute mediating between people, and to the systems in which these relations are put into practice (Gledhil, 2000). Of all the possible angles to be studied in this framework, we focus here on the state and its manifestations such as the government, the president, and the police, insofar as those were the most significant concepts for the research subjects within their daily life practices. Although developmental psychology has its own productions regarding the conformation of these concepts and their history in the discipline (compiled for example in Castorina & Aisenberg, 1989; Lenzi, 2014), on this occasion, we will focus on the revision of the ethnographic fieldwork's results, leaving the dialogue with psychology for other writings, already in production.

At this point, we believe that the ethnographic approach (Guber, 2008; Rockwell, 2009) is an ideal tool for this research, with its tradition of recovering diversity parting from equality, and its careful observation of the subjects' being and acting in the field. This does not only refer to an intercultural analysis, but also to the differences arising within the scientist's group of belonging, developing the ability to exoticize what is familiar and opening a reflective path on one's own continuities and transformations in cultural practices. As stated by Colángelo on this matter: "It is the articulation of these two dimensions—diversity and inequality—that enables the analysis of childhood social problems in all their complexity" (2003, p. 3), through ethnography.

That is why this research was constructed upon four years of field work in one of the MTL's squatted houses, focusing on what the children did, said, and hid, on their games and conversations, although always attentive to the general social relations making up the daily lives of all human groups. This record of the life in the squatted house allows for the recovery of all the voices and perspectives composing it, in their continuity and modifications, as well as in the power relations within it. From this perspective, anthropology has made an important contribution to the acknowledging of boys and girls as valid actors, subjects of their own history (Fonseca, 1998; García Palacios, 2012; Pires, 2007; Szulc, 2015), passing from a research upon them to a research *with* them (Hecht, 2007).

Regarding these studies, we should not forget that "doing anthropological research with children is, first and foremost, doing anthropological research" (Cohn, 2005). In this framework, ethnography allows for an access to multiple situations of children interacting with each other, with adult subjects, and with the social world (Rockwell, 2009), since it enables the registration of what is said and of what is done, but not said (Guber, 2008). Within ethnography, there are different possible tools that we used to exhaustively record the meanings children give to the world they live in: field observation and production of records, interviews (colloquial and semi-structured conversations), drawings (as an end in itself, and also as a means, working on them in interviews), games, requesting specific written texts, and the use of audio-visual media.

In this research, ethnography is linked to the epistemological principles of the clinical method (Castorina et al., 1984), originated in the constructivist tradition of developmental psychology. This method consists of conducting an interview with each child, regarding the object of knowledge, in this case the city, trying to comprehend the logics operating in each of the responses. Hence, the interviewer asks for explanations and provides counter-arguments in order to reconstruct the reasoning underlying the subjects' statements. This way, we can get closer to understanding their knowledge of politics.

Without ignoring criticisms of the clinical method (cited in Duveen, 2000; Delval, 2001), we highlight the effort made by interviewers to go beyond considering the responses to problems provided by children as "right" or "wrong," in order to understand the logic they use when formulating their responses. Hence, the researcher's interpretation and the dialogue with the subjects is key to the reconstruction of these logics, as study objects. This methodological dialogue has proven to be more than fruitful when it comes to examining knowledge construction in everyday practices, with regard to various social objects (García Palacios, 2012; García Palacios & Castorina, 2014; Shabel, 2018).

THE GOVERNMENT, THE PRESIDENT, AND THE POLICE IN THE SQUATTED HOUSE

From the daily records and clinical interviews of the twenty children between 8 and 15 years old, living in the MTL's squatted house in Almagro, we have been able to reconstruct some of their concepts regarding politics, expressed as either more violent or negotiating conceptions of the state, in accordance to each case, differentiating three conceptions, distinctly naming them the government, the president, and the police. Now, we will analyse the daily practices that construct meanings regarding these concepts, trying to comprehend what subjects know on the issue, in relation to what adults know, and to the multiple social discourses circulating on the matter.

The Government

One afternoon in 2015 I stopped by *the house* to congratulate Andrés (8)[3] on his birthday, and I ran into Natalia (12), who was going out to walk her dog, quite large and threatening:

Paula: Nati! How strange, you walking the dog, you hate him.

Natalia: (laughs) Yes, I do hate him, but we need to hide him, since actually we can't have pets here, and the government is coming today.
                                         — *(Records, August 2015)*.

That day I learned that the City Government sends social workers from the Ministry of Development to control the houses' state. The professional that I met a few hours later that afternoon, told me herself: "We're here to check that everything is well." Although not frequently, when necessary, the boys and girls participate in setting up the scene, they take the dog out, remove the curtains from the doors (which are prohibited according to the government's housing parameters), and that day they do not play in the hallways. This complicit silence, especially installed by adults and children for the occasion, is part of what Lave and Wenger (1991) call a community of practice, political in this case, aiming to show what is expected from them in order to preserve their home.

On these occasions, women clean while telling the girls how to collaborate, and asking the boys to please go sit somewhere in the house and watch TV at a very low volume. Hence, when the social worker is about to arrive, seemingly always with advance notice, the rooms have been transformed. The same afternoon that I met Natalia, I stopped by Mirta's place, and she invited me to step into her room:

Mirta tells me that the school called her because of an issue regarding Jeremías (8), that he is not reading well, that half of the year has passed, and that the teachers are worried. While we talk, she sweeps the room, throws everything she gathered in the dustpan into a small bag, which she then closes and leaves next to the door. She asks me to check if the bathroom is clean enough and I say it's impeccable. She arranges the chairs by the table and begins to put away the clothes she has just taken off of the clothesline, while we continue the conversation. Meanwhile, her two daughters are in the kitchen washing the dishes, and her four boys, among whom is Jeremías, huddle on the couch watching TV, arguing about which channel to watch.

---

[3] All the children's names have been changed to preserve their identity. Next to each name, in parentheses, is the age of each subject.

— (Records, August 2015)

In the words of Lave and Wenger (1991), the term community of practice "implies participating in an activity system, where the participants share an understanding of what they are doing and what it means in their lives and to their communities." (1991, p. 95). And this is how Natalia explained it later in the conversation, when speaking of the purpose of her actions: "They check if everything is clean, if they threw away the garbage, and so we clean." In the previous fragment, she says that who comes to see their conditions, is "the government," which at her home is understood as a control agent, for whom it is necessary to behave in an extraordinary manner.

But the state can also translate into less obvious practices, referring to the same state control in the daily lives of boys and girls, as in Mauricio's (11) explanation on the functioning of the Movement's meetings, in which "there is a notebook they then give to the government, everything is written down there for them to see." This explanation given by Mauricio in his clinical interview (March 2016), refers to the minutes book used in the co-op meetings, in which the resolutions reached at each meeting are written down, and which, indeed, is then delivered to the City Government.

Although the children do not actively participate in the Movement's meetings, they do know a great deal about what happens there, as the women of *the house* discuss these issue openly in the kitchen and in the *tendedero*. In addition, they frequently comment on what they heard or were told, and upon that they build their own hypotheses of how the relation between *the house* and the state works. This means that the world's meanings produced by subjects are always "committed to the meanings that others have made and are making" (Toren, 1990, p. 979), so we need to analyse them in the context of the link between these relations.

Apart from talking about the government, the children use the names of the City and Buenos Aires to refer to the state in its most bureaucratic manifestations regarding *the house*, as Jaime did in his clinical interview:

Jaime:—The house used to be a school. And then I don't know what happened and no one ever went to that school again. And a man bought the school and made a house out of it. Then he wanted to sell it and the MTL was asking for a house and they gave us that house. And so the owner was no longer the owner because now it is a house of the MTL.

Paula: But who gave it to the MTL?
Jaime: The City. (...)
(...)
Jaime: They pay things, gather the money and give it to Buenos Aires.
—(Interview, February 2016)

Here, the state appears in its negotiating version, to whom utilities are paid, with the accompanying accountability, and on whom permanence in the house depends. This notion is also expressed in the adults' discourse, just as Iris (42), Jaime's mother, explained in this informal conversation that I had with her one afternoon, while doing fieldwork:

> I'm exhausted Pauli, yesterday we had a co-op meeting, we finished at about two o'clock, and today at six o'clock I had to get up for the boys. Yesterday we wanted to go to sleep, but this Friday we have to present the whole file to the City, with all the numbers, it's all so difficult, I don't understand anything, but we have to present it.
> — *(Records, April 2015)*.

For many years, Iris one of the heads of *the house,* and spent many nights at late meetings, doing the numbers and discussing MTL's resolutions, for which her daughter Rosa (8) reproached her on more than one occasion in my presence. Not by Jaime, however, he has always taken great pride in everything that his mother does in the organisation. This means that the socio-historical contexts of each subject approach or move away certain objects of knowledge, but they do not determine the meaning that each child builds regarding these objects (García Palacios, 2012), as it is in everyday practice, with its constant renewal, that the becoming of those meanings is consolidated.

Andrés, 8 years old, also situates state power as the negotiation partner regarding the property of *the house*: "Humahuaca used to be a school, but the government said there couldn't be a school with rooms. That's why they gave it to the MTL (...), and now they come and see if we pay." What is interesting here is that in discourses regarding the government, the state and the president, adults are often very confrontational, using phrases like "this crappy government is going to starve us all," "we should go and remove this government," but in practice it is an actor they negotiate with. In this sense, we highlight the originality of children's hypotheses about the world surrounding them, which draw on the world's materiality, social discourses, and their own experience, to produce each subject and group's interpretation (Shabel, 2018).

The marches regularly organized by the Movement "so that they don't take us out of our home" (Barbara, 8), and the adults' ongoing concern for the lack of money to pay for utilities, as required by the City Government requires in exchange for their staying in *the house*, rounds off the context in which children construct knowledge regarding the state:

> Giselle (9) and Ema (10) are sitting in the hallway on the first floor, playing cards. They play a couple of rounds with a logic that I do not understand, and write their points on a piece of paper with their names on it. They laugh, while talking about the game and its rules. Then, we hear the front door and I see a woman, living in the house, coming up the stairs. I don't know her name, but we've seen each other many times, and we greet each other. She pauses for a few moments to read the billboard on the wall, showing various announcements, including last month's utility bills, on which the rooms owing money are highlighted in red. While she is looking at the billboard, another woman, Susana (45), comes out of her room and they

greet each other. They comment on the utility payments and one of them raises her voice, a little frustrated, and exclaims, "How is it possible that Irene is always owing money!" The girls abandon the game for a few moments and look at Susana, then look at each other, laugh a little, as if they had heard a secret, and then keep playing. Susana notices this, and also my presence. She greets me, and then continues on her way to the kitchen

— *(Records, October 2016).*

The graphic representation of the mediation we propose as a category condensing children's knowledge regarding the state, is the wall of the corridor of the first floor, serving as the place's billboard, on which the announcements inform on marches, meetings, and who is late paying utilities, as the state's permanent presence in *the house*, with whom children have a daily relation on which they construct knowledge.

There, the state becomes a material connection with the subjects, in a bond that turns the families into debtors and itself into the eternal collector. It is also within these bonds that boys and girls construct a concept of the state that contains negotiating on the property and permanence of families in *the house*, in a relation of exchange. However, it is an unequal, if not impossible exchange, because in general there is not enough money to pay for everything that Buenos Aires demands, and a possible eviction becomes a daily source of concern among adults and boys and girls of the squatted house.

The announcements on the billboard on the first floor are, perhaps, the clearest proof that the money is never enough, as the names of the defaulting families are highlighted in red, after which the referents of *the house* pay visits to the rooms to remember the debts. All those practices put into play by the organisation in order to comply with the severe agreement proposed by the state as a negotiator, occur while the boys and girls play in the corridors or watch TV in their rooms. Then, they discuss who owes money to *the house*, and even use it as an offense mechanism when a problem arises regarding that week's football goals:

Teo (10): Hey, hey, hey, that was a goal, man!
Mauricio (11): No, what goal? I caught it with my hands and pushed it to the stairwell!
Teo: What a cheater, just like your dad, who cheats on the house and doesn't pay what he owes!
Mauricio: What? You don't know a thing, my dad pays everything he owes.

— *(Records, October 2016).*

Although this conflict was resolved between the boys in a few seconds, it reveals they understand the payments families must make for *the house*, and the generalized debts this reality implies to a population without fixed income, and without much state aid. We can say, then, that state presences and absences are shaping conceptual notions about what the state is, and what it does within the movement, of which children are part (Shabel, 2018).

The President

Negotiation practices are combined with threats and violence in the event of a possible eviction, something that is also known by the boys and girls:

Jaime: They talk about the territory and all that, about the order in the house (in reference to the Movement's meetings). And if the house is in poor condition and the president finds out, they throw us all out of the house.
Paula: Who?
Jaime: The police, because they didn't listen to who gave the order to keep the house clean"

— *(Interview, February 2016).*

Just like the rest of the boys and girls of *the house,* Jaime uses the figure of the president as the one who directly gives orders to vacate and close the spaces, without any type of negotiation. He distils a concept of what we call an evicting state, as opposed to the previous situations, in which staying in the house was a possibility throughout the exchange. In this case, power is conceived as overwhelming and absolute, severe in its decision to evict, shut down, and "throw out" whoever is occupying the space, as Candelaria (11) explained to me one afternoon when I was doing fieldwork at *the house,* on the eve of the elections: "If Macri[4] wins, they will close my house and we will have to leave" (records, August 2015).

In all cases, the president, or Macri, is related to a figure that closes houses and schools, the idea of a president who evicts the poor who cannot pay for the house's utilities or school fees is repeated in different areas:

We have to vote for Scioli[5] because we are poor, because we can't pay for school and we go to a free school. But in private schools people take care of things, they don't break them, if you go there, you see that everything is clean, nothing broken, no stains, we misbehave. When I was little, I also used to misbehave, we break things, we dirty them, but not in private schools, because they know that if they break things they have to pay for them, and that's why they are careful. That's why Macri is right, but we poor people have to vote for Scioli. We have to learn, because if we are left without school, perhaps our children will understand that we have to take more care of things, but we ourselves will no longer be going to school, we're all going to be idiots

— *(Records, October 2015, Jaime, 13).*

At this point, we wish to highlight how children's lives are influenced by the various junctures, electoral in this case, the concerns generated by public discourses, and their own elaborations about what they hear in the media, at school,

---

[4] Mauricio Macri, candidate for president for the alliance Cambiemos, the main opposition to the Peronist government that held power at that time, and against whom the ruling party would compete in the October elections of that same year.

[5] Daniel Scioli, presidential candidate for the Peronism, the ruling party at the time.

and, especially in this context, what they hear from the political organisations in which their family and social lives are embedded. Macri's negative evaluation by adults, as a threat of economic crisis and pauperization of their daily lives, was a recurring theme in *the house* during the second half of 2015. The concept of the evicting state is being shaped, then, through a diversity of scenarios frequented by the subjects in that particular time and space.

Following these circumstances, the person *Macri* has been connected to the figure of the president, negatively constructed on itself, as Zacarías (8) told me, already in 2016, one afternoon we were playing in *the house*. While building a castle with blocks, he made two dolls interact: "This is the king of the castle and this is the president, but this one (the latter) we're going to throw out of the castle, because he's bad." Once again, the context acts as a catalyst for the meanings constructed regarding the world (Valsiner, 2014), since it brings us closer to or further away from various objects of reality to be known, already socially signified in certain ways, producing new knowledge in each subject or group's singularity, always in relation to the knowledge circulating in this context, but never identical (García Palacios et al., 2018; Toren, 1999).

The Police

This evicting state, expressed in the president and in Macri, is completed with the figure of the police, as those responsible for carrying out the eviction and the closing of *the house*:

> I get to the house around two in the afternoon. It is February, and the children are on vacation, so they are at the front door playing soccer and trying to get some air to alleviate the terrible heat. Although it is not very common to find them playing outside the house, in the summer, without classes, all routines are modified a little. Mauricio (12) sees me coming from the corner and tries to throw the ball in my direction, shouting, "Catch it Pau!" I try my best to catch it, but the ball deviates and ends up bouncing in the street, close to a passing car. The driver has a scare, stops the car, and gets out, but when he sees that the boys are responsible for the mess, he calms down, insults a little in a low voice, and gets back into the car. As they see him drive away, they have the following conversation:

Paola (16) (while holding her younger brother, Valen, in her arms): What are you doing, are you crazy? What if he calls the police?
Mauricio (12): Why would he call the police? He's already gone.
Paola: And what if he had called them? What if more police came to get us out of the house because of you?
Teo (11) (Paola's brother): What if they came with guns and shot us all to get us to leave (gestures he has a gun and shoots. He laughs, it seems more likely that he is teasing his sister than saying something he thinks might happen).
Andrés (9): If the police come they will throw us all out.
Jeremías (7): But we will tell them that it wasn't us.

Paola: With that face of yours, who's going to believe that it wasn't you? (Everyone laughs)
— *(Records, February 2017).*

Within the attentive perspective provided by ethnography, there are two circumstances that we wish to add to this analysis in order to unravel the paths of the meaning they construct regarding the police institution. First, there are the stories of imprisoned relatives, in which the prison staff is referred to as the police, as those who keep control over the loved ones, as explained by Roberta (23), regarding the conversations between her son Dalton (4) and his father: "They talk at night because they share a cell phone between three people, and his turn is at night, which is when it's calmer, when the cops, the policemen, are lazy and don't check on them so much" (field record, November 2015). Jaime (14) tells me about a similarly hostile situation when visiting his mother, recently imprisoned in Ezeiza:

It is Thursday, a holiday, and there is a teachers meeting at the "Tere." I get there early, and Helena (26) and Estefi (29) are already at the door, chatting in the sun. Jaime (14), Natalia (15), and a friend of theirs from school walk by. They say hello and talk with us for a while. I take the opportunity to ask Jaime about his mother, and he answers:

Jaime: The other time that we went there, you know, the first time, the police didn't let us through, they checked everything and they didn't let us through because there were missing some papers, and we had gone all the way out there, we got up very early, like six o'clock, you know, and we went there on the bus and all, but they didn't let us in.
— *(Records, February 2018).*

Here, the police is presented as an obstacle in the relations between boys and girls and their imprisoned relatives, being who decide whether or not they can enter to see their mothers and fathers, if they can take the cake they brought for their birthday, or give them the new perfume they bought to celebrate their release drawing near. This category, like all of them, is constructed in various contexts of the subjects' daily lives, which in this case always present conflict and opposition, and the police holding power over the children's actions and their relations with others.

The confrontation with the police is also repeated in the adults' stories on their confrontations with them during various evictions, as Irene (39) and Dafne (38) tell me:

Irene: It reminds me of before, when we had to face the police all the time. I remember when I was already in the Movement, I was pregnant and we went out and resisted the police. They were much worse than now, because before, we used to squat houses all the time, and they would come and throw us out by force, using tear gas, hitting us (...). Daf-

ne:—And we weren't even fighting for the house before, it was just for the food bag, for a box of things, it wouldn't even occur to us to fight for the house.
— *(Records, April 2016).*

The concept of an evicting state appears in the form of the police, always in violent episodes, which, while belonging to the past, make up the present context of the families and children: "Children are historical subjects with a collective past that is also expressed in circulating meanings, which are appropriated making up knowledge, even when adults do not explicitly state them, or even deny them" (García Palacios et al., 2018, p. 266). This means that the revision of the records revealed the children's (common) sense, in which the concepts regarding the state are related to *the police*, as being the one that closes, shuts down, and evicts the squatted property. And while circulating through the various spaces, they put these senses into play, reinforcing or modifying them on each occasion.

The state practices of eviction and negotiating with the Movement on the permanence in *the house* produce relations between the MTL and the state, from which the subjects construct their knowledge. Also, the children converse with various state presences in other scenarios, more or less on a day-to-day basis, such as school and prison. Within these social frameworks they build their own meanings regarding the world, always in relation to the adult world, but far from being a mere copy of it (Rabello de Castro, 2002).

CONCLUSIONS

Based on the daily practices in *the house,* such as meetings and visits of Social Development, the children of the MTL construct concepts regarding various aspects of reality, as in this case is the state. Every concept produced around them is a framework of meanings that they construct in a permanent dialectic with their context, which we sought to analyse throughout this work.

We can see, then, that while the movement's adults blame Macri or the government, interchangeably, for the possible closure of the house, the children believe that the police and the president are responsible for a possible eviction of the property, and that the Buenos Aires government is the bureaucratic agent levying taxes and demanding explanations in exchange of permanence. This microhistory of conceptualizations allows us to approach the meanings constructed by children regarding their social reality, resulting in an original hypothesis of the group and each of the subjects, in which, however, the tracks of meaning can be traced in a permanent movement of what continues and what is transformed.

We would like to particularly emphasise that, since daily life practice is a source of knowledge, the material conditions in which the families live, are also part of the knowledge they construct on the state, since "they are concrete instances of social relations, structuring the conditions under which children construct their own understanding of the categories that adults use to refer to the world" (Toren, 1999, p. 86). Just as the state materializes in various practices, so does it in the materiality of the living conditions, upon which children produce their knowledge.

Throughout this research, the children have proven to be active subjects in the production of meaning regarding the reality surrounding them, and in this cognitive production they also dispute the cultural meanings of the different social objects, in a dialectic between the two levels. Finally, this leads us to discard the concepts of transmission and internalization when considering the meeting points between individual and society, in order to understand the relations between children and the social production of life.

REFERENCES

Carli, S. (2009). *La cuestión de la infancia. Entre la escuela, la calle y el shopping* [The childhood Issue. Between the school, the street and the shopping centre]. Paidós.

Carman, M. (2005). La ciudad visible y la ciudad invisible: El surgimiento de las casas tomadas en Buenos Aires [The visible city and the invisible city: The emergence of the casas tomadas in Buenos Aires], *Población & Sociedad, 12*(1), 57–91.

Castorina, J. A., & Aisenberg, B. (1989). Psicogénesis de las ideas infantiles sobre la autoridad presidencial. Un estudio exploratorio [Psychogenesis of children's ideas about presidential authority. An exploratory study]. In J. A. Castorina (Ed.), *Problemas en psicología genética* [Problems in genetic psychology] (pp. 76–98). Miño y Dávila.

Castorina, J. A., Fernández, S., & Lenzi, A. (1984). La psicología genética y el proceso de aprendizaje. [Genetic psychology and the learning process] In J. A. Castorina, L. S. Fernández, A. M. Lenzi, H. M. Casávola, A. M. Kaufman, & G. Palau (Eds.), *Psicología genética* [Genetic psychology]. Miño y Dávila.

Cohn, C. (November, 2005). O desenho das crianças e o antropólogo: reflexões a partir das crianças mebengokré-xikrin [Children's drawing and the anthropologist: Reflections from the mebengokré-xikrin children]. *VI Reunião de Antropologia do Mercosul (RAM).* Universidad de la República

Colángelo, M. A. (November, 2003): *La mirada antropológica sobre la infância. Reflexiones y perspectivas de abordaje* [The anthropological view of childhood. Reflections and perspectives of approach]. International Seminar *La Formación Docente entre el siglo XIX y el siglo XXI,* La Plata University, Buenos Aires, Argentina.

Comisión Económica para América Latina (CEPAL) & United Nations International Children's Emergency Fund (UNICEF). (2005). La pobreza infantil en América Latina [Child poverty in Latin America], *Desafíos* 1, United Nations

Duveen, G. (2000). Piaget ethnographer. *Social Science Information, 39*(1), 79–97.

Fernández Álvarez, M. I. (2015). *Hacer juntos(as). Dinámicas, contornos y relieves de la política colectiva* [Doing together. Dynamics, contours and thickness of collective politics.]. Biblios.

Fonseca, C. (1998). Quando cada caso NÃO é um caso. Pesquisa etnográfica e educação [When every case is NOT a case. Ethnographic research and education], *Revista Brasileira de Educação, 10,* 58–78.

García Palacios, M. (2012). *Religión y etnicidad en las experiencias formativas de un barrio toba de Buenos Aires* [Religion and ethnicity in the formative experiences of a Toba neighborhood in Buenos Aires]. Doctoral thesis specializing in Anthropological Sciences, University of Philosophy and Letters, Universidad de Buenos Aires

García Palacios, M., & Castorina, J. A. (2014). Studying children's religious knowledge: Contributions of ethnography and the clinical-critical method. *Integrative Psychological and Behavioral Science, 48*(4), 462–478.

García Palacios, M., Shabel, P., Horn, A., & Castorina, J. A. (2018). Uses and meanings of "context" in studies on children's knowledge: A viewpoint from anthropology and constructivist psychology, *Integrative Psychological and Behavioral Sciences, 52*(2), 191–208.

Guber, R. (2008). *El salvaje metropolitano* [The metropolitan savage]. Paidós.

Hecht, A. C. (2007). De la investigación sobre a la investigación con. Reflexiones sobre el vínculo entre la producción de saberes y la intervención social [From research on to research with. Reflections on the link between the production of knowledge and social intervention.], *Runa. Archivo para las Ciencias del hombre, 27*, 87–99.

Lave, J. (1988). *Cognition in practice: Mind, mathematics and culture in everyday life*. Cambridge University Press.

Lave, J., & Wegner, E. (1991). *Situated Learning: Legitimate peripheral participation*. Cambridge University Press.

Lenzi, A. (2014). Desarrollo cognoscitivo y formación de conocimientos políticos en niños y adolescentes [Cognitive development and the formation of political knowledge in children and adolescents]. *Revista de Psicología-Segunda época, 11*(1), 78–90.

Manzano, V. (2013). *La política en movimiento* [Politics on the move]. Prohistoria.

Padawer, A., Scarfó, G., Rubinstein, M., & Visintín, M. (2009). Movimientos sociales y educación: debates sobre la transicionalidad de la infancia y de la juventud en distintos contextos de socialización [Social movements and education: debates on the transitionality of childhood and youth in different contexts of socialisation]. *Intersecciones en antropología, 10*(1), 141–153.

Pires, F. (2007). Ser adulta e pesquisar crianças: explorando possibilidades metodológicas na pesquisa antropológica [Being adult and researching children: exploring methodological possibilities in anthropological research]. *Revista de Antropología de San Pablo, 50*(1), s/p.

Poli, C. (2007). Movimiento Territorial Liberación: su historia. Piquetes, organización, poder popular [Territorial liberation movement: Its history. Pickets, organisation, people's power], *Cuaderno de trabajo N° 77*. Centro Cultural de la Cooperación.

Rabello de Castro, L. (2002). A infância e seus destinos no contemporâneo[Childhood and its destinies in contemporary times]. *Psicologia em Revista, 8*(11), 47–58.

Santillán, L. (2009). La crianza y educación infantil como cuestión social, política y cotidiana: una etnografía en barrios populares del gran Buenos Aires [Child rearing and education as a social, political and everyday issue: An ethnography in poor neighborhoods of Greater Buenos Aires]. *Anthropologica, 27*(27), 47–74.

Shabel, P. (2018) "I learn as i please": The construction of children's knowledge in, and about, a Buenos Aires Neighbourhood. *Children and Society, 32*(2), 417–428.

Szulc, A. (2015). *La niñez mapuche. Sentidos de pertenencia en tensión* [Mapuche children. Senses of belonging in tension]. Biblos.

Toren, C. (1990). *Making sense of hierarchy: Cognition as social process in Fiji.* London School of Economics.

Toren, C. (1999). *Mind, materiality and history. Explorations in Fijian Ethnography.* Routledge.

CHAPTER 9

THE RIGHT TO PRIVACY IN SECONDARY SCHOOL

Ideas of Adolescents

Mariela Helman, Axel Horn, and José Antonio Castorina

INTRODUCTION

The right to privacy is a legal attribution to children and adolescents, as written in the *Convention on the Rights of the Child* (UN, 1989). This produces a rupture with the previous legal conceptions, since they are now given active or participation rights, such as freedom of opinion or privacy, and not only passive or protective rights such as food, health or education (García Méndez, 1994). In this way, minors are considered subjects of rights, expanding their public participation. These rights are recognised as unconditional, with no other condition than that of being girls, boys or adolescents in order to enjoy them.

The privacy barrier protected by the *Convention* is the product of a long historical journey that goes from the Middle Ages, where public and private spaces mingled (there was no private space belonging to each person), to the establishment of the first European courts, where a personal space outside the intervention of others began to be formed (Aries, 1989; Elias, 1998). Thus, the right to privacy is constructed upon the—prior—admission of an area free from the actions of others, and of which a person has complete availability, being thus an active subject in the usufruct of his rights. Also, in as much object of knowledge, the right to privacy belongs to the domain of social knowledge, a field studied by Piagetian psychology (Helman & Castorina, 2007; Horn & Castorina, 2008).

This work is situated in a critical perspective, developed within Piaget's psychology (Barreiro, 2012; Castorina, 2005; Castorina & Faigenbaum, 2000), according to which conceptualisation does not only depend on constructive individual activity, but is also subject to the social context's constraints, emphasizing those resulting from participation in institutions and the appropriation of common sense beliefs.

Certain currents of developmental psychology have tried to explain the child's construction of a concept such as intimacy, understanding it as the subject's solitary elaboration of the object it tries to know (La Taille et al., 1991), and referring to an *expectation of treatment* (Leiras, 1994) regarding his private aspects. However, research carried out by this team has shown that at school this expectation is often canceled when the child violates school rules. That is, the right is not considered as unconditional—as established by *The Convention*—but is thought of as depending on certain school conditions that the child must meet, or, as mentioned in an other work (Helman, 2010; Helman & Castorina, 2005), as a right earned by being a good student. From our line of research, we have postulated that school practices condition the construction of children's ideas regarding their rights. The conditions we have identified are linked to certain characteristics of school practices. For example, in those cases in which the subjects recognize that the school adults should not disclose the students' personal information, this recognition of their right vanishes if the teacher did so in order to help him or her, or if the student has poor school grades.

In other words, the studies carried out by Helman and Castorina (2007), and broadened by Horn and Castorina (2008), showed that children's ideas concerning their rights are painstakingly acquired in a context of institutional actions, such as directives or gestures by school authorities, aimed at students (Helman & Castorina, 2005, 2007). Helman's research addresses rights in school context, selecting the right to privacy, education, and free expression to study the children's perspective. Horn's works focused specifically on the right to privacy, articulating the collected material with observations from the classroom context. This made it possible to compare the produced categories, while at the same time defining practices related to the work of school authorities, which in many cases naturalized the practices in which this right is violated. Also, although less frequently, we found practices contemplating and protecting this right. In these approaches the analysis of individual productions intertwine with an exhaustive study on institutional contexts (Horn & Castorina, 2010; Horn et al., 2013). One of the conclusions of these works is that the children's first conceptual approach to the right to privacy at school depends on the compliance with school regulations. These results allow us to state that institutional practices constrain the construction of children's ideas regarding their rights, and that the recurrence to this conditioning indicates that the concept of rights is not yet consolidated. If it were, it would "resist" as an expectation of treatment, even in situations considered as bad behaviour (Helman, 2010). These constraints operate in relation to the process of interaction between subject and object of social knowledge (Castorina & Lenzi, 2000), enabling and at the same time limiting the elaboration of children's concepts (Castorina & Faigenbaum, 2000). This is, they do not determine the constructive process itself, since the subjects' intellectual activity is not negated, but occurs only in certain socio-institutional conditions. One of this article's purposes is to define whether the concept of constraints continues to be fruitful when defining the relations between subject and object of social knowledge, or whether it is necessary to incorporate other components into that epistemic relation. We will return to this question in the section addressing to the discussion of the results.

Exploration of the different research works led to the study on the conceptualisation processes of the right to privacy, in the context of middle school, seeking to explore the ideas of older subjects participating in school practices very different from those of primary school subjects. In this framework, the possibility of exhaustively studying the construction of the right to privacy in the context of middle school, is relevant for the following reasons: first, because it is safe to assume that in school practices, as well as in the organisation of the middle school itself, the adolescents' personal information is treated differently than in primary school, thus enabling the development of other ideas about the right; secondly, because beyond the assumption that adolescents recognize and appreciate privacy, it is necessary to specify what privacy in the school context means to adolescents, and what conceptualizations—if any—exist regarding this right, leading us to identifying the level of justification attributed to it by the subjects; finally, and without confirming any evolutionary thesis, it can be expected that the adolescents' growing interest in a life with increasing degrees of autonomy, as proposed by our culture, will enable the production of other ideas about the right to privacy.

First, this work aims to present some characteristics of secondary school as an institution, in order to situate the study on the ideas of adolescents. Then we present the research process, and analyse the interviews we carried out, distinguishing common and novel elements with respect to previous research. Finally, we draw some conclusions about the meaning of previous analyses and the emergence of new problems.

MIDDLE SCHOOL AS A FRAMEWORK FOR COGNITIVE ELABORATION

The purpose of this work is not to exhaustively characterize the secondary level, but to recover some of its central matters in order to better understand the type of school practices related to our topic of research. These considerations regarding certain characteristics of the school institution allow us to draw a more specific outline of the context in which subjects produce social knowledge concerning their rights. Also, cultural changes of the recent years, including the debate of concepts such as youth participation and political formation, among others, make us reconsider the context as a constraint of cognitive production.

At present there is a broad consensus regarding criticism of secondary school as it was historically understood (e.g., Miranda, 2013; Southwell, 2018; Terigi, 2008). Middle school is mainly experiencing a crisis of significance: what is secondary school "good for"? This resulted in Latin American governments pursuing changes in this level's institutions for a long time.

In our country, the enactment of the Law on National Education (2006) reinstated social debate on secondary education, posing the enormous challenge of access, permanence and completion of this level, under conditions that guarantee quality learning for all adolescents. The policies implemented in response to the requirement of secondary education's universalization take place within complex scenarios of social, cultural, and institutional transformations (Miranda, 2013). The elaboration of new legal texts[1] implies a relevant repositioning of the state. In turn, these legal instruments and the discourse on social and educational inclusion have been translated into actions and strategies materialized in plans, programmes, and projects.

The obligatory nature involved in this change of law requires a revision of the institutional conditions. While secondary school incorporated only the population's middle layers, its pedagogical proposal, organizational format and *curriculum* acquired legitimacy. The fact that many students could not finish secondary school was not considered a problem of the level, since it was accepted that it was not "for everyone." However, realizing these necessary changes is a complex task, given that the middle school's organizational pattern features three elements making up an *iron tripod* that seems difficult to remove: the classification of curricula, the designation of teachers by specialty, and the organisation of the teaching job in class hours (Terigi, 2008). The challenges of incorporating excluded adolescents and young people into middle school are opposed to the limits of its historical formats.

From the perspective of rights, we ask ourselves in what way the teachers' working conditions favor the inclusion and recognition of each student. Does teaching by class hours, implying belonging to several institutions, carry the risk of making a quick, and therefore often superficial and fragmentary assessment of the students? This means fewer opportunities to know each one's trajectory. On the other hand, what conditions does the tension between secondary school "for a few" or "for all," still present in the representations of teachers and community, generate in order to guarantee the rights of all students?

---

[1] *Ley de Financiamiento Educativo* [Law on Educational Financing] (2005), *Ley de Formación Técnico-Profesional* [Law on Technical-Professional Formation] (2005), and fundamentally the *Ley de Educación Nacional* [Law on National Education] (2006).

If there is consensus regarding the level's universality, as there is in primary school, and even so, these rights are conditional, as shown in our research, how can the regulatory frameworks of institutional life function if there is no general agreement that each student has the right to be in secondary school?

Our work belongs of the tradition studying the development of children's ideas in their very production context; that is, in this case, the school. As we said, the theoretical perspective places this production in the context of youth participation in social practices. For this reason, a reference to studies addressing the analysis of everyday school life is relevant for our study object. In this regard, a line of research and intervention works on international and national level tends to provide pedagogical answers to various conflictive situations in everyday school life. Some studies on "school violence" (D'Angelo & Fernández, 2011) allow for the distinction between "violence at school" (episodes that happen at school but in which the latter merely functions as a sounding board for social interactions typical of the context in which it is inserted), and violence resulting from institutional mechanisms produced within the framework of the relations of the school community, that is, violent practices or practices accentuating situations of social violence. Therefore, concepts such as "school conflict" and "school environment" (Kornblit, 2008) are introduced, aiming to conceptually capture phenomena that demand urgent responses in the schools' day-to-day life.

According to some studies (Benbenishty & Astor, 2005; Welsh et al., 1999), the conflict is mainly related to the school's institutional factors, being less relevant individual psychological aspects or social characteristics. This contradicts the common assumption of a direct correlation between violent communities and violent schools. Some of the institution's characteristics seem to be particularly closely related to an increase of conflict: inconsistency in activities of and decisions by teachers or directors, a lack of clarity in the rules and their application or arbitrariness, etc.

In our country, studies on school violence, such as those by Kaplan (2006) and Castorina and Kaplan (2006, 2009), among others, have focused on the middle level of the educational system. They emphasised symbolic violence, like a "soft violence," not visible to the institution members, and often affecting the adolescents' school trajectories. This form of domination does not rule out forms of participation and discussion that may question it (Castorina & Kaplan, 2006, 2009). In general, these studies include the so-called "social environment of the school" as a significant aspect, defined by the perceptions of the different actors participating in the institution, although studies directly addressing practices and interactions arising at school are less frequent.

Teachers themselves recognize the existence of questionable ways of treating the students (authoritarian, derogatory or discriminatory manners; difficulties to hear the adolescents' problems; more or less explicit underestimation). Students, for their part, recognize these manners in the day-to-day relations between teachers and students (intimidating screams, humiliations), and associate situations of violence at school with the teachers' failure to teach content. The adolescents also mention recurring situations of humiliation, harassment or ridicule among peers (D'Angelo & Fernández, 2011).

More recent studies also address perceptions of everyday school life at secondary level. In a statistical survey on school environment, violence and conflict in secondary schools, carried out by the National Ministry of Education, we find similar data, although the students' appreciation for the school space stands out (Argentine National Ministry of Education, 2014[2]). The study reveals the degree of conflict, and what the school environment looks like from the students' perspective. Results show that in general the students know and agree with the rules, but have little participation in their elaboration—beyond the current regulations promoting the construction of school coexistence agreements—a fact that coincides with other studies (Southwell, 2018). Regarding the participation bodies (assembly, coexistence council, classroom council, student centre, body of delegates), students know the body of delegates best. This is interesting, since this instance is usually more mediated by adults than, for example, the student centre, of which the adolescents themselves define the dynamics.

Outside these institutional levels, we considered another participatory aspect related to what we call "hearing," that is, the perception of students regarding the degree of being taken into account, the sense of freedom to express their opinions, the comfort and confidence they experience at school. These imply a highly valued expectation of treatment by the students towards the adults. It is noteworthy that, while the challenge of strengthening participatory instances in schools persists, students feel—in their majority—that they are taken into account, heard, that their opinions are considered, just as the results of the aforementioned research described. These experiences are not necessarily related to participation in formal instances, they are two different aspects of participation.

In turn, Southwell (2018)[3] proposes to address school dynamics to analyse institutional ways of enabling intergenerational relations, as well as ways of being recognised at school[4]. This study allows us to observe certain generational controversies regarding the meaning given by adults and adolescents to different

---

[2] Objective of the work: This research report contains the results of the survey carried out in November 2014 by the 'Observatorio Argentino de Violencia en las Escuelas del Ministerio de Educación de la Nación' [Argentine Observatory of Violence in Schools of the National Ministry of Education], whose general objective was to survey the perception of 2nd and 5th year students of secondary schools, both state and private schools, of the country's 24 jurisdictions, regarding coexistence, conflict, and violence in their institutions. Study carried out on 26,600 students. Nationwide.

[3] Intergenerational relations and educational positions: tensions in today's secondary school.

[4] Research project PIct ANPcyt-uNIPE N° 0097, Escuela media y cultura contemporánea: vínculos generacionales, convivencia y formación ciudadana' [Middle School and Contemporary Culture: Generational Relations, Coexistence and Civic Education], carried out between 2012 and 2016. Fieldwork in four schools of Buenos Aires Province. The research focused on the ways in which institutions favour or hinder certain forms of intergenerational relations.

components of school experience, such as, for example, justice of school rules, respect, or even the very significance of secondary school.

According to this and other studies (Litichever, 2014), this educational level faces the challenge of a change in the ways coexistence is regulated, from a disciplinary model to a participatory one. However, these old manners are still in force at schools: the participatory model is still more of a project than it is a reality in concrete practices. Hence, there is evidence of a certain distance between what is proposed in regulations and what actually happens at school: on the one hand, certain regulations propose a conception of coexistence enabling dialogue and participation of school actors, seeking to generate a more inclusive school; on the other hand, the realization of the school coexistence system is opposed to these ideas: the rules actually in force are similar to those demanded by the disciplinary model, therefore the behaviours that are most punished are related to the maintenance of hierarchies and not to the revision of institutional relations.

Hence, the expiration of the traditional way of conceiving adolescents and school life coexists with the absence of real and broader participation spaces in school dynamics. The approach of inclusion, recognizing and respecting diversity, supplants that of homogenisation. This respect determines new conditions for the regulation of school life: these basically propose the inclusion of all subjects, but also demand respect for the characteristics of each student (learning pace, diversified school programmes, consideration of each student's particularity). We insist, these new, current conditions require the renewal of regulation modalities of institutional life, in order to extend rights and guarantee various forms of student participation, which is not easy to achieve.

Considering the outlines of our research object, we explore in what ways the regulation of school practices intervenes in the ideas developed by the students on the right to privacy. In other words, can we link the right's conditional nature to the students' perception that in school they are often humiliated, ridiculed and harassed? Is the fact that children's ideas enable the authorities to "violate" their right to privacy related to the intention of avoiding greater evil, mistreatment and ridicule among peers, seeming to be a central aspect of their concerns, as shown in different studies?

Widely accepted interpretations in our culture understand children as full subjects of rights, and a legal correlation was established with the approval of a set of national laws[5] that reflect, while installing, manners of perceiving children and adolescents, as well as an understanding of coexistence and its problems. In turn, this new conception requires the construction of a new authority in adults, in a democratic institutional culture, reinforcing its pedagogical and institutional char-

---

[5] N° 26,206, N° 26,061, N° 26,877, N° 26,892) and resolutions of the *Consejo Federal de Educación* [Federal Council of Education] (N° 93/09, N° 174/12, N° 188/12, N° 217/14, N° 226/14, N° 239/14), and the conformation of the *Sistema de Protección Integral de Derechos de Niños, Niñas y Adolescentes* [System of Integral Protection of the Rights of Children and Adolescents] (Law N° 26,061)

acter. This should result in more student participation, a formative, non-punitive penalty system based on progressive responsibility, collective elaboration of coexistence agreements, and several forms of accompaniment of school trajectories, among other issues.

In the case of middle school, the aforementioned tension (for some/for all) is combined with others arising from the coexistence of different conceptions regarding childhood and youth. For example, the right to protection is widely accepted and generally recognised, while the right to participation is controversial. At schools, the latter collides with more traditional conceptions of authority that, even from the perspective of safeguarding these rights, allows for significant differences in its materialization. This interpretation is consistent with what the abovementioned studies reveal: students generally acknowledge feeling heard and contained by the school (protection rights) but indicate little action when it comes to the development of standards or devices such as student centres (participation rights).

From our constructivist perspective, what we mentioned regarding the various tensions in disciplinary practices and participation in middle school raises the question of how these tensions intervened in young people's cognitive development of the right to privacy. Whether we may consider them as constraints for the construction of subjects' ideas, or whether their participation in such production is more vital, an issue we will take up in this article's final discussion.

In other words, does the authorities' increased safeguarding of protection rights prolong the conditioning found in children of primary school? And, on the other hand, does the lower presence of participation rights in school practices have an influence on young people's ideas regarding the possibility of claiming the fulfilment of their rights? Finally, is it possible to redefine the constraints on knowledge conceding a more prominent place to the teachers' social practices and social representations, in addition to the relations between subject and social object?

ADOLESCENT'S IDEAS

Between 2014 and 2016, we interviewed middle-class adolescents from 13 to 16 years old, attending public schools of the "CABA" [Autonomous City of Buenos Aires]. This research combined the use of observations from different school spaces, in order to characterize everyday practices regarding intimacy, with clinical interviews. We used non-participant observation as a methodological instrument to obtain first-hand empirical data regarding school life events. Based on the obtained data, we drew up categories using the constant comparative method, highly relevant when establishing relations between phenomena, behaviour and beliefs of the subjects involved (Goetz & Lecompte, 1988).

Here we exclusively address the interviews' analysis, given its methodological importance, although we recognize its incompleteness and temporariness, leaving a categorization of the observations for future work. The interviews were conducted individually, based on the guidelines of the Piagetian clinical-critical method (Delval, 2001; Piaget, 1926), to explore and reconstruct adolescents' ideas on their right to privacy in school context[6].

The following questions guide the analysis of the conducted interviews[7]: what are the characteristics of adolescents' ideas regarding their right to privacy at school? Are their features similar to those found in the samples of children from primary school? Can we point out differences? What might be the cause of continuity and transformation? Developments in the characteristics of adolescent thought? Participation in other types of school practices? A combination between the two?

The analysis of the conducted interviews reveals a few characteristics of the knowledge on the right to privacy at school:

1. Certain continuities in relation to the ideas of primary school students. In particular, the ideas regarding the legitimacy of the authority's actions to safeguard or violate the right in question are similar to those of younger children, according to previous samples.

We asked the following questions to the subjects: how does a teacher know whether he or she can or cannot intervene in a certain manner? (Read a message on a student's phone, read a note circulating in the classroom, disclose a student's problem, etc.). Where does this authorization or prohibition to act in a certain way "come from"? What we try to find out is whether, from a youthful perspective, these acts safeguarding or violating rights are thought from a more objective framework (a rule, law, or right) than the one of the reciprocity expected in interpersonal relations. In the case of primary school students, this dimension is remarkably foreign to them: the subjects do not understand the question or give explanations based on common sense, or on knowledge acquired by their own experience with school authority or life. For example, "She knows she shouldn't read the phone, because it is something that everybody knows, you shouldn't do that, the teacher wouldn't like it herself if someone were to spy on her" (Dalia, 10 years old).

In general, we did not find great differences with respect to the arguments given by subjects of middle school, as can be seen in the following interview fragment:

"If the teacher had FB he wouldn't like for someone to watch it without his permission"... Interviewer: Does it come from somewhere that she—the teacher— is not

---

[6] In the course of the interviews, different narratives were presented, typical situations of institutional life, in which an authority discloses some personal aspect of the student. Parting from these narratives, the subjects were asked to identify whether or not privacy is at stake, and whether the right in question is either respected or violated.

[7] The interviews were carried out by bachelor students of the *Licenciatura de Ciencias de la Educación de la Facultad de Filosofía y Letras* [Educational Sciences of the University of Philosophy and Letters], within the framework of the Research Credits Work implemented by the Chair of Piaget's psychology of that university, during the second term of 2016. The sample was of twenty subjects, between 14 and 16 years old.

allowed to do that? (Disclose a student's personal problem). "No, I think she just makes her own decisions. But I think she should talk to some higher authority and see what they can do with the group. Whether to discuss it in the group or to talk to this boy, to the pedagogical advisor, the school psychologist..." ... "I think she does the first thing that comes to her mind. But I couldn't say because I really don't know." (Lucas, 15 years old)

Also, we did not observe important differences regarding actions the subjects can carry out when their right to privacy is violated. Systematically, the youngest children believe there are no possible sanctions for the authorities violating their privacy. The argument they maintain is that the damage is already done (disclose a personal problem to the whole group, read the content of a note circulating between students in class, for example), and when facing this, the only option is the student's anger or discontent. They do not consider it a possibility for institutional authorities to be punished for such actions. For example, if the teacher reads the content of a note passed between students, they cannot do anything, as maintains one of the subjects: "Well... no, because if they raise their voice something extreme may happen. The teacher yelling at them or something like that. That's it, to me they can't do anything." (Sofía, 14 years old)

Clearly, there is continuity with regard to the arguments stated by the youngest subjects. They also make justifications that focus on the authority's protective nature (performing certain acts involving the crossing of limits concerning private information for the good of the students or to avoid greater evil). The conditioning of the right to privacy is even considered to be in accordance with the areas in which conflictive situations arise. In general, the teachers seem to own the classroom while recess belongs more to the students; and this property enables more intrusion into personal space. These characteristics were already found and described in primary school boys and girls (Horn & Castorina, 2010)

2. Continuities or transformations? Adults have the obligation to protect young people; the novelty is the adolescents mentioning problems proper of their age. In the studies on elementary school subjects, on some occasions situations were presented that implied conflicts of rights between the right to privacy and the right to physical integrity. In the sample taken in popular class, some children stated that if a student has a very serious problem at home, the school authorities should know about it in order to intervene. This was an argument that had not appeared in the middle class subjects. We believe these situations are conflicts of rights, where the protection of minors "weighs more" than the respect for privacy, an issue that normatively functions this way. In fact, school authorities are obliged to intervene in situations where rights are violated.

Based on these findings, we incorporated these types of situations into the interviews, and once again found, in the sample of middle school students, a predominance of the minors' protection over the subjects' privacy. This is interesting because, as the study involves adolescents, the examples they mention are different, and relate to young people's concerns and to certain issues proper of our era, such as the denaturing and rejection of gender related inequalities (for example, the identification of violent dating). For example, Zoe (16 years old), when analyzing a situation in which a young woman tells the course tutor that a friend is in a potentially dangerous relationship, states: "Her friend was not wrong, it is important that the school tutor finds out, because they have to help her ... maybe she is not yet ready to speak out and stays in this toxic relationship ... she has to feel comfortable to be able to say it. But it is important for her to speak out, or for a friend to tell, so that they can help her to get out."

The meanings that we find are directly related to the cultural and social processes of recent years, and, at the same time, in them we still see the different place occupied by youth and adults when it comes to protecting and guaranteeing the rights of the former. Martina (13.7 years old) maintains that "the adults are the ones who can do something greater, not the classmates, they can listen to her, contain her, but the adults can do something more...." These considerations are compatible with the aforementioned studies, in which adolescents report feeling heard and taken into account by their teachers at middle school.

3. We noticed some significant differences in the sample of subjects from middle schools compared to those from primary school, regarding the conception of the right to privacy. The immediate recognition of the right implied in the different narratives particularly stands out. While the youngest subjects did not recognize the right to privacy in these situations, even as an expectation of treatment, older children seem to recognize it instantly when the situation arises. These different interpretations evoke Piaget (Piaget & Garcia, 1982), for whom the observables were not a "given" but assimilated into the frameworks of meaning available to a subject. When presented the empirical situations, primary school subjects first focus on the non-compliance with school regulations, while those in middle school emphasise the violation of privacy by school authorities.

For example, when faced with a situation in which two students hand each other a piece of paper during class hours, and the teacher intercepts it and reads its content, we find this type of appreciation: ."... What the teacher did was wrong. Because what was on that piece of paper was something private of the girl and her classmate." (...) ."... Their problem may be a private subject and she shouldn't read it. To me, she should do what my teacher did, which was throw the letter in the trash" (Martín, 16 years old). Meanwhile, in the samples of studies carried out on elementary school students, the responses frequently argue that, for example, "what the girls did is wrong, because they can't send messages during class hours, this way they don't pay attention and they won't learn what the teacher explained"

(Abril, 9 years old). On many occasions, only after being presented the counter-argument do the subjects "visualize" or interpret the situation as an observable related to privacy.

As we have mentioned, these types of responses are frequent in the sample of middle school subjects, repeatedly indicating a noticeable difference. For example, when faced with the situation in which students lock their cell phone when the teacher asks them to hand it over because they were sending messages to each other during class hours: "I think this is right because they are protecting what they are talking about. The teacher has no right to infringe their privacy. As I said before, it may be a very private matter concerning one of them, and the teacher has no right to know." Also ."... a cell phone is one's property, and the teacher doesn't have the right to read it, well, anyway they locked it, but still, the teacher has no right to read what's on the phone" (Felipe, 15 years old).

The same happens with the narrative in which the teacher discloses a student's family problem to the rest of the class: "I think that what the teacher does is wrong, because if he has a family problem and tells the teacher about it, maybe he just doesn't want to tell his classmates ... (...) Maybe he just wants her to know and doesn't want to tell the others." (Micaela, 14 years old)

> ...If the boy didn't want to tell, she shouldn't either. Because it seems to me that personal situations are private. And also, sometimes children can't understand a child of their same age, especially if they are very young. (...) Well ... it seems to me that unless the boy wants to tell it, she can't say anything without consent (...) (María Sofia, 15 years old).

> "This is a bad start. To me, that's wrong. Because it's an issue that only the boy should tell to whomever he wants." "Because it's the boy's private matter. (...) And to me the teacher was simply wrong, because it's a private matter and well, maybe the boy doesn't trust everyone, like me ... (laughs), and maybe he didn't want some other kid to know. The situation was exposed, when maybe he wanted it to stay private, and talk about it with the teacher only" (Azul, 16 years old).

The previous examples reveal how the subjects notice the issue of privacy immediately, and we could say that it is almost the first thing they "see," in the sense of the aforementioned constructed observables, and according to the situations presented to them. It is what they emphasise when interpreting the narratives.

In the situation described in the narrative of the message circulating during class hours, there is a tension between the respect for privacy and the compliance with school regulations, since in fact the students are breaking a rule. We have already characterized this tension as an element that conditions the right to privacy (Helman & Castorina, 2005, 2007). In the youngest subjects, it is almost a constant that the transgression of school regulations implies losing the right to privacy for those boys and girls. The argumentative sequence is usually the following: children can have things where adults do not interfere, but if they circulate in the classroom, during class hours, that right loses its value as such. For them, the most important issue seems to be that the classroom is the teacher's property, or that a school rule has been broken. Adolescents, on the other hand, while in doubt due to the fact that the students are in class, end up stating that it is more important that the content of these messages be safeguarded. Clearly, they seem to have another way of considering the problem, in which respect for privacy prevails over non-compliance with school regulations.

Furthermore, there is evident progress in the way of explaining, relating, speaking, and arguing about the issues proposed by the narratives. In other words, the observables are broader compared to the younger subjects, more elements are included—laws, rights, intimacy, privacy, etc., are mentioned spontaneously—and more complex relations are established between them. In our opinion, the fact that the subjects of this sample are from middle school, that is, older, also intervenes in how they conceive the object of knowledge. Of course, it is not a matter of a maturational ability or a natural competence "of recognizing rights," but rather are these arguments related to diverse social interactions and experiences. On the other hand, adolescents have more powerful cognitive instruments allowing them to structure this experience in a more advanced manner; that is, they can isolate the variables producing a phenomenon, formulate hypotheses and contrast them, examine whether they are true or false, etc. (Delval, 1983), and are capable of producing much more thorough verbal inferences. Above all, they are able to produce abstractions regarding their own elaborations with respect to rights, they can explicitly thematize the issues, reflect on their own actions, and even on those carried out upon them. What is more, the intersubjective activity in the classroom, including the relation of recognition regarding the teacher or their peers, supposes a reflective activity for it to be conceptualized.

DISCUSSION ON THE RESULTS

It is interesting to return to the ideas we find in adolescents. In short we can say that we identify certain persistence in the difficulty of recognizing the legality of rights governed by public norms. Adolescents, just like younger children, sustain an interpersonal legality. That is to say, they interpret the teachers' actions regarding their rights as being sustained by personal decisions or general expectations of treatment, rather than being supported by legal norms or rights recognised and declared beyond the school. In our team's first research on school authority (Castorina & Lenzi, 2000) we have stated that the children's explanations revolve around certain organizing hypotheses. We identified a passage in the development of these ideas, in which the youngest children explain authority by the *owner hypothesis* (the principal exercises her authority because she bought the school, or its owner assigned her this task) to an explanation of the oldest children of the sample, who sustain school authority by the *position hypothesis*, being able to identify that it is not the person who is the holder of the position, but the latter a symbolic space occupied by the former. To younger children, the domain or entities constituting authority are people and relations of an interpersonal nature. In turn, to the older subjects the domain is constituted by observable entities such as the concrete actors being part of the school, but also by theoretical entities such as "positions," "functions" or "norms." Acts of authority are therefore explained through criteria transcending personal aspects.

We might think that respect for rights is part of the generalized and impersonal norms regulating school practices, as conceived by the older subjects. However, regarding the right to privacy, we find a continuity between children and adolescents in which school authorities seem to act according to personal and individual criteria, without a clear normative regulation that demands responsibility regarding these rights from the authorities, and that is reminiscent of the most primitive versions of school authority. This may be connected to the difficulties experienced by both younger children and adolescents, when thinking about possible steps they can take when teachers violate their right to privacy. It is safe to assume that this persistence is sustained in a version of a certain institutional paternalism or protective perspective, also found in the abovementioned research on authority.

This last question is relevant because data suggest, although this should be specifically researched in order to be confirmed, that there is a coexistence of strict logical thought, or an intellectual activity revolving around the abstractions of the norms, at the same time that norms embodied in persons are sustained, a social belief that is hegemonic at school. As if this belief's force were imposed on the subjects' thought, and they could not detach or abstract the norms from the persons.

We would like to emphasise the novel aspects of adolescent thought, since it allows us to return to a relevant question for the constructivist perspective and the theoretical discussions raised in the introduction: how is a novelty produced that does not depend on the subject's purely individual and intellectual activity? A novelty we found, is the use of arguments with a greater degree of coherence, and also a better identification of the problem mentioned by the interviewer: middle school subjects immediately recognize that the raised situations involve privacy issues. However, this greater clarity, both of understanding the problem and of maintaining their position, does not directly lead them to imagine the unconditionality of the right to privacy. In other words, we see that adolescents' intellectual activity works systematically when it comes to the right to privacy, even enabling the experiences' thematical organisation, but this does not lead them to think more objectively about the right: at times, they argue a conditioned perspective of rights using logical tools.

This research offers the opportunity of reconsidering the concept of constraints (Castorina & Faigenbaum, 2000), which we do not reject, but wish to reposition in a more complex relation with the subject and the object of knowledge. Subjects construct their ideas regarding the right to privacy in a context of social and institutional practices (including teachers, their decisions as authority, and their social representations). Hence, it is preferable to establish the interactions between subject and object as units of analysis and include institutional practices. We suggest that the analysis take into account three components: the subject, the object of knowledge, and the social practices in which the knowledge is produced. In other words, the concept of constraints takes on a novel perspective by proposing a ternary unit of analysis, transcending the Subject-Object duality, and enabling the study of multiple interactions between the components of the unit of analysis, its dynamics of oppositions and articulations.

We suggest then that future studies on the construction of social knowledge take into account these three dynamically articulated components. Children's ideas regarding the right to privacy are the product of inferential processes of meanings, a dialectic of integration and conceptual differentiation of the object of knowledge, but taking into account that these ideas emerge from the subjects' own social experience in relation to the institution's teaching activity and the teachers' social beliefs on children and adolescents' rights.

In other words, the social practices carried out in a given institution, with certain norms, or in a social context that also includes identity positions related to social representations (which have not been researched in this work) are a third element of the constructive relation between subject and object of knowledge. In this way, by simultaneously studying the formation of ideas regarding the right to privacy in the subject's relations with the object and its social conditions, the concept of constraint loses a remainder of "exteriority" when it comes to cognitive construction.

In this article, the institutional context in which adolescents elaborate their ideas was reconstructed based on other research in which various coexistence problems of middle school were studied. It is significant that in secondary schools the most frequent way of taking the adolescents' voice into account, is through the school authorities hearing the students, or through less organized mechanisms such as course delegates, instead of through the formation of student bodies such as the student centre, or experiences of norm construction where adolescents play a greater role, without having others interpreting or representing their voice. In other words, we find a certain consistency between the most protective ideas on the legitimacy of the actions carried out by school authority, and the lack of preponderance of practices defining normative agreements in which they participate as subjects of rights. The analysis of a crucial aspect of the unity we have defined remains pending for future work: we are referring to the observations we made regarding school practices, and also to new research that considers the cultural and institutional changes in which adolescents played a predominant role. For a few years now, adolescents have been developing much more participatory experiences in several institutions (through school squatting, student coordinators, the participation—through representatives—in discussions with ministers of education regarding changes in curriculum, etc.). These are not present in the experiences mentioned in the references of this article. What remains a question is the effect of these experiences on the development of ideas regarding their citizenship rights, including the right to privacy.

We believe that state policies implemented to guarantee these rights are necessary but not sufficient, since there is aspects of experiences lived on a daily basis that must be governed by these principles, in the areas where adolescents participate, that is, in this case, at school (Korinfeld, 2016). The regulation of school life and the characteristics of the authority figures have been modified according to new scenarios and demands. The new school culture proposes the adolescents' comprehensive participation in the institution, in the elaboration and implementation of a coexistence system, collectively agreed upon (Levy, 2016).

According to what we have stated in this work, it is very promising and interesting for the field of education to study the teachers' social representations of the right to privacy and other citizenship rights, as well as those of secondary school students. It is reasonable to argue that some of the teachers' social representations, focused on the school's protective nature, operate as a true epistemological obstacle for adolescents to know and exercise their right in the school space.

Finally, we want to point out that many policies aimed at youth revolve around the idea of *participation*. To carry out such a policy involves conceding a protagonism generally denied to younger generations. "Adding the students" voices to the issue of administering and regulating school life is a process of democratization that breaks with authoritarian or despotic conceptions' (Levy, p. 117, 2016). And this is a central aspect of our approach, also supported by the data from this research: school practices are the starting point for the elaboration of ideas regarding students' rights. If school practices consider children and adolescents as full subjects of rights, as protagonists in the development of normative and coexistence agreements, this may lead to the possibility of them believing they own these rights, and subsequently demanding they be respected.

REFERENCES

Argentine National Ministry of Education. (2014). *Relevamiento estadístico sobre clima escolar, violencia y conflicto en escuelas secundarias según la perspectiva de los alumnos* [Statistical survey on school climate, violence and conflict in secondary schools according to the students' perspective]. Observatorio Argentino de Violencia en las Escuelas del Ministerio de Educación de la Nación' [Argentine Observatory of Violence in Schools of the National Ministry of Education].

Aries, Ph. (1989). Por una historia de la vida privada [History of Private Life]. In Ph. Aries & G. Duby (Eds.), *Historia de la vida privada. Del Renacimiento a la Ilustración* [History of private life. Passions of the renaissance] (pp. 7–19). Taurus.

Barreiro, A. (2012). El desarrollo de las justificaciones del castigo: ¿conceptualizacion individual o apropiación de conocimientos colectivos? [The development of justifications for punishment: individual conceptualization or appropriation of collective knowledge] *Estudios de Psicología, 33*(1), 67–77.

Benbenishty, R., & Astor, R. (2005). *School violence in context. Culture, neighborhood, family, school and gender*. OUP

Castorina, J. A. (2005). La investigación psicológica de los conocimientos sociales. Los desafíos a la tradición constructivista [The psychological investigation of social knowledge. Challenges to the constructivist tradition]. In J. A. Castorina (Eds.) *Construcción conceptual y representaciones sociales. El conocimiento de la sociedad* [Conceptual construction and social representations. Knowledge of society] (pp. 19–44). Miño y Dávila.

Castorina, J. A., & Faigenbaum, G. (2000). Restricciones y conocimiento de dominio: hacia una diversidad de enfoques [Constraints and knowledge domain knowledge: Towards a diversity of approaches]. In J. A. Castorina, & A. Lenzi (Eds.) *La formación de los conocimientos sociales en los niños. Investigaciones psicológicas y perspectivas educativas* [The formation of social knowledge in children. Psychological investigations and educational perspectives] (pp. 155–177). Gedisa.

Castorina, J. A., & Kaplan, C. (2006). Violencias en la escuela: una reconstrucción crítica del concepto [Violence at school: A critical reconstruction of the concept]. In C. Kaplan (Dir.) *Violencias en plural. Sociología de las violencias en la escuela* [Violence in the plural. Sociology of violence at school] (pp. 27–54). Miño y Dávila.

Castorina, J. A., & Kaplan, C. (2009). Civilización, violencia y escuela. Nuevos problemas y enfoques para la investigación educativa [Civilization, violence and school. New problems and approaches for educational research]. In C. Kaplan (Ed.), *Violencia escolar bajo sospecha* [Suspected school violence] (pp. 29–54). Miño y Dávila.

Castorina, J. A., & Lenzi, A. M. (2000). Las ideas iniciales de los niños sobre la autoridad escolar. Una indagación psicogenética [Children's initial ideas about school authority. A psychogenetic inquiry]. In J. A. Castorina & A. M. Lenzi (Eds.), *La formación de los conocimientos sociales en los niños. Investigaciones psicológicas y perspectivas educativas* [The formation of social knowledge in children. Psychological investigations and educational perspectives] (pp. 19–40). Gedisa.

D'Angelo, L. A., & Fernandez, D. R. (2011). *Clima, conflictos y violencia en la escuela* [Climate, conflict and violence at school]. UNICEF-FLACSO.

Delval, J. (1983). Crecer y Pensar. La construcción del conocimiento en la escuela [Grow and think. The construction of knowledge at school. Pedagogy notebooks]. *Cuadernos de Pedagogía*. Editorial Laia.

Delval, J. (2001) *Aprender en la vida y en la escuela* [Learn in life and in school]. Morata.

Elias, N. (1998). *El proceso de la civilización. Investigaciones sociogéticas y psicogenéticas* [Civilizing process state formation civilization. Sociogenetic and psychogenetic investigations]. Fondo de Cultura Económica.

García Méndez, E. (1994). *Derecho de la Infancia-Adolescencia en América Latina: De la Situación Irregular a la Protección Integral* [Childhood-Adolescence Right in Latin America: From Irregular Situation to Comprehensive Protection]. Forum Pacis.

Goetz, J. P., & Lecompte, M. D. (1988). *Etnografía y diseño cualitativo en investigación educativa* [Ethnography and qualitative design in educational research]. Madrid.

Helman, M. (2010). Los derechos en el contexto escolar: relaciones entre ideas infantiles y prácticas educativas [Rights in the school context: Relationships between children's ideas and educational practices]. In Castorina J. A. (Ed.), *Desarrollo del conocimiento social: prácticas, discursos y teoría* [Development of social knowledge: practices, discourses and theory] (pp. 215–235). Miño y Dávila.

Helman, M., & Castorina, J. A. (2005). La institución escolar y las ideas de los niños sobre sus derechos [The school institution and children's ideas about their rights]. *Revista del Instituto de Ciencias de la Educación, 13*(23), 29–39.

Helman, M., & Castorina, J. A. (2007). La institución escolar y las ideas de los niños sobre sus derechos [The school institution and children's ideas about their rights]. In J. A. Castorina (Ed.), *Cultura y conocimientos sociales: desafíos a la psicología del desarrollo* [Culture and social knowledge: challenges to developmental psychology] (pp. 219–241). Aiqué.

Horn, A., & Castorina, J. A. (2008). Las ideas infantiles sobre el derecho a la privacidad en la escuela [Children's ideas about the right to privacy at school]. *XV Anuario de Investigaciones, 15*(2), 197–206.

Horn, A., & Castorina, J. A. (2010). Las ideas infantiles sobre la privacidad: una construcción conceptual en contextos institucionales [Children's ideas about privacy: A conceptual construction in institutional contexts]. In J. A. Castorina. (Ed.), *Desarrollo del conocimiento social: Prácticas, discursos y teoría* [Development of social knowledge: practices, discourses and theory] (pp. 191–214). Miño y Dávila.

Horn, A., Helman, M., Castorina, J. A., & Kurlat, M. (2013). Prácticas escolares e ideas infantiles sobre el derecho a la intimidad [School practices and children's ideas about the right to privacy]. *Cadernos de Pesquisa, 43*(148), 198–219.

Kaplan, C. (2006). *Violencias en plural. Sociología de las violencias en la escuela* [Violence in the plural. Sociology of violence at school]. Miño y Dávila.

Korinfeld, D. (2016). Espacios e instituciones suficientemente subjetivados [Sufficiently subjectivized spaces and institutions]. In D. Korinfeld, D. Levy, & S. Rascován. *Entre adolescentes y adultos en la escuela. Puntuaciones de época* [Between adolescents and adults at school. Period scores] (pp. 97–122). Paidós.

Kornblit, A. (2008). *Violencia Escolar y Climas Sociales* [School Violence and Social Climates]. Buenos Aires: Biblos.

La Taille, Y., Bedoia, G., & Giménez, P. (1991). A construção da fronteira moral da intimidade: O lugar da confissão na hierarquia de valores morais em sujeitos de 6 a 14 años. [The construction of the moral frontier of intimacy: The place of confession in the hierarchy of moral values in subjects aged 6 to 14 years] *Psicologia: Teoria e Pesquisa, 7*, 91–110.

Leiras, M. (1994). *Los derechos del niño en la escuela* [The children of the school]. UNICEF Argentina.

Levy, D. (2016). Convivencias Escolares [School Activities]. In D. Korinfeld, D. Levy, & S. Rascován (Eds.), *Entre adolescentes y adultos en la escuela. Puntuaciones de época* [Between adolescents and adults at school. Epocal scores] (pp. 153–184). Paidós.

Ley de Educación Nacional n° 26.206 [Law on National Education] (2006).

Litichever, L. (2014). La Convivencia como modalidad de resolución de conflictos [Coexistence as a conflict resolution modality], *I Encuentro Internacional de Educación: Espacios de investigación y divulgación. 29*, 30 y 31 de octubre de 2014—Facultad de Ciencias Humanas—UNCPBA Tandil—Argentina.

Miranda, E. (2013). De la selección a la universalización. Los desafíos de la obligatoriedad de la educación secundaria [From selection to universalization. The challenges of compulsory secondary education], *Espacios en Blanco, 23*, 9–32.

Piaget, J. (1926). *La representación del mundo en el niño* [The representation of the world in the child]. Morata.

Piaget, J., & García, R. (1982). *Psicogénesis e historia de la ciencia* [Psychogenesis and history of science]. Siglo XXI.

Southwell, M. (2018). Vínculos intergeneracionales y posiciones docentes: tensiones en la escuela secundaria contemporánea [Intergenerational links and teaching positions: Tensions in contemporary high school]. *Revista Ensambles, 4*(8), 69–85.

Terigi, F. (2008). Los cambios en el formato de la escuela secundaria argentina: por qué son necesarios, por qué son tan difíciles [Changes in the Argentine high school format: why they are necessary, why they are so difficult]. *Propuesta Educativa, 29*(15), 63–71.

UN. (1989). Asamblea General de las Naciones Unidas. *Convención sobre los derechos del niño* [*Children's rights convention*]. CRC.

Welsh, W., Greene, J., & Jenkins, P. (1999). School disorder: The influence of individual, institutional and community factors. *Criminology, 37*(1), 73–115.

BIOGRAPHIES

José Antonio Castorina, PhD in Education. Emeritus Professor at the University of Buenos Aires and Research National Scientific and Technological Research Council (CONICET-Argentine) and Honoris Causa Professor at National University of Rosario (Argentine). He has been engaged in research problems related to the psychology of social knowledge development in children and on the epistemological problems of the social representations theory and developmental psychology.

Alicia Barreiro, PhD in Educational Sciences and Postdoctoral Studies in Social Sciences, Magister in Educational Psychology. She is a Professor of Genetic Psychology and Epistemology at the University of Buenos Aires, and an endowed researcher at the National Scientific and Technological Research Council (CONICET-Argentine). Academical Coordinator of the Master Cognitive Psychology and Learning (FLACSO-Argentine). Member of the Directive Board of the Jean Piaget Society and Associate Editor of the journal *Papers on Social Representations*. Her research interests are focused on the construction of social knowledge and moral development of children, adolescents and adults, combining social and developmental psychology approaches.

AUTHORS

Tomás Baquero Cano. Master student in Interdisciplinary Studies of Subjectivity at the University of Buenos Aires. Professor Assistant in Theory and Technique of Groups II at the Faculty of Psychology, University of Buenos Aires. His research focuses on the historical conditions of the construction of knowledge and subjectivity, in dialogue with philosophy, especially through the thought of Michel Foucault and Giorgio Agamben.

Daniela Bruno. PhD in Educational Sciences from the University of Buenos Aires. Master in Political Science and Sociology from the Latin-American Faculty of Social Sciences, Argentina. Researcher at the National Council of Scientific and Technical Research. Teacher at Social Psychology I, at Faculty of Psychology, University of Buenos Aires.

Mariana García Palacios. PhD in Anthropology from University of Buenos Aires (UBA). Researcher of CONICET at the Anthropology and Education Program (Institute of Anthropological Sciences, UBA, professor of the Department of Anthropology (UBA) and executive editor of the journal *Cuadernos de Antropología Social*. She obtained several scholarships for study abroad (El Colegio Mexiquense and CAPES-Brazil) and postdoctoral research (FMSH-France, DAAD-Germany and UNESCO). Since 2006, she has been conducting ethnographic fieldwork with the Toba/Qom population. Her main areas of research are: childhood, education and interculturality, formative experiences and construction of socio-religious knowledge.

Mariela Helman. Professor at the Department of Education, Faculty of Philosophy and Letters, University of Buenos Aires, Argentina. Teacher of Subject Ethics, Human Rights and Construction of Citizenship in Primary School at IFD N° 7 José María Torres. Member of the technical team of the Acceleration Program and the Shared Project Program of the Ministry of Education of CABA, aimed at primary schools in the jurisdiction. He participates in various training projects for teachers and management teams at the primary level in different jurisdictions. Her research focuses on the construction of children and adolescents about their rights at school, in articulation with the analysis of school practices.

Axel Horn. PhD in Education from the Faculty of Philosophy and Letters of the University of Buenos Aires and Master in Critical Pedagogies and Socio-educational Issues. He is currently Assistant Professor of Genetic Psychology at the Faculty of Psychology of the National University of La Plata and Researcher at the Nacional Council of Scientific and Technological Research (National University of José C. Paz). He has researched the construction of children's ideas about the right to privacy at school and worked on the relationship between neurosciences and educational practices in high school.

Paula Shabel. PhD. in Anthropology from the University of Buenos Aires. Researcher at the National Council of Scientific and Technological Research and is a member of the team "Niñez Plural." Her research topics focus on the political participation of children and adolescents in the urban space and the processes of knowledge construction that occur in these practices, always from an ethnographic approach.

Cristian Parellada. PhD in Psychology from the National University of La Plata (Argentine) and Assistant Professor at the same institution. His research focuses on the construction of historical knowledge, specifically on the study of the mechanisms of production and appropriation of historical maps both in textbooks and by students.

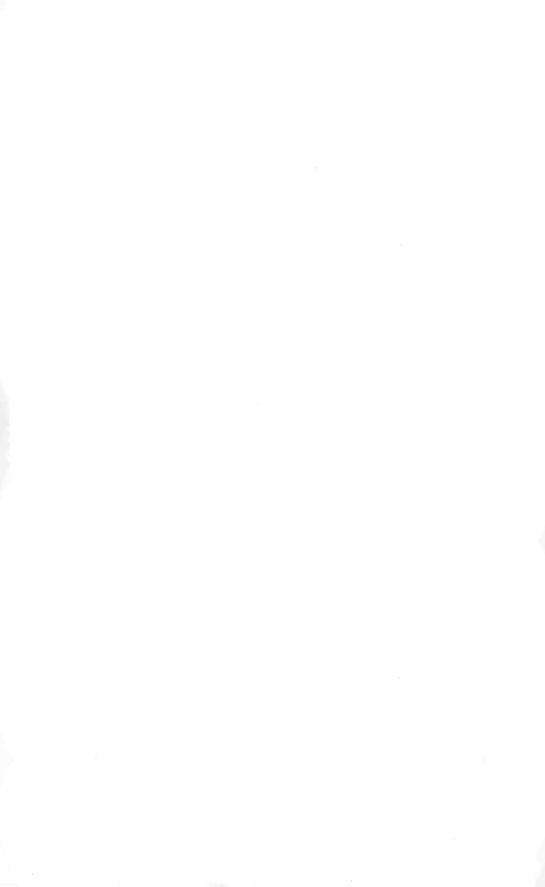

Printed in the United States
by Baker & Taylor Publisher Services